# Theoretical population geography

# Theoretical population geography

**Robert Woods**

Lecturer in Geography,
University of Sheffield

**Longman**
London and New York

Longman Group Limited
Longman House
Burnt Mill, Harlow, Essex, UK

*Published in the United States of America
by Longman Inc., New York*

*First published 1982*

**British Library Cataloguing in Publication Data**

Woods, Robert
    Theoretical population geography.
    1. Anthropo-geography
    I. Title
    909         GF50

    ISBN 0-582-30029-0

**Library of Congress Cataloging in Publication Data**

Woods, Robert.
    Theoretical population geography.

    Bibliography: p.
    Includes index.
    1. Population geography.    I. Title.
    HB1951.W663        304.6        81-2842
    ISBN 0-582-30029-0        AACR2

Printed in Singapore by
Singapore National Printers Pte Ltd

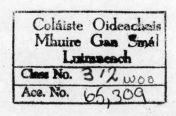

for Alison and Rachel

# Contents

# Contents

# List of figures

# List of tables

# Preface

Anyone who attempts a discussion of 'theories' and 'population geography' is obliged to begin by outlining definitions and drawing some distinctions. As regards the definitions, 'geography' is used here as a term to refer to that discipline which employs the 'spatial perspective' as its dominant mode of enquiry. It studies spatial relationships, patterns, processes and movements, what their causes are and what they in turn influence. The spatial perspective may be accompanied by the temporal or it may be temporarily abandoned in favour of the economic, social, political, physical or biological perspectives, but it will eventually re-emerge as the focal method and the most important arbiter of relevant questions. Population geography is, therefore, the study of population using the spatial perspective. Within the study of population there are core and peripheral issues. Those at the centre are concerned with the distribution and structure of population; with mortality, fertility and migration; what causes them to be as they are, why they change over time and through space; and with how and why they themselves affect other economic, social, political and environmental issues. At the periphery lie issues which are central to other specialisms, such as urbanisation and social segregation.

One important distinction which is made here is that between models and theories, and thus between modelling and theorising. All theories are models, but not all models are theories. Theories provide means of solving 'how' and 'why' questions whereas models may simply deal with 'how'. Models can be predictive without being explanatory; they have a strong representational emphasis.

The questions raised in the following pages will be concerned mainly with the core issues of population geography and the ways in which theories have been and can be constructed as aids to their understanding. Chapter 1 deals with the questions of how and why population grows. It distinguishes between biological and socio-economic interpretations and concludes by contrasting the work of Malthus and Marx on population. Whilst the first chapter has a temporal emphasis, the second discusses the use of pure demographic theory to distinguish spatial pattern and the third considers spatio-temporal variations in population characteristics, especially mortality and fertility, together with theories which assist in the explanation of those variations over time and through space. Migration theories are discussed in Chapter 4 from the standpoint of the individual and the group. Chapter 5 treats two 'grand theories' which are available to geographers, namely those of the demographic transition and historical materialism, both of which attempt to account for global changes of a revolutionary nature.

These discussions are motivated by two objectives: firstly, to stimulate the construction of theories in population geography at a variety of levels and, secondly, to demonstrate how geographers as social scientists can make important contributions to the core issues in population studies via their spatial perspective, by empirical analysis and by theorising.

The possibility of realising these objectives has been enhanced by the help of a large number of people to whom I would like to express my thanks. My colleagues in the Sheffield Population Research Group, particularly David Grigg, Alan Nash, Chris Smith, Paul White and John Woodward, have provided critical stimulus. More exacting tasks with text and diagrams have been performed by Carole Elliss and Wendy Mann, Paul Coles and Rosemary Duncan. Any errors of omission or misinterpretation that remain must, of course, be attributed to the theories themselves, upon which there can be no conclusions.

Robert Woods
Sheffield
January 1981

# Acknowledgements

We are grateful to the following for permission to reproduce copyright material:

The Hogarth Press Ltd and St John's College, Oxford for the poem 'Time and Again' from *Selected Poems* by R.M. Rilke translated by J.B. Leishman; The Princeton University Press for our Fig. 3.21 from a Fig. on p. 31 of *The Contraceptive Revolution* by Charles F. Westoff and Norman B. Ryder. Copyright (c) 1977 by Princeton University Press reprinted by permission of Princeton University Press.

# 1
# Theories of population growth

An abstract law of population exists only for plants and
animals, and even then only in the absence of any historical
intervention by man.

Karl Marx, *Capital*

There are three ways in which a population can grow: when
natural increase exceeds net emigration; when net immigration exceeds natural decrease; and when there is both natural increase and
net immigration. But the factors which affect the contributory variables of mortality, fertility and migration are extremely complex and
are as yet little understood either individually or in combination.
Why do some populations increase faster than others? Why do particular groups of females have more offspring than others? How are
diseases communicated and what is their influence in restraining the
growth of population? These and other similar conundrums are of
fundamental importance for the study of population structures.
Attempts to solve them require the construction of models and
theories which are intended to help in the process of simplification
and explanation. Because of the importance of theory construction
for the analysis of population structure and distribution, it will be
necessary to discuss some of the different ways of developing
theories, their strengths, weaknesses and complexities, before the
main question to be posed in this chapter can be tackled, namely,
'How and why does population grow or decline?' The results of this
general discussion may then be applied to the specific problem of
constructing theories to explain population growth.

## Systems and theories

It must not be imagined that the characteristics of a population are the simple direct outcome of processes which can be
accounted for in terms of a variety of causes. The quantitative and
qualitative aspects of a population will have reciprocal influences not

only on other populations, but also on individual members of the same population. For example, economic development in human societies can be both enhanced and dampened down by rapid population growth, whilst in animal populations chronic overcrowding can initiate genetic mutations and even lead to reduced fecundity. The interplay of factors which cause population growth to occur and the influence of that growth on the organisation of society make a full understanding of the demographic system unlikely. As a consequence of its complexity it is necessary to 'break in' to the overall system at some specific point and to deal with sub-systems which comprise only a limited number of interacting variables. The two main sub-systems will therefore focus on 'what causes population to . . .' and 'what influence population has on . . .', population as effect and cause. However, within these sub-systems there are yet more associations which need to be isolated. Change in fertility could be taken as the definitional criterion for a sub-system, for instance, which would make the pattern of fertility the outcome to be explained by its associations with a number of other causal variables within the sub-system. In this case, the effects of changes in fertility on the organisation of society or on the other demographic factors would be temporarily removed from discussion. Apart from this 'systems closure' approach it is also common for variables to be 'held constant'. For instance, the influence of migration can be removed while the interaction of mortality and fertility is studied.

Once a system of enquiry has been identified, it becomes important to establish the level of generality which is to be aimed for and to select a methodology by which that aim may be realised. What kind of theories are required? How are they to be constructed? These are the questions which need to be resolved.

Most social scientific theories have the following form: they contain *theoretical statements* from which *empirical statements* can be logically deduced and which can be related to observations; that is, they are verifiable. Causal theories contain theoretical statements about the association between two or more *variables*, variables which have *observable values*. For example, the three variables $A$, $B$ and $C$ may be connected in a variety of ways. If $A$ causes $B$ and $B$ causes $C$ then the following representation is appropriate

$$A \rightarrow B \rightarrow C.$$

Similarly, $A$ and $B$ in combination may cause $C$

$$(A + B) \rightarrow C$$

or *A* and *B* could be causally related to *C*, but unrelated to one another

Clearly these are very simple examples yet they all rely on the term *cause* (→) for their meaning. *Cause* can be used to refer to the necessary and only pre-condition for the existence of a phenomenon; a sufficient condition; or even a contributory condition. In social scientific enquiry it is unlikely that any meaning other than the last-mentioned will be an unrealistic one, for associations and connections which are in reality like those shown above are trivial. Causal theories have to be constructed using proxy or surrogate variables which are contributory, although necessary, pre-conditions for the existence of a phenomenon. *A* and *B* must stand in for *D* to *Z*, some of which may not as yet be identified as having connections, or if identified they may not have observable values. Despite problems encountered in the definition of *cause* social scientists have extended the range of empirical statements to include positive, negative and two-way associations between variables. For instance, although *A* is a cause of *C* the observed value of *C* is inversely related to that of *A*, whilst *B* and *C* are causally and reciprocally interrelated in a positive fashion, thus

Such causal empirical statements have been elaborated to include whole series of causal variables whose relationship with other variables can be hypothesised. The following gives an example

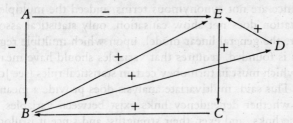

which can also be written in matrix form

|  | | | To | | |
|---|---|---|---|---|---|
| Causal link | A | B | C | D | E |
| A | − | | | | − |
| B | | | | + | + |
| From    C | | + | | | |
| D | | | | | + |
| E | | + | | | |

Here all the variables, but $A$, are in some way causally related to other variables, although variable $E$ is the destination of the most causal links. Much more sophisticated causal empirical statements have been developed by social scientists, but all are in some sense the product of systems closure and the holding of certain variables constant.

The above brief outline raises a number of additional questions, three of which will be posed here. How may empirical statements be verified? Are there different kinds of theoretical statements? Where do the theoretical statements come from in the first place?

The sociologist Hubert M. Blalock (1961, 1969) has offered a means of translating empirical statements about variables whose values are *measurable* into statistically testable statements. For example, the above matrix expresses the relationship

$$E = f(A, B, D)$$

which it is possible to write in terms of a multiple regression model

$$E = \alpha - \beta_1 A + \beta_2 B + \beta_3 D + \varepsilon.$$

Here one takes $E$ to be the dependent variable; it depends upon three independent ones $(A, B, D)$ but is inversely related to $A$ and positively related to $B$ and $D$. The step from the empirical statement, which is embodied in the matrix of causal links, to the additive multiple regression equation is not a straightforward one because it requires that a number of assumptions be made. Causality and dependence are not synonymous terms, indeed the multiple regression equation does not show causation, only statistical association. Further, the general linear model, upon which multiple regression analysis is founded, requires that variables should have measurable values which must in turn obey certain statistical rules (see Johnston, 1978). This said, multivariate analysis does provide a means of establishing whether dependency links exist between variables, the signs of those links, and even their strengths; and since it is illogical to expect causation without dependence at least part of the verification process is achieved by its use.

Although variables may have observable values these need not necessarily be measurable. In consequence statistical testing is often an inappropriate means of verifying empirical statements. Many human characteristics which are legitimately the subject of theoretical statements are essentially qualitative. People's attitudes, superstitions, fears and desires are crucial aspects of any interpretation of their behaviour yet these are also rather nebulous attributes which defy both precise definition and measurement. Similarly, many of the 'world theories' of the social sciences contain variables which are themselves whole theoretical systems. The term *modernisation* epitomises this problem; it implies material, ideological, economic, social and political changes which are themselves the focus of complex theoretical statements. Many 'grand theories' of social change are expressions of belief rather than the source of testable empirical statements, yet it is certain that the quality of derivative theories would be much reduced without, for example, the imagination of Freud or the historical vision of Marx.

One way out of this maze would be to follow Robert K. Merton and attempt to develop *theories of the middle range*. These are not all-embracing unified theories which explain all observed regularities nor are they propositions of the most unsophisticated sort, rather they involve abstractions which are, 'close enough to observed data to be incorporated in propositions that permit empirical testing' (Merton, 1967: 39). These middle range theories, Merton advises, should be *special theories* applicable to limited conceptual ranges which can gradually be merged to create even more generalised grand theories. Once we readopt the empirical verifiability criterion for the construction of theories we are able to base the verification process on the foundation of statistical testing, provided we are willing to deal with dependence rather than cause and can measure as well as observe.

The problem of theory verification has, however, been cast in a rather different mould by the work of Karl Popper. He emphasises the role of falsification – theories are to be rejected if they can be falsified although only temporarily accepted if they cannot (see Popper, 1965; Harvey, 1969: 39; Gregory, 1978: 35). Theories must therefore be tested although it is not always clear whether as a result one has falsified or temporarily accepted. *A* causes *B* – the introduction of a family planning programme causes fertility to decline – is a theoretical statement which can be tested empirically, it is falsifiable, and indeed has been found to be false in the case of the Nigerian population (Caldwell and Caldwell, 1977; Caldwell and Ware, 1977), but in most instances the statement is valid, if not very helpful. To reject on the strength of one counter-example would be in this case to fly in the face of common sense, although even this objection seems to be controversial (Popper, 1972: 32–105). Popper's falsifiability criterion does pose new and practical problems for the social scientist, but its emphasis on how the mechanism of theory testing should work is nonetheless important.

Hay (1979) has taken a different tack by suggesting a means of assessing whether a theory is *useful* or not. Hay's criterion is based on a positive answer to the question, 'Does this theory contribute an explanation of a part of the observed variation which would otherwise remain obscure?'; in contrast to a question like, 'Does this theory *totally* explain the observed variation?' (Hay, 1979: 9).

The verification issue also has disciplinary and ideological elements. Contrast the views of development economist Leibenstein and sociologists Hindess and Hirst. Leibenstein (1954: 5) argues that, 'one of the primary objectives of theory construction is the careful formulation of a set of interrelated ideas from which it is possible to deduce meaningful theorems, by which we mean simply a body of conceivably refutable propositions'. This should lead to, 'one or more non-trivial theorems or propositions that can be put in such form as to be conceivably falsifiable by empirical research' (p. 6). But to Hindess and Hirst (1975: 3), 'Our constructions and arguments are theoretical and they can only be evaluated in theoretical terms – in terms, that is to say, of their rigour and theoretical coherence. They cannot be refuted by any empiricist recourse to the supposed "facts" of history' (but see Hindess and Hirst, 1977: 41).

The question 'How may empirical statements be verified?' is therefore an extremely complex one. Its answer depends upon the form of the theory under discussion (nature of the variables, etc.) and the rigour of the criteria one wishes to use, for instance, in translating cause into dependence. Answers to this question will vary depending on the kind of theory which is being constructed. Whilst the physical sciences tend to deal with deterministic theories the social sciences are usually relegated to the imprecision of probabilism. Empirical statements are really probability statements which rely for their verification on the observation of the joint occurrence of measurable variables. This is the inductive-statistical approach to theory building; it is the cornerstone of positivism in geography and as such it has become the target of many hammer-wielding critics.

Two points regularly made by these critics question, firstly, the logic of inductive reasoning that moves from the particular to the general usually by repeated observation or experiment (i.e. although in *n* trials *A* → *B* it need not necessarily do so in the *n* + 1th trial) and, secondly, that these inductive-statistical theories are counter-revolutionary. This point is made by Harvey (1973: 120–52) and illustrated by reference to the Negro ghetto. Most geographical theories relating to ghetto formation are of the inductive-statistical form. They attempt to identify the causal links which make ghettoes as they are, the association between the causal variables being implicitly assumed to be invariant and in consequence the ghetto being the only possible outcome. In contrast, a revolutionary theory seeks to establish a network of variable association which would lead to the destruction of the Negro ghetto. Emphasis is transferred from theorising over what *is* to that which *should be*; the ethical neutrality of interpretation is abandoned for the commitment to change.

The kinds of theories mentioned above are not exhaustive, but they do indicate the variety that is available to the theorist. His choice of approach will be conditioned by the particular problem at hand, by the tradition of his intellectual discipline and even by his own personality. However, the question 'Where do the theoretical statements come from in the first place?' still remains. As usual there is no one answer. Theoretical statements are rarely divinely inspired today. Most are born of intuition, speculation, or from the reconstituted debris of theories which have been rejected or only temporarily accepted, or have been thought insufficiently revolutionary. Theory construction, although somewhat diffuse, can follow certain general guidelines which counsel the listing of relevant variables drawn from any one of the above sources; their precise definition in an observable or, ideally, a measurable form; the elaboration of an empirical statement which will contain causal links between the variables; and, finally, the specification of a method of statistical testing, falsification or critical assessment which will enable one to judge the value of the particular theoretical statement as an intellectual tool.

The theories constructed and employed by population geographers have tended to be of the inductive-statistical variety and as such they have usually specified the dependency relationship between measurable variables. 'Migration between two places depends upon the characteristics of the interacting places, the intervening places and the potential migrants themselves' is one example in which once the characteristics have been defined precisely the resulting empirical statement can be tested using multivariate analysis (see Ch. 4). Such statements are typical of the use of middle-range theory in geographical studies. However, population geography has also taken to itself at least one grand world theory, namely that of the demographic transition which deals with changes in mortality, fertility and migration both over time and through space. It is a theory which is only partially testable because it not only contains statements about the past and the present, but it also predicts changes for the future (see Ch. 5). Verification also raises problems for behavioural theories in population geography. This category of theories deals with the association between attitudes, behaviour, and the organisation of society which is often observable in spatial patterns (i.e. at its simplest the $A \rightarrow B \rightarrow C$ causal chain). It has proved particularly valuable in studies of the motivation for migration and the links between prejudice, discrimination and spatial segregation, but because it deals with both psychological and sociological variables it tends to express the observable rather than the measurable. Nevertheless, these theories are crucial for the understanding of the behaviour patterns of individuals in population geography, even though they have to be critically assessed rather than statistically tested (see Ch. 4; White and Woods, 1980). During the 1970s the construction of revolutionary theories was begun in population geography. Most of these attempted to deal with the vexed problems of distribution of and access to resources, overpopulation and underemployment. Harvey (1974), for instance, has discussed the population-resources problem and the contribution to the debate made by Robert Malthus, David Ricardo and Karl Marx. Only Marx's dialectical materialism, Harvey argues, provides a dynamic analysis which is explicitly ideological. Here the emphasis is on altering the 'social organisation of scarcity' rather than reducing numbers. Although Harvey's (1974) analysis is destructive – it is unclear how the implications for distribution are to be effected – his work has placed both the supposition of ethical neutrality and the new-Malthusianism in sharp perspective and has cleared the way for a constructive revolutionary theory of population-resources.

It is evident from the above that population geographers in their attempt to construct theories have taken to heart Wrigley's advice that, 'Perhaps the most sensible attitude now as at other times to adopt towards the question of method in geography is to be eclectic – to use whichever method of analysis . . . appears to offer the best hope of dealing with the problem in hand' (Wrigley, 1965: 17).

The central question to be posed in this chapter is, 'How and why does population grow or decline?' The task of providing an answer will be approached with the aid of the guidelines described above. Controlling factors will be discussed, their definitions and association examined as the first stage in the construction of theories of how the size of populations change over time. However, growth or decline is not simply monotonic; there have been cycles of population change which will require separate theoretical treatment. Finally, we shall return to the work of those two most influential of nineteenth-century social scientists – Malthus and Marx – to see whether they were able to provide satisfactory answers to the question.

## Factors controlling population growth

Whether a population grows or declines is controlled by the relative balance of mortality, fertility and migration, which are in turn influenced by six groups of factors: biological, environmental, economic, social, political and technological (see Sauvy, 1969).

Biological factors are responsible for both a population's physiological and epidemiological characteristics. The maximum number of offspring a female can have is determined by biological factors, as is the sex ratio at birth. The age at menarche and menopause controls the number of years a female is potentially fecund, whilst the propotion of potentially fecund who are actually sterile is also largely the result of biological influences. Physiological variables establish maxima and minima between which the normal pattern of reproduction is to be found (see Parkes, 1976; Cavalli-Sforza and Bodmer, 1971).

The aetiology of diseases is an important influence on mortality patterns. Man's ability to first understand and then control the incidence and impact of infectious diseases have been relatively new-found skills. For example, bubonic plague ravaged the population of western Europe for over 300 years without being scientifically explained whilst in the nineteenth century the significance of tuberculosis declined seemingly without the aid of medical practice (McKeown, 1976). The dramatic impact of newly imported diseases on a population lacking any resistance has often been recorded, but it was particularly important as an adjunct to the colonisation of the New World (McNeill, 1977). Certain epidemic diseases have therefore had a significant influence in creating demographic crises, whilst the endemic nature of others in particular areas has led to the maintenance of relatively high mortality. Smallpox and influenza are typical of the former class of disease, cholera and malaria are examples of the latter.

Whilst the biological factor is particularly important for its influence on reproductive performance and mortality conditions, the environmental factor also influences the propensity to migrate. An examination of a map showing the distribution of world population makes it clear that there are some very negative areas for human settlement – mainly those areas experiencing very high or very low temperatures in the tropical and polar regions – but that most of the rest of the globe's land surface is well populated. Obviously there are differences between Kansas and Bengal, but there are economic, social and historical reasons for them and not simply environmental ones. Climatic fluctuations and the vicissitudes of weather have also had substantial indirect influences on population growth, particularly by generating short- and long-term crises in populated areas (Lamb, 1972, 1977: 423–549). Subsistence crises in particular have been related to harvest failures which are themselves a function of late springs, wet autumns or seasonal droughts (Le Roy Ladurie, 1972). During such crises mortality, especially amongst the young and the old, is usually heightened, rural emigration is accentuated and fecundity is often reduced.

The environmental factor is also responsible for a number of other hazards which can have locally devastating consequences. Of these flood and earthquake are possibly of most importance. The Hwang Ho, for instance, has gained a notorious reputation as 'China's sorrow' and despite centuries of canalisation 10 million people lost their homes and 50 milion were directly affected by the floods of 1931 (Kolb, 1971: 109). The environment imposes more subtle checks and barriers such as the limits on the growth of crop varieties which indirectly influence the level of rural population density attainable; rice and wheat cultivation provide a contrast on this point (Braudel, 1973: 66–120). The natural environment also restricts and channels the movement of people, information and the spread of technological innovations (Hägerstrand, 1967). In short, although one would not wish to return to using the concepts of the environmental determinists it is undoubtedly true that the character and vagaries of the natural environment do impose constraints, inflict unpredictable dangers and provide opportunities to which man has adapted himself, succumbed and taken advantage to varying degrees at different times and in different places.

That human societies are divided into 'classes', 'status groups' and 'parties' was one of the most important contentions of the German sociologist Max Weber (Gerth and Mills, 1948: 180–95). Although this basis for stratification has not been accepted wholeheartedly (see Runciman, 1968; Freund, 1968: 167) it is important in focusing attention on the economic, social and political dimensions of social organisation. Whilst no one, including Weber, would claim that these strata are mutually exclusive one is forced to recognise that the economic relationships which create classes – the disposal of goods or skills for the sake of income – are not the same as the ascriptive processes of prestige allocation which create distinctive status groups, or the mechanisms which determine the distribution of political power in society. Economic, social and political factors are essential, although interrelated, aspects of the wider demographic system and as such they must be treated as distinct and separate influences.

The time-honoured adage that population grows in response to the demand for labour has all the characteristics of an overworked half-truth: it is simple, eminently reasonable, yet presents only one side of the problem. Certainly, the massive demand for labour by the expanding American economy in the nineteenth century did lead to emigration from the Old World just as the industrial revolution in Britain created the opportunity for rural–urban migration, but there can be population growth without there being a demand for labour, whilst labour shortages can be chronic without inducing population growth or redistribution (Simon, 1977). The essence of the argument is that one is to regard fellow human beings, and even one's as yet unborn offspring, as though they are commodities – consumer durables, for instance – the supply of which will be adjusted to demand, even if this means the creation of population surpluses or shortages and the necessity for transport. Who one is will be very important here.

The economic factor also has a considerable, if indirect, influence on population growth through the standard of living. The inverse relationship between improving living standards and mortality has often been observed, particularly as it works through better diet, clothing and housing to ameliorate the worst excesses of those diseases which stem from undernourishment and poverty. Fundamental changes in the economic system associated with the agricultural, manufacturing and tertiary stages of development put strains on the structure of population as it adjusts from rural to urban and from manual to cerebral styles of life and modes of employment. These pressures may have influences on the desire to regulate fertility and certainly are important for generating both higher population turnover and longer distance 'betterment' migration.

It is not always easy to make a precise division between the

influence of economic and social factors. For example, although
'class' is usually defined in practice in terms of occupation, the resulting combinations are placed in a hierarchy defined by levels of prestige which makes them 'status groups'. The terms 'socio-economic
groups' or 'social classes' are therefore used to express the ideology
that sub-populations with similar occupations and degrees of prestige
have similar life styles and consumption patterns; have the same attitudes and behave in a similar fashion; and that inter-class is significantly greater than intra-class variation. The social class factor is
most important in accounting for differential population growth.
Mortality, fertility and migration patterns are all empirically related
to differences in class.

The pure social factor can be thought of as expressing a large
variety of variables, the cultural, religious, linguistic, ethnic and racial characteristics of a population which can all be important in giv-
ing it a distinctive demographic structure. Such attributes are often
used as signs of inferiority or superiority and are thus potential
means of self or imposed isolation, which can itself have a variety of
demographic and spatial expressions. American Negroes and central
European Jews, for example, are two populations with cultural and
ethnic identities which have been used to separate them from white
America and gentile Europe. The oppression involved has also established demographic distinctions between minority and majority. The
relative standing of women, the form of marriage pattern; the organisation of family groups, whether nuclear or extended; together
with the inheritance laws are all ways in which social roles are
formed and norms established. These roles and norms can mean the
difference between, on the one hand, a society having monogamous
marriages that are contracted when bride and groom are in their late
twenties or thirties, where nuclear families are formed which use
primogeniture as the rule for the transfer of property and, on the
other, a society with early marriage, extended families and partable
inheritance. The fertility of females in the first-mentioned society is
likely to be lower than that of those in the second, although which of
the contributing variables is the most important in creating the
tendency remains to be seen.

The social factor is naturally an extremely important influence in both fertility and migration patterns. It embodies the system
of values that groups use to order their day-to-day existence,
together with the more intangible interpretations they may place on
the reasons for that existence. Such group values place obligations
and constraints on members which lead them to behave in a more or

less similar way. For example, they force them to marry; have children, not too many but not too few; and to form separate households away from parents and in-laws. The individual may choose not to conform, but social ostracism might be the result of such defiance. In this context demographic behaviour can be regarded as but one part of the wider ambit of social behaviour.

The potential migrant is also susceptible to group pressures and restraints, since the mechanism of chain migration is an extremely powerful one which is even capable of generating a 'migrating mentality'. This force is not confined to truly nomadic populations, but is equally applicable to twentieth-century urban Americans and Caribbean islanders. In making migratory moves individuals often use their social networks to gather information about possible destinations. Once the decision to move has been made and the venue chosen they are also used to gain access to both accommodation and employment. The active migrants are then joined by passive migrants, who in time often establish an immigrant colony within which the values of the homeland are gradually adapted to the new social and economic environment with its consequent influence in changing demographic patterns. This sequence of events, whilst not universal, has been observed frequently enough to provide a valuable example of the close interrelationship between social, economic and demographic variables, all of which change during the sequence.

The political factor is also an expression of an assortment of variables which are connected with resulting population patterns and with other causal factors. Nationalism, for instance, cuts across geographical, cultural and class barriers; it creates sentiments of an all-pervading nature and establishes the most significant of economic units. The distinctive government policies enacted in these separate nation states are bound to influence the size and structure of the populations which inhabit them. Immigration can be controlled; settlement in the frontier encouraged; family planning promoted; a national health service established – all of which will alter the make-up and distribution of a country's population. Similarly, at the local scale planning authorities can radically influence the distribution of population by their control over the location of new employment, the housing market and the provision of education, medical and social services facilities. All of these components are regarded as a reflection of the distribution of power in society and its translation into a system of differential allocation of benefits, rewards and compensations.

The technological factor can be thought of as comprising

four aspects – invention, practical development, adoption and mass use – which are, to varying degrees, responses to stimuli from the other factors. Advances in medical, transport, agricultural and industrial technology have all contributed to rapid population growth in the past 200 years by, respectively, reducing mortality via chemotherapy; allowing large-scale international migration by passenger ship and train; by preventing subsistence crises; and by improving living standards. Medical advances in the field of oral contraception technology have meant that birth control can now be practised effectively by the many millions of women who wish to space out their children's births and to limit their completed family size. However, these developments have not been ubiquitous nor have they always been wholly beneficial. The ever-widening gap between the technologically advanced Western states and those in the Third World means that health services are differentially distributed and there are wide disparities in living standards, both having important implications for long-term, rapid population growth.

It will be apparent from the above that these six factors are by no means independent of one another. New contraceptive methods will not be widely used and thus have an impact in reducing fertility, unless there are favourable social and economic conditions for their adoption, such that available methods are seen as the means of obtaining a desirable objective. Although long-distance migration is often spurred on by economic motives its mechanism is very much a behavioural one with social, political and even psychological components. As a final example, it can be shown that mortality responds to what are often chance variations in the biological and environmental factors, but it can also be affected by man's attempts to directly lengthen his average lifespan and by the way in which he organises his socio-economic environment.

A summary outline of part of the demographic system is shown in Fig. 1.1. The dashed lines are used to symbolise the possibility that those boxes within them are also associated, but in some unspecified manner, whilst the sets of straight lines show causal links from, firstly, the factor combination box and, secondly, from the purely demographic factors to the 'population growth and distribution' box. (Frederiksen (1969), Mabogunje (1970) and Schofield (1976) provide additional examples of demographic systems.)

Figure 1.1 represents the first and most easily completed stage in the construction of theoretical statements in population geography. The second stage requires one to be more precise about

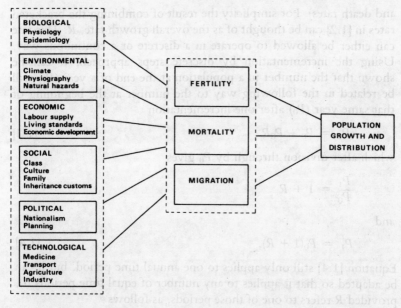

**Fig. 1.1** Demographic relationships

the variables concerned and to specify the form of the causal links involved. This stage can be aided by recourse to the inductive approach which helps to elaborate both forms of population growth and the processes likely to be involved. Firstly, it addresses itself to the 'how does population grow?' problem and then, secondly, to 'what processes are involved in that growth?'

## The form of population growth

The basic demographic equation tells us that a population will change between time $t$ and $t + n$ because of the addition of the number of births and immigrants and the subtraction of deaths and emigrants. Thus

$$P_{t+n} = P_t + B_{t,t+n} - D_{t,t+n} + IM_{t,t+n} - EM_{t,t+n}. \qquad [1.1]$$

If a single time period is considered, say a calendar year, then the size of a population will change from $P_0$ to $P_1$ in the following way

$$P_1 = P_0 + P_0 (b - d + im - em) \qquad [1.2]$$

where $b$, $d$, $im$ and $em$ are birth, death, immigration and emigration rates respectively ($b$ and $d$ in parts per 1,000 would be the crude birth and death rates). For simplicity the result of combining the bracketed rates in [1.2] can be thought of as the overall growth rate, $R$. This rate can either be allowed to operate in a discrete or a continuous way. Using the incrementation by discrete steps approach, it can be shown that the number in a population at the end of a year ($P_1$) will be related in the following way to the number at the beginning of that same year ($P_0$) after one incrementation

$$P_1 = P_0 + P_0R \qquad [1.3]$$

which after division through by $P_0$ gives

$$\frac{P_1}{P_0} = 1 + R$$

and

$$P_1 = P_0(1 + R). \qquad [1.4]$$

Equation [1.4] still only applies to one annual time period, but it can be adapted so that it applies to any number of equal time periods ($t$), provided $R$ refers to one of those periods, as follows

$$P_t = P_0(1 + R)^t \qquad [1.5]$$

and, for example,

$$P_{2000} = P_{1980} (1 + R)^{20}.$$

$R$ may be found from

$$(1 + R) = t\sqrt{\frac{P_t}{P_0}} \qquad [1.6]$$

or

$$\log_e(1 + R) = \frac{\log_e\frac{P_t}{P_0}}{t}. \qquad [1.7]$$

The relationship shown in [1.4] deals with growth, or decline if $R$ is negative, in discrete and equal time periods, but it is more realistic to treat time in its continuous form. Population change over time could then be regarded as a function of population size itself. Using the language of calculus

$$\frac{\delta P}{\delta t} = f(P)$$

which expands to the power series

$$\frac{\delta P}{\delta t} = a + bP + cP^2 + dP^3 + \ldots$$

and since when $P$ is 0, a is also 0

$$\frac{\delta P}{\delta t} = bP + cP^2 + dP^3 + \ldots \qquad [1.8]$$

By considering only the first and most simple term one obtains

$$\frac{\delta P}{\delta t} = bP$$

and

$$\frac{\delta P}{P} = b\delta t$$

integrating both sides

$$\int \frac{\delta P}{P} = \int b\delta t$$

that is

$$\log_e P = Rt + C$$

where $C$ is the constant of integration.
Taking exponents gives

$$\exp(\log_e P) = \exp(bt + C)$$

and     $P = e^{bt}$.

This is a general expression of unlimited exponential growth which can easily be made specific to population change between time zero and time $t$ by introducing $P_0$ and $P_t$ and by substituting R for b. Therefore

$$P_t = P_0 e^{Rt} \qquad [1.9]$$

or

$$\log_e P_t = \log_e P_0 + Rt \qquad [1.10]$$

and

$$R = \frac{\log_e \dfrac{P_t}{P_0}}{t} \qquad [1.11]$$

The expression in [1.9] is that of exponential growth. A special case of this growth rule gives a geometrical series

$$P_t = P_0 e^{(\log_e R)t} \qquad [1.12]$$

which is

$$P_t = P_0 R^t. \tag{1.13}$$

The incremental and continuous rates which are found by [1.7] and [1.11] will not give precisely the same result when similar $P_0$, $P_t$ and $t$ values are substituted. For example, if $P_0$ is 10,000, $P_t$ is 50,000 and $t$ is 10 then the discrete growth rate is 0·1746 and the continuous rate is 0·1609; whilst the former would be required for incremental growth the latter would be sufficient if growth were continuous.

The process of population growth is therefore a matter of the balance between $b$, $d$, $im$ and $em$ in [1.2] which creates the overall growth rate, $R$. This point, together with its various consequences, can be illustrated by considering the growth potential of a number of populations. Table 1.1 gives ten cases and Fig. 1.2 shows the effect of these $Rs$ over 200 time periods when $P_0$ is set at 100 and $im - em$ is assumed to equal zero. Although the USA (1970s) and the Sweden (1788–92) populations have similarly low growth rates these are the result of combining very different fertility and mortality experiences; birth and death rates are, respectively, low and high. England and Wales (1861) provides an example of what can happen if the death rate falls. The rate of world population growth was estimated to be 1·9 per cent *per annum* in the 1970s, which would give a doubling time of 36 years. India (1960s) Kenya and Mexico (1970s) have growth rates substantially higher than the world's $R$ of 0·0190, but

**Table 1.1** Examples of population growth rates, $R$

| Population (1) | CBR* (2) | CDR* (3) | $R$† (4) |
|---|---|---|---|
| USA, 1970s | 14·7 | 8·9 | 0·0058 |
| Sweden, 1788–92 | 33·6 | 27·7 | 0·0059 |
| Australia, 1970s | 17·3 | 8·1 | 0·0092 |
| England and Wales, 1861 | 34·6 | 21·6 | 0·0130 |
| World, 1970s | 32·0 | 13·0 | 0·0190 |
| India, 1960s | 42·0 | 18·6 | 0·0234 |
| Kenya, 1970s | 48·7 | 16·0 | 0·0327 |
| Mexico, 1970s | 42·0 | 8·6 | 0·0334 |
| Doubling every 100 years | — | — | 0·0069 |
| Doubling every 25 years | — | — | 0·0277 |

* The crude birth rate ($b \times 1,000$) and the crude death rate ($d \times 1,000$)
† Assuming that $im - em = 0$
*Data sources*: United Nations *Demographic Yearbooks*; Keyfitz and Flieger (1968); Cassen and Dyson (1976)

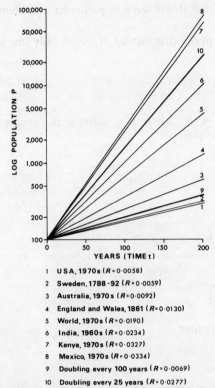

**Fig. 1.2** Population growth curves
*Data sources*: United Nations *Demographic Yearbooks*; Keyfitz and Flieger (1968)

they are the result of different combinations of birth and death rates. India's $R$ is lower because the death rate is higher, whilst although Kenya's $R$ is the highest of the three populations its death rate is also higher than that of Mexico, so that Mexico's $R$ leads to the most rapid population growth. The implications of these different $R$s remaining constant for 200 years are made clear in Fig. 1.2 where the straight line semi-logarithmic plots denote exponential increase.

The crucial point, however, is that $R$ is unlikely to remain constant for long periods. Will the population of the world in the year 2000 be 6,380 millions? The population of Sweden in 1970 was 8,076,903 and not 6,249,929; that of England and Wales in 1971 was 48,749,575 and not 84,127,478; in the former $R$ increased at some stage in the preceding 180 years and in the latter $R$ declined between 1861 and 1971. Whilst $R$ cannot simply be regarded as constant over time it is quite possible that it will vary in particular and identifiable ways.

For example, suppose that instead of taking only one term in [1.8] two are considered

$$\frac{\delta P}{\delta t} = bP + cP^2.$$

If $c$ is allowed to equal $-b/K$, where $K$ is some upper asymptote to which population grows, then

$$\frac{\delta P}{\delta t} = bP - \frac{bP^2}{K}$$

and

$$\frac{\delta P}{\delta t} = bP\left(1 - \frac{P}{K}\right)$$

or

$$\frac{\delta P}{\delta t} = bP\left(\frac{K - P}{K}\right).$$

After integration this becomes

$$P = \frac{K}{1 + e^{-bt}}$$

which is a general equation expressing rapid growth initially, but as $P$ tends towards $K$ the rate of growth is reduced until it reaches zero. It can be made both specific and consistent with the terms already used by introducing $P_0$ and $P_t$ and by substituting $R$ for b. Thus

$$P_t = \frac{K}{1 + P_0 e^{-Rt}} \qquad [1.14]$$

This equation, which expresses what is known as *logistic growth*, was originally derived by the Belgian scientist Pierre-Francois Verhulst (1804–49), but its wide-scale use for both theoretical and empirical purposes probably owes more to its rediscovery by Pearl and Reed (1920), Pearl (1925), Lotka (1925) and Yule (1925). Its importance lies in its summary of the effects of density dependence. Unlike [1.9], [1.14] does not show $R$ to be constant over time; $\delta P/\delta t$ is affected by the size of $P$ in the latter, but not in the former, with the result that population growth is restrained as $P$ approaches some critical size ($K$ in [1.14]). $R$ is still the result of $(b - d + im - em)$, but as $P$ rises $b$ and $im$ may be reduced, while $d$ and $em$ are increased.

Two questions stem from these observations. How valuable is the logistic growth curve in describing population change over time? The second question, on the processes involved in such growth, will be tackled in the next section. The answer to the first question depends upon which particular population is under examination. Experiments with various animal populations, especially the fruit fly *Drosophila melanogaster* have shown that [1.14] is very useful because under experimental conditions *im* = *em* = 0, the environment remains constant and, in consequence, *b* and *d* have to change as *P*, and thus population density, increases. In *Drosophila melanogaster* responses seem to include a reduction in the number of eggs laid per female and increased adult mortality as access to food becomes restricted by numbers (see Hutchinson, 1978: 21–33). Although the results of similar experiments with *Homo sapiens* would be interesting, fortunately none has been attempted. Over the past 200 years the growth of a number of national populations has tended to be distinctively logistic in form. Figure 1.3 shows, for example, semi-logarithmic plots of population growth in the USA since 1970 and Sweden and Japan since 1750. None of the curves is simply a straight line as they would be if exponential growth were in operation. Rather, the curve for the USA shows increase that is at first rapid, but which ultimately begins to fall off. This is the typical pattern expected from logistic growth.

Employing a procedure outlined by Croxton, Cowden and Klein (1968: 274–80; De Sapio, 1976: 416–55 gives alternative methods) it is possible to fit a general curve to the one for the USA shown in Fig. 1.3. Croxton *et al.* rewrite [1.14] in the following way

$$P_t = \frac{K}{1 + 10^{(\delta + \beta t)}} \qquad [1.15]$$

which with 1800 as the origin, *t* expressed in units of 10 years and *K* in millions, gives

$$P_t = \frac{229}{1 + 10^{(3.7411 - 0.3085t)}} \qquad [1.16]$$

Equation [1.16] predicts that the population of the USA in 2000 will be 211 millions, which seems unlikely since that enumerated in 1970 was 204 millions. Repeated attempts to fit the logistic curve to American population growth have always shown that estimates of *K* were too low and that shown in [1.16] seems to be no exception. However, it cannot be denied that the logistic growth curve does give a better summary of most numerical changes in hu-

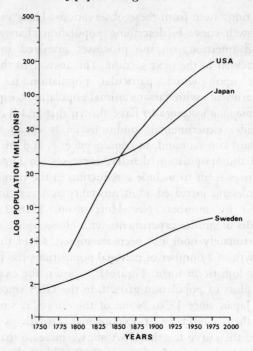

**Fig. 1.3** Population growth curves for Sweden, Japan and the USA

*Data sources*: Mitchell (1975: 23); United States Bureau of the Census (1975: 8); Taeuber (1958); United Nations *Demographic Yearbooks*

man population over time; it is certainly more realistic than the exponential growth curve, merely because it also allows for change in the rate of growth.

The curve for Sweden shown in Fig. 1.3 does not appear to conform to one simple logistic pattern, nor does it quite match the exponential. That for Japan shows both a period of demographic stagnation and one of exponential growth. There is obviously a need for a set of growth curve models which will allow *R* to vary, but in a variety of predetermined ways. Exponential and logistic growth are merely two of the more simple forms which could be taken by population growth over time.

## The process of population growth

The second question that needs to be asked is, 'What mechanisms are responsible for population growth?' The inductive approach is at its most vulnerable here because of the equifinality problem. Given that a logistic curve fits the growth of a particular population over time, one is left to infer what processes could have caused that pattern to be established, and since a number of different processes can lead to similar outcomes it is difficult to be certain whether the causes isolated are in fact the most important. Where experimentation is possible, as in the case of *Drosophila melanogaster* mentioned above, one may be reasonably certain what mechanisms are at work because all the variables involved can be controlled and observation is relatively straightforward. Most animal populations pose far greater interpretative problems than *Drosophila*, whilst human populations represent the most complex of demographic systems.

The important mechanisms controlling $R$ for animal populations have been outlined by Lack (1954, 1966) and Clark *et al.* (1967: 33–56). Following Lack (1966: 2–3) we may divide these into three. First, density-dependent factors are responsible for the maintenance of a degree of balance in numbers by leading to changes in the reproductive rate; the death rate, due to food shortages, predation or disease; and even to self-regulating behaviour associated with territoriality. Environmental change may establish new levels of $K$ which will in turn influence these density-dependent factors to check $R$ or allow it to increase. Such concepts are associated with the name of their most persistent advocate. A. J. Nicholson, but they have been summarised in a most succinct form by Lack himself. 'Birds and other animals can increase in numbers with great rapidity but are usually held drastically in check. Nearly all animal populations fluctuate irregularly between very restricted limits. Their comparative stability must be due to controlling factors which are density-dependent' (Lack, 1954: 20). Secondly, there are density-independent factors which are linked with short-term random changes in, for example, weather patterns. If these factors are of prime importance in regulating growth, as Andrewartha and Birch (1954) have argued, then the ability of members of a population to change the conditions in which they live by migration also becomes significant. Thirdly, density-dependent factors are taken to be the most important, but density itself is not regarded as beyond the control of certain animals which, by means of spatial dispersion and constraints on breeding, regulate their numbers below the limit set by food supply. The existence of social behaviour capable of such regulation has been propounded by Wynne-Edwards (1962, 1965). These three sets of factor combinations embody the range of influences which control animal population numbers. They all work through the balance of $(b - d + im - em)$, but lay relatively greater emphasis on $b$, $d$ or $im$ and $em$; and on external controls or induced adaptation. In Nicholson's theory $d$ is of prime regulatory importance and is determined by food supply, although $b$ can also vary; for Andrewartha and Birch $d$ is randomly influenced; whilst for Wynne-Edwards $b$ can be lowered so that $d$ will not oscillate violently.

Lack's (1966) own studies of bird populations have tended to show that the most important control on them is density-dependent mortality and that starvation outside the breeding season is particularly significant in this context. He comments that, 'when a bird is introduced to a new region and becomes established there it at first increases rapidly, which shows that it is capable of rapid increase, but eventually its numbers level off; which shows that the capacity for increase has been checked, evidently by factors which operate more strongly at higher than lower densities of population. Thereafter the introduced species, like those native to the region, tends to fluctuate, in most cases irregularly, between limits that are small compared with what is theoretically possible' (Lack, 1966: 3). Wynne-Edwards's ideas are treated with some sceptism and whilst random shocks can obviously have a great influence on numbers in the short-term it is pressure on food resources that is the dominant long-term regulator of population size. In general, therefore, density-dependent $d$ is the most important control on the size of animal populations so that as $P_t$ tends towards $K$, when $P_t < K$, $d$ will be increased and $R$ will be diminished. In practice it is also possible for $P_t > K$, in which case $d$ will remain high and $R$ will be negative until $P_t \leqslant K$.

Although this description of animal population does not do full justice to the subtleties of the matter it nonetheless serves to illustrate how it is possible for such populations to approximate the pattern of logistic growth through the mechanism explicit in the causal chain: environment (food supply) $\rightarrow K \rightarrow R$. What are the processes operating in human populations? For example, why has the growth of the American population apparently approximated to the logistic form?

The birth, death and migration rates for the American population are shown in Fig. 1.4 together with $R$. They reveal that in this particular case net immigration has been a most important contributor to the rate of population growth, but that variations in both $b$ and $d$ have also had a substantial influence on $R$. (Bogue (1969: 127–46) provides a concise outline of the development of America's population, but see also the papers reprinted in Vinovskis

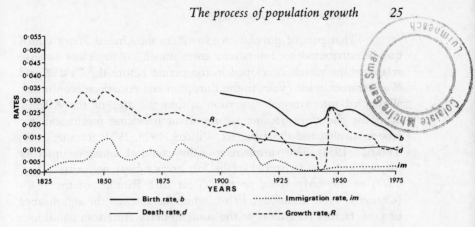

**Fig. 1.4** Birth, death, immigration and growth rates for the USA
*Data sources*: United States Bureau of the Census (1975); United Nations *Demographic Yearbooks*

(1979).) During the late nineteenth and twentieth centuries the death rate fell persistently and significantly while the birth rate also fell to a low point in the 1930s, since which time it has oscillated about a relatively low level. Is this the result of density-dependent controls? In a sense one could argue that the immigration restrictions imposed in the 1920s were a response to perceived overcrowding, but the changes in mortality and fertility which are reflected in *d* and *b* certainly were not. Mortality fell because the private and public health of the population was improved, diet became better balanced and medical science was able to both cure and prevent many fatal illnesses (Hermalin, 1966; Rao, 1973; Preston, Keyfitz and Schoen, 1972). The variables influencing the pattern of changing fertility, which is only partially reflected by *b* in Fig. 1.4, are far more difficult to specify, but declining child and then infant mortality, rising economic and social aspirations, together with increased availability and effectiveness of birth control methods are factors which are normally thought to be influential (Whelpton, Campbell and Patterson, 1966; Ryder, 1969; Rindfuss and Sweet, 1977). The impetus to establish a low fertility pattern was more likely to have been the recent acquisition and desire to retain material benefits, than the pressure of poverty resulting from a clash between population numbers and resources. Once low fertility had been established then temporal and spatial patterns could emerge which were the product of short-term economic fluctuations. (These points will be taken up in the following section and in Ch. 3.)

That part of population growth in the United States which can be attributed to migration, owes much to the close inverse relationships which developed in the period before the First World War between trade cycles in the European and American economies. Westward international migration within the area of the Atlantic economy therefore became an important balancing mechanism for labour surplus and shortage (see Willcox, 1929, 1931; Jerome, 1926; Thomas, 1954). This simple relationship could of course be upset by major European disasters like the 'last great subsistence crisis' (Post, 1977) of the early 1800s or the 'Great Irish Famine' of the 1840s (Cousens, 1960; Kennedy, 1976), which heightened the significance of push factors regardless of the contemporary American condition. The growth of the American population since 1790 is ultimately a matter of restrictions imposed on massive immigration; voluntary restraints applied to marital fertility; and medical control being developed and adapted for the limitation of mortality. The combined effects of these restrictions, restraints and controls began to be felt in the 1920s and 1930s when, as Fig. 1.4 shows, $R$ first started to decline. It is this reduction in $R$ through lower $d$, $b$ and $im$ that gives America's population curve its logistic form. Although the processes involved in establishing this time series are very complex, it cannot be reasonably argued that they involve a true density-dependent, $K$-related element. The United States case is therefore a prime example of how the pattern of growth over time can appear to take a form which, if it had been related to another population, would have implied completely different causal processes.

The example of Japanese population increase, which is also illustrated in Fig. 1.3, raises similar problems. The case seems to be a simple one of the exponential growth of a population that in the eighteenth and early nineteenth century was static. However, the processes lying behind this pattern are extremely difficult to unravel. Figure 1.5 shows, in generalised form, the rates $b$, $d$ and $R$ for Japan during the period 1875–1975. Whilst $R$, which summarises ($b - d + im - em$), varies quite markedly over the hundred years it does so within narrow bounds, and when rates are averaged out over 25 year periods an approximately constant value of $R$ is obtained. The birth and death rates by contrast reveal rather different trends. The Japanese birth rate increased from the 1870s to the 1920s and then began to fall. The post-war 'baby boom' was only a temporary reversal and the most dramatic decline in $b$ occurred during the 1950s. The death rate shows a three-stage pattern – increase, plateau, decrease – in which the most rapid change has occurred since the 1920s.

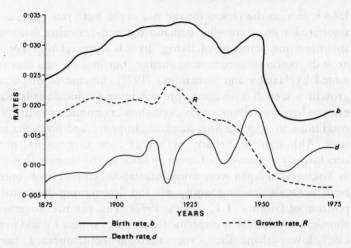

**Fig. 1.5** Birth, death and growth rates for Japan
*Data sources*: Taeuber (1958); United Nations *Demographic Yearbooks*

Figure 1.5 only applies to the years since 1875, because it was only after the Meiji Restoration of 1868 that reasonably reliable vital statistics were registered on a systematic and comprehensive basis. In the Tokugawa era (1600–1868) national surveys of the commoner population were made, but estimates of birth and death rates have to rely solely on local village population registers. The family reconstitution studies which have used these registers have tended to show that in the eighteenth and the first half of the nineteenth centuries *b* and *d* both ranged from 0·015 to 0·030, while *b* occasionally exceeded 0·040 (see, for example, Hanley and Yamamura, 1977: 211; T.C. Smith, 1977: 40). The low levels of *b* and *d* when compared with those shown in Fig. 1.5 suggest that the Tokugawa era in pre-industrial Japan was significantly different from the Meiji, since birth and death rates were both lower and tended to balance one another out (hence the shape of the curve for Japan in Fig. 1.3). However, in the Meiji period birth and death rates were rising, but with *b* always higher than *d*. Since the 1930s and 1940s *d* and then *b* have both fallen back to, and in the case of *d* well below, average Tokugawan levels, even though overall values of *R* have not been altered by these modern developments.

Interpretations of the curves for *b* and *d* are many and various. One traditional theory stresses the impact of economic stagnation and famine in Tokugawan Japan which it links with the practices of abortion and infanticide. The rapid economic growth after

1868 is seen as the reason for the rise in the birth rate because it was associated with a growing demand for non-agricultural labour and an improving standard of living. In this interpretation population growth responds to economic change, but in a counter-theory presented by Hanley and Yamamura (1977) the control of population growth is seen as a necessary pre-condition for industrialisation, because when it combines with even slow economic growth it creates conditions in which living standards improve and *per capita* income rises. Although the validity of one of these theories has not been conclusively demonstrated there is evidence to suggest that villages in Tokugawan Japan were using infanticide as a means of controlling birth intervals, limiting family size and determining the sexual composition of families (T.C. Smith, 1977). This practice, together with abortion, meant that age-specific fertility was similar to, and in many-cases lower than, that experienced in contemporary European villages, where age at marriage was the prime indirect regulator of fertility. Social behaviour of this kind was certainly an important contributory factor in keeping the Japanese population static for over a hundred years.

Theories to account for the rising and falling curves of the trajectory are less controversial. Certainly the economic expansion of the Meiji period did permit controls to be relaxed and the birth rate to rise, whilst in the 1920s and 1930s government disapproval of birth control measures meant that the relatively high levels of $b$ which had been reached would be temporarily maintained. Since the Second World War the birth rate has declined dramatically, due partly to the legalisation of abortion in 1948, but also to the increased availability of birth control methods and the growing desire for smaller families which accompanied general prosperity and female involvement in the labour force (Taeuber, 1960; Mosk, 1977, 1979).

The case of Japanese population growth over the last 200 years is therefore an interesting one, for the multiplicity of processes that contributed to the static and exponential stages are intractable and in consequence not fully understood. It illustrates well the point that population growth can remain exponential ($R$ is virtually constant) when $b$ and $d$ are both increasing, both static, and both declining. Unlike the American case, international migration has not been of great importance nor has there been an initial period of rising birth and death rates. However, there are distinct similarities in the way $d$ has changed since the 1930s.

The American and Japanese examples are only two from a large number that could be used to show the different forms of population change over time and to illustrate the plethora of mechanisms that create those changes. They demonstrate that any general answer to the question, 'How and why do populations grow or decline?' is likely to be only a partial one; that location in time and space make the experiences of individual human populations unique; and that whilst it might be possible to say 'how' the combination $(b - d + im - em)$ has given rise to $R$, theories that treat the 'why' element of the question are as yet simple in structure and relatively weak in explanatory power. Nevertheless, one is forced to face the additional problem that the representations of population change over time shown, for example in Fig. 1.3, are themselves merely parts of much larger series which contain not one but a group of cycles. The next section considers examples of these growth cycles and addresses itself to their general form and the processes that have led to their creation.

## Population growth cycles

Following the work of J. D. Durand it is usual to represent the growth of world population by a smooth curve which in its final stage is exponential in form. However, it is more likely that world population has increased in a series of cycles and that at times there has been actual decline. Figure 1.6 shows world population growth since 400 BC according to Durand's (1967; see also Durand, 1977) estimates and compares them with those made by Biraben (1979). Similar patterns of cyclical growth have been illustrated by McEvedy and Jones (1978: 342–51) in their *Atlas of World Population History*. They identify three cycles which they call *primary* (10,000 BC–AD 500), *medieval* (500–1400) and *modernisation* (post-1400). The years 500 and 1400 are used to symbolise periods of population decline when, McEvedy and Jones suggest, population growth had reached and even exceeded some upper limit which had in consequence led to the establishment of a dramatically higher level of mortality. The medieval prayer *A bello, fame, et peste libera nos Domine* reveals three of the ways in which these periods of crisis manifest themselves: war, famine and plague. The coincidence of events in Europe and China, together with the high proportion of the world total which the combined population of those two regions comprised, has tended to give the course of world population growth this distinctively cyclical form. (The form and cause of the *modernisation* growth cycle will be discussed more fully in Ch. 5.)

The growth of population in England and Wales also pro-

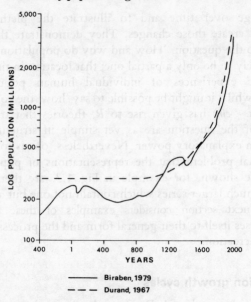

**Fig. 1.6** World population growth curves
*Data sources*: Durand (1967); Biraben (1979)

vides an example of cyclical change. Figure 1.7 shows the time series
that can be created from a variety of estimates for the period since
1250, some of which are of dubious reliability. Hatcher (1977: 71),
for instance, estimates that the population in 1300 was similar to that
in 1650, that is about 5·5 millions. Three cycles are also in evidence
here. The first ends around 1400; the second continues until the
eighteenth century; and we are still in the third today. Since we can
assume that in general *im* = *em* and if it does not then *im* < *em* the
form of the curve in Fig. 1.7 must largely be the result of the balance
between birth and death rates (*R* = *b* − *d*). Apart from the latter half
of the fourteenth century, the curve consists of alternating periods
when *R* is approximately zero and when *R* is well in excess of zero −
that is, it may be looked on as a series of connected logistic growth
curves each of which represents a cycle.

In theory there are four main ways in which a logistic type
cycle can occur. These are shown in Fig. 1.8. The birth rate remains
static while the death rate declines and then increases (Fig. 1.8a); *b*
increases followed by *d* (Fig. 1.8b); *d* declines and is followed by *b*
(Fig. 1.8c); and *b* increases and then declines while *d* remains static
(Fig. 1.8d). The variants in Fig. 1.8 treat cases where *b* = *d* at the

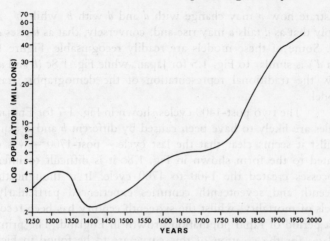

**Fig. 1.7** Population growth curve for England and Wales
*Data sources*: Wrigley (1969: 78); Lee (1973: 606); Tranter (1973: 41 -2); *Population Censuses of England and Wales, 1801 to 1971*

beginning and at the end of the cycle, but in Figs. 1.8a and 1.8d, *b* and *d* resume the same level at the end as they had at the beginning, whilst in Figs. 1.8b and 1.8c new levels are reached after the *b* = *d* stage. Several variations are possible on these four basic patterns; four are shown in Figs. 1.8a and 1.8d. Here *b'* and *d'* respectively

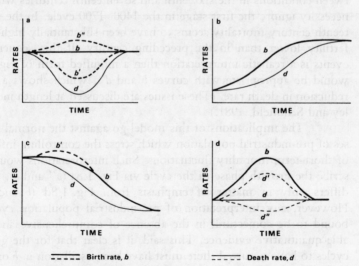

- - - - Birth rate, *b*      - - - - Death rate, *d*

**Fig. 1.8** Population growth cycles
*Source*: based on Cowgill (1949)

illustrate how *b* may change with *d* and *d* with *b*, while *b''* and *d''* imply that as *d* falls *b* may rise and, conversely, that as *b* rises *d'* may fall. Some of these models are readily recognisable. Figure 1.8d (*b* and *d'*) is similar to Fig. 1.5 for Japan, while Fig. 1.8c (*b* and *d*) is by now the traditional representation of the demographic transition model.

The two post-1400 cycles shown in Fig. 1.7 for England and Wales are likely to have been caused by different *b* and *d* sequences. Whilst it seems clear that the last cycle – post-1700 – was closely related to the form shown in Fig. 1.8c it is difficult to infer what processes created the 1400 to 1700 cycle. It is thought that the fifteenth and seventeenth centuries experienced particularly high levels of mortality, whilst the sixteenth century has been recognised as a period of rapid population growth in England. The prime candidates for the creation of this curve are to be found in Figs. 1.8a and 1.8d. During the sixteenth century the death rate may have fallen to a relatively lower level and life expectancy at birth may have been in the low forties, but there are also grounds for arguing that the birth rate rose to give a mean completed family size for women married before age 25 of over seven. The evidence for these assertions comes mainly from the results of family reconstitution studies which use Anglican parish registers for individual villages (see, for example, Wrigley, 1966a, 1972a). They rely on comparisons between conditions in the sixteenth and seventeenth centuries which of necessity ignore the first stage in the 1400–1700 cycle. In the seventeenth century mortality seems to have been substantially higher and fertility lower than in the preceding century. If this sequence of events is a realistic interpretation then a modified form of Fig. 1.8d would be appropriate with curves *b* and *d''*, which shows a slight reduction in death rate. (These issues are discussed at length in Wrigley and Schofield, 1981.)

The implications of this model go against the normal analyses of pre-industrial population which stress the controlling influence of short-term mortality fluctuations. Such interpretations would describe the growth phase of the cycle via Fig. 1.8a (*b''* and *d*), which differs only in matter of emphasis from Fig. 1.8d (*b* and *d''*). However, any interpretation of pre-industrial population cycles is bound to be conjectural in the absence of comprehensive and reliable quantitative evidence. This said, it is clear that for the growth cycles to have occurred there must have been oscillation in *b* or *d*, or both. There must have been stretches of good years when plague and other epidemic diseases were not as rife and periods of good harvests when agricultural improvements were made and when new land was brought into cultivation, when the production of food was adequate or even abundant. It would appear that the thirteenth and sixteenth centuries in England and Wales were such times. These 'times of feast' were also suitable for earlier marriages which in turn meant that the birth rate increased. The delaying of first marriages for females to the mid- or late-twenties was one of the most effective means of social control that pre-industrial societies could exert on their fertility and as is becoming increasingly more obvious, one which was used to good effect in western Europe from at least the sixteenth century onwards (see R. M. Smith, 1978; and more generally Dupâquier, 1979).

The 1400–1700 population growth cycle in England and Wales is, therefore, a difficult one to explain. The mechanisms which caused its first and third stages were essentially dominated by high death rates with lower life expectancy. Although the second stage was partly a response to falling $d$, it was also, and perhaps most significantly, influenced by rising $b$. The form and underlying mechanism of the post-1700 cycle are fundamentally different. In this cycle new levels of fertility and mortality have been reached in the twentieth century which are inconceivable in any former period. However, even the mechanisms underlying these changes are highly controversial.

The course of change in birth and death rates since vital registration began in 1837 is known. The pattern appears to be similar to that of Fig. 1.8c, but it has been suggested that the period of rapid population growth which began in England and Wales in about 1750 was induced by a rise in the birth rate, which would mean that the whole cycle could be represented by Fig. 1.8d ($b$ and $d'$). The major protagonists for this point of view have been Krause (1967, 1969) and Habakkuk (1972). Their argument is that the process of industrialisation and economic expansion led to a demand for labour which in turn created conditions favourable to a reduction in the age at first marriage and hence a rise in the birth rate. Krause (1969: 127) refers to the view that the death rate declined in late eighteenth-century England as a 'statistical mirage', but there are many who, following G. T. Griffith (1926), have taken the view that the current cycle of population growth in England and Wales was initiated mainly by a fall in the death rate. Few would now agree wholeheartedly with Griffith that this secular decline was linked with medical advances and the establishment of hospitals. Razzell (1965) argues that inoculation against smallpox led to a significant mortality decline, whilst McKeown and Brown (1955) stress the importance of rising living standards and improvements in diet (see also Razzell, 1974). Whilst it seems that a major cause of the take-off of population growth in this period was declining $d$, a view endorsed by Lee's (1974, 1978) demographic simulations, it is also more than likely that $b$ rose at the same time, a point which has emerged from reverse projections undertaken by members of the Cambridge Group for the History of Population and Social Structure (Wrigley and Schofield, 1981). In these circumstances it is appropriate to represent the pattern of change by Fig. 1.8c ($b'$ and $d$).

If the above account of the pre-vital registration phase of the current population growth cycle is based on estimates which are made like 'bricks without straw', as Glass (1965a) has remarked, then the construction of theories to explain the post-1837 aspect of the cycle ought to be more straightforward. It is not. We may follow McKeown (1976, 1978) and argue that mortality fell in the second-half of the nineteenth century largely because of improvements in living standards and particulary diet which affected the incidence of such infectious diseases as tuberculosis, but it must be remembered that only 30 per cent of the decline in mortality from 1848–54 to 1971 occurred before 1901 (Woods, 1979: 69), and that for certain groups, particularly infants, mortality did not even begin its secular decline until the twentieth century. Our analysis of mortality decline in England and Wales, together with that already mentioned, must take into account the important roles of chemotherapy, advances in surgery and anaesthetics, and the development of efficient medical institutions for the cure and prevention of illness. These advances have had a major impact on the population of Western scientifically advanced countries since the first advances were made in germ theory in the 1880s. By the 1980s in England and Wales life expectancy is approaching its biological maximum, so that mortality is likely to remain extremely low in the future.

Theories to account for the decline of fertility in England and Wales must be highly sophisticated to be at all realistic. Most of those put forward have stressed one or more of the following: the significance of relative economic pressure on the middle classes; the increasing availability of mechanical and subsequently chemical means of birth control; the declining economic value of children; and the growing economic value of women's time as more and more of them enter the labour force. But despite rigorous analyses of class, regional and socio-economic fertility differentials there is as yet no single comprehensive theory to account for the changes in *b* which have brought about the final stage of the post-1700 cycle (see, for example, Innes, 1938; Glass, 1938; and Ch. 3).

The examples used here to illustrate the phenomenon of growth cycles suggest that there is no one guiding principle which can be called upon to account for the onset and subsequent cessation of rapid population increase. Clearly the density-dependent mechanism, which affects the regulation of animal numbers and generates the often observed logistic curve, does not have the same direct relevance to human populations which have a far greater degree of control over their own food supply, environment, fertility, mortality and mobility. Without this control animal populations are unable themselves to alter *K* which means that natural, or man-induced, environmental change must be the ultimate arbiter of the level to which population can rise. Although Western man now possesses this controlling ability his power has by no means always been so profound. For this reason it is quite conceivable that there have been periods of 'ecological climax' when available resources were unable to provide for the needs of populations, but it is also the case that there have been periods of heightened disease activity which were unrelated to population size or environmental conditions. Under these circumstances the pleasing regularity of line which population growth cycles display is entirely deceptive. Their causes are most complex depending as they do upon particular combinations of the factors shown in Fig. 1.1.

The vague and extremely imprecise models and theories which have been invoked above to help answer the question 'How and why does population grow or decline?' must be specified far more precisely before they can be tested, evaluated or rejected. The inductive approach and emphasis on the reverse link between form and process do provide a rudimentary starting point. Subsequent chapters will make the additional simplifications which are necessary before objective evaluation via measurement can be employed. But they will also introduce the complications associated with viewing populations as combinations of age groups, together with the spatial component, so that populations can be seen to grow over time in a spatially differentiated fashion. To remain for the moment with the 'how' and 'why' question in the time dimension we will turn to the works of Malthus and Marx and to the influential and opposing theories and 'laws' which they propounded by way of answers.

## Malthus and Marx on population growth

I think I may fairly make two postulata.
First, That food is necessary to the existence of man.
Secondly, That the passion between the sexes is necessary and will remain nearly in its present state.

These are the first statements in the argument presented by Malthus in his *An Essay on the Principle of Population, as it affects the Future Improvement of Society, with remarks on the speculation of Mr. Godwin, M. Condorcet, and other writers* which was published anonymously in London in 1798. (The quotations used here are from the edition by Flew, 1970.) From them Malthus makes the following deductions.

Assuming then my postulata as granted, I say, that the power of population is indefinitely greater than the power in the earth to produce subsistence for man.

Population, when unchecked, increases in a geometrical ratio. Subsistence increases only in an arithmetical ratio. A slight acquaintance with numbers will shew the immensity of the first power in comparison of the second.

By that law of our nature which makes food necessary to the life of man, the effects of these two unequal powers must be kept equal.

This implies a strong and constantly operating check on population from the difficulty of subsistence. This difficulty must fall somewhere and must necessarily be severely felt by a large portion of mankind.

The consequences for mankind of 'this natural inequality of the two powers of population and of production in the earth' are misery and vice. Therefore, it is impossible for a society to exist, 'all members of which should live in ease, happiness and comparative leisure; and feel no anxiety about providing the means of subsistence for themselves and families'.

Consequently, if the premises are just, the argument is conclusive against the perfectability of the mass of mankind.

Here we have the object of Malthus's argument in the *First Essay*, to prove the imperfectability of mankind and hence to demonstrate the error in the utopian views expressed by William Godwin and the Marquis de Condorcet (see Glass, 1953: 84).

Although Malthus extended, elaborated and modified these logical ideas in subsequent editions of the *Second Essay* (1803), in pamphlets and in his *Principles of Political Economy considered with a view to their practical application* (1820), the *First Essay* of 1798 expresses the essence of his contention that human society is imperfectable and his reasons for coming to such a conclusion. However, Malthus is obliged to demonstrate why unchecked population growth is geometrical and subsistence increases arithmetically. He does this by taking an example, the population of the United States, which he says doubles every 25 years, and making it a general rule.

> This ratio of increase, though short of the utmost power of population, yet as the result of actual experience, we will take as our rule, and say, that population, when unchecked, goes on doubling itself every twenty-five years or increases in a geometrical ratio.

In his article on population for the *Encyclopaedia Britannica* (1824) and in *A Summary View of the Principle of Population* (1824; reprinted in Glass, 1953: 115–81), Malthus subsequently showed why his estimate of the United States' growth was valid and that its magnitude could not be attributed to immigration (Rubin, 1960; Coale, 1979). Malthus is less sure of his contention that agricultural production can only grow at maximum by an arithmetical ratio because any expansion in the production of land in excess of such a ratio, 'would be contrary to all our knowledge of the qualities of land'.

The implication of the combination of these two ratios, which can be expressed simply as

$$P_t = P_0 R^t \qquad [1.13]$$

or

$$P_t = P_0 e^{(\log_e R)t} \qquad [1.12]$$

for the geometrical series and

$$F_t = F_0 + R(t-1) \qquad [1.17]$$

for the arithmetical series, where $F$ is the level of subsistence (Lloyd, 1969: 23), is illustrated by the example of 'this Island', that is, Great Britain, which in the 1790s was estimated to have a population of 7 millions. The following progression would therefore be possible, assuming that the level of subsistence matches the size of population in year one.

| Year | 1 | 25 | 50 | 75 | 100 |
|---|---|---|---|---|---|
| Population (millions) | 7 | 14 | 28 | 56 | 112 |
| Level of subsistence able to support (millions) | 7 | 14 | 21 | 28 | 35 |

After a century this would leave a population of 77 millions 'totally unprovided for'.

It is not Malthus's contention that this will happen, he merely claims to use the example to show the imbalance in the power of populations and the level of subsistence to increase over time. It demonstrates the inevitability that checks will be imposed on population growth to keep it in line with the level of subsistence. Such checks, which are referred to as misery and vice in the *First Essay*, work in the following manner.

> The constant effort towards population, which is found to act even in the most vicious societies, increases the number of people before the means of subsistence are increased. The food therefore, which before supported seven millions must now be divided among seven millions and a half or eight millions. The poor consequently must live much worse, and many of them be reduced to severe distress. The number of labourers also being above the proportion of the work in the market, the price of labour must tend toward a decrease, while the price of provisions would at the same time tend to rise. The labourer therefore must work harder to earn the same as he did before. During this season of distress, the discouragements to marriage, and the difficulty of rearing a family are so great that population is at a stand. In the meantime the cheapness of labour, the plenty of labourers, and the necessity of an increased industry amongst them, encourage cultivators to employ more labour upon their land, to turn up fresh soil, and to manure and improve more completely what is already in tillage, till ultimately the means of subsistence become in the same proportion to the population as at the period from which we set out. The situation of the labourer being then again tolerably comfortable, the restraints to population are in some degree loosened, and the same retrograde and progressive movements with respect to happiness are repeated.

The effect of the operation of this mechanism would be to create oscillations in population growth about the long-term arithmetical increase in the means of subsistence. These checks to geometrical population increase, which Malthus also refers to as preventive and positive checks, both enable a population to limit its growth via what he calls in the *Second Essay* and subsequent editions moral restraint, that is the postponement of marriage and the increase in celibacy, and force it to do so either directly through higher mortality associated with subsistence crises or indirectly as a consequence of a reduction in the demand for labour. This last-mentioned aspect has been seen as the key to Malthus's interpretation of population; it is the 'effectual demand' for labour that determines the rate of population growth (Spengler, 1972). In the *Second Essay* and the *Principles of Political Economy considered with a view to their practical application* (1820) this argument is made more forcibly and the view is expounded that whilst the level of subsistence establishes the true upper limit to population growth, before that limit is reached it is the current and prospective demand for labour which, because they affect access to the means of subsistence and the propensity to marry, regulate a population's growth rate.

Reactions to Malthus's writings have rarely been equivocal. Petersen (1979), for instance, provides a modern and largely sympathetic evaluation. To Keynes the *First Essay* was a work of 'youthful genius', the importance of which, 'consisted not in the novelty of his facts but in the smashing emphasis he placed on a simple generalisation arising out of them' (Keynes, 1933: 119). To Marx and Engels they were anathema. But how valuable are they as an account of the mechanisms which control population change over time? By setting aside his rhetoric, bravura and consciously polemical style, the accusations that he was an apologist for the conditions of the working people, a plagiarist and a counter-revolutionary, one can still examine the logic of Malthus's arguments in a more or less objective manner.

Davis (1955: 542) has outlined four elements which are important in the appraisal of theoretical statements, including those made by Malthus.

1. A frame of reference.
2. A set of deductive propositions which concern the relationships between variables defined in the frame of reference.
3. A set of empirical propositions verified by disciplined observation. (The empirical statements discussed earlier in this chapter.)
4. Crude empirical propositions based only on common-sense observation.

The problems Malthus tackles – the determinants and consequences of population growth – require the precise specification of the variables involved in a frame of reference. This is not accomplished; rather we are presented with two 'postulates', one of which is reasonable, the other dubious. The sex drive is variable in man and certainly the effects of the 'passion between the sexes' are by no means constant. The deductions Malthus makes from these 'axioms' lack any logical value. They are statements of belief bereft of scientific substance. 'The argument says, in effect, that a population can double every 25 years, because there are actual cases on record; but that subsistence cannot increase that fast because there are no cases on record' (Davis, 1955: 550). However, if the level of subsistence controls the rate of population growth then food supply must also be capable of doubling every 25 years. In his defence it could be claimed that Malthus merely wished to put forward an example to illustrate his point on the discrepancy between the power of geometrical and arithmetical series. Although this was the stated intention the language he used gave the impression that it was a general principle when Malthus knew full well that it did not apply to 'this Island'.

In the *Second Essay* and subsequent works Malthus attempted to establish what are termed 'empirical propositions' in Davis's scheme and in doing so he treated a set of ideas which was essentially deductive as though it was inductive in origin. Malthus's deductive propositions are invalid because they do not stem logically from his 'postulata'. It is on this ground that the claim to be scientific must be invalidated and the propositions quoted above rejected.

Malthus's framework also contains statements on the mechanisms which check population growth (Flew, 1970: 31). These were ultimately described as vice, misery and moral restraint and were thought to span the range of possible influences; although in the *First Essay* 'vicious customs with respect to women, great cities, unwholesome manufactures, luxury and war' were also included in the list but were in some way subsumed under the misery and vice headings. Through the moralistic phraseology one can, however, perceive the outline of what could be translated into a hard economic theory. When the growth of the labour force exceeds the demand for labour there will be a relative abundance of labour, thus depressing wage rates and reducing living standards, which in turn will put pressure on the propensity to marry and the ability to maintain a family. When population growth exceeds the growth in the level of subsistence there will be a positive check to that growth as a result of malnutrition, starvation and higher mortality in general. In the former and the latter sequences of events new levels of growth will ultimately be reached which will be in keeping with labour demand and level of subsistence respectively. In terms of the discussion presented earlier in the chapter, this scheme implies the existence of two

$K$ values, one set by labour demand ($K'$) and the other by food supply ($K''$). It is possible for $K' \geq K''$ although it seems Malthus visualised that in general $K' \leq K''$. Unlike the theories related to the growth of animal numbers $K''$ could change over time, that is $K''$ could be set equal to $F$ in [1.17], whilst $K'$ also changes, but in a manner which is always inversely related to the growth of labour supply.

This homeostatic system in which negative feedback plays such an important role can be criticised in a number of ways. First, as has already been remarked, $K''$ need not increase arithmetically. For example, Engels in his *Outlines of a Critique of Political Economy* (1844; see especially Engels, 1959: 184–8) stresses the contribution of science – which he claims also grows geometrically – to the increase in the means of subsistence.

> The area of land is limited – that is perfectly true. But the labour power to be employed on this area increases together with the population; and even if we assume that the increase of output associated with this increase of labour is not always proportionate to the latter, there still remains a third element – which the economists, however, never consider as important – namely, science, the progress of which is just as limitless and at least as rapid as that of population (Engels, 1844; reprinted in Meek, 1953: 63).

Second, the preventive check, upon which Malthus laid so much stress in his principle, specifically excluded the possibility of birth control methods being widely employed; delayed marriage was to be the main regulator of overall fertility. Whilst it can be argued that this view is valid for Malthus's period, at least in Britain, by 1900 fertility had been reduced in most West European countries because methods of birth spacing and family limitation were being employed within marriage. The very low level of population growth in the West today has been achieved by the effective use of birth control which has in fact made the postponement of marriage a redundant demographic regulator (see Ch. 3). Although Malthus opposed the use of birth control on moral grounds it is ironic that its wide-scale use has meant that fertility can now become far more closely attuned to economic fluctuations than it could have by the use of his preventive check alone (see, for example, Easterlin, 1968; Ermisch, 1979).

Third, Malthus's emphasis appears to be – population growth → labour surplus → checks to population growth – so that combined with a labour surplus is a falling standard of living.

Population growth and rising living standards should therefore be roughly inversely related (Petersen, 1964: 37 and 86). But if living standards rise why should not marriages be contracted at a younger age and in consequence the rate of population growth accelerated? Malthus regards universal education and the 'desire of bettering our condition' as contributing factors here; factors which will presumably negate the force unleashed by the 'passion between the sexes'. Obviously there are some problems regarding the regulatory mechanism in Malthus's system which have never been convincingly resolved. Some of these inconsistencies stem from their author's notorious facility for changing the emphasis of his ideas from the *First Essay* to the *Second Essay* and its subsequent editions, but others owe their origin to the confusion of polemic, moral tract and scientific discourse.

Davis (1955: 541) has attempted to place the importance of Malthus's *Essays* in their modern context: 'Malthus's theories are not now and never were empirically valid, but they nevertheless were theoretically significant and, as a consequence, they hold a secure place in intellectual history'. Here, as ever, there are grounds for controversy. To Le Roy Ladurie (1974: 311), 'Malthus was a clear-headed theoretician of traditional societies, but he was a prophet of the past; he was born too late in a world too new'. An epitaph which would, in a sense, be appropriate to Karl Marx, but for the role of V. I. Lenin.

Marx's views on population growth are best summarised in the section entitled *The Progressive Production of a Relative Surplus Population or Industrial Reserve Army* which appears in *Capital* (1867; see Marx, 1976: 781–94). Marx argued that it was essential to have a theory of population and labour force regulation specific to the capitalist system; that there could be no one eternal or natural law of population, as Malthus had claimed, but that such 'laws' must always be linked with the dominant contemporary mode of production, which has been defined as, 'a specific set of forces of production (human labour, materials and machinery) patterned into a specific set of relations of production (relationships of property, and work-relationships)' (Maguire, 1979: 159). Hence each mode of production has its own economic and demographic laws. But although Marx was concerned with identifying and analysing the conditions particular to the pre-capitalist modes of production in *The German Ideology* (1845–46) and the papers that have come to be known as *Grundrisse*, neither he nor Engels developed laws of population peculiar to the communal, ancient, feudal, Asiatic, or, for that matter, the socialist modes of production. Marx did, however, argue that population growth could have had a role in the transition between modes; that the growth of urban centres was a particularly significant aspect of feudalism, and hence of the initiation of the capitalist mode, the transition to which was partly brought about by tensions between town and country (see Hobsbawm, 1964; Marx, 1964).

Under capitalism, based as it is on competition and private ownership of property, the demand for labour is inversely related to the accumulation of capital and since with competition the increase in capital is liable to violent fluctuations – 'periods of average activity, production at high pressure, crisis, and stagnation' – there are bound to be oscillations in the demand for labour which will in turn lead to the temporary, but repeated, production of a *surplus population* simply because the supply of labour increases more quickly than the demand for workers.

> The working population therefore produces both the accumulation of capital and the means by which it is itself made relatively superfluous; and it does this to an extent which is always increasing. This is a law of population peculiar to the capitalist mode of production . . . (Marx, 1976: 783).

This surplus population becomes an *industrial reserve army* of 'unemployed or semi-employed "hands"'. The movement of wage levels is solely determined by the changing proportion of the working population that is in this industrial reserve army and not by fluctuations in the absolute number in the potential labour force itself. This critical proportion is controlled by the successive expansion and contraction of capital. The birth and death rates and the sizes of families are in turn inversely related to the level of wages, that is, to 'the means of subsistence at the disposal of different categories of worker' (Marx, 1976: 797). The more prone the members of a class are to be part of the surplus population the lower will be their average wage level and the higher their birth and death rates. Marx's theory of population is therefore very much a theory of labour, founded as it is in the conditions that apply to the capitalist mode of production which specifically identifies the condition experienced by different categories of workers. The variables: capital accumulation, labour demand, proportion in the surplus population, wage levels, and demographic rates are closely linked in a system articulated by access to and variation in the means of employment. (Mandel, 1970, provides an introduction to these concepts.)

Obviously there are major differences between the theories of Malthus and Marx as they affect population, but there is also some common ground. At least in his *Second Essay*, and to some extent in the *First Essay*, Malthus was aware of the importance of labour demand as a population regulator. Some of the criticisms he levelled at 'this baboon', as Marx once referred to 'Parson Malthus' (Marx, 1973: 606), were therefore based on the principle of population to be found in the *First Essay*, the one which gave greatest weight to the control exerted by the level of subsistence. Both men seem to have been aware of the inverse relation between rising wages and falling birth and death rates, but, as was remarked earlier, this notion is by no means conspicuous in Malthus's writings.

Malthus and Marx, together with Engels, differ most fundamentally on three matters. First, their ideological perspectives are poles apart. Malthus held opinions which were essentially conservative. Individuals and families should be encouraged to be self-reliant; self-interest should be the guiding rule, with marriage, the family, private property and inheritance the focal points of society. Marx, the 'bourgeois ideologist', saw the ownership of private property at the root of most of society's evils. Malthus's conclusions on human inperfectibility had to be thrown over as a step towards the removal of the capitalist mode of production. Second, Malthus took as the starting point for his principle the effect of population growth and its repeated clashes with the level of subsistence; population was the independent variable in his system. Marx, on the other hand, saw the creation of a surplus population, with all that entailed, as being dependent upon the existence of the capitalist mode of production. Malthus's is a theory of population, Marx's a theory of labour. Third, Marx's theory was related to a particular economic system; it would not operate under feudalism or socialism, whilst Malthus's concepts were deemed to be universally applicable.

The theories of Malthus and Marx, as they concern population, have both been proved inadequate because they fail to accommodate the possibility that population could grow and that living standards could improve almost continuously over a long period of time. Labour substitution – unskilled for skilled, children for adults, females for males – does not automatically lead to a secular decline in real wage levels as Marx argued. The exponential increase in population has not led to diminution in the 'effective demand for labour' nor to successive subsistence crises, although these have occurred at certain times and places. In fact the major reason for the growth of world population in the late nineteenth and the twentieth centuries has been the falling death rate which has not, until recently been accompanied by a falling birth rate.

Unlike ordinary men, both the good and evil that Malthus and Marx did have lived on. Their writings have had theoretical and practical implications which have shaped seemingly irreconcilable views on the nature of the relationship between population and socio-economic development. Both Darwin and Keynes acknowledged the importance of Malthus's ideas for their own biological and economic theories, while the current state of Soviet Marxist–Leninist population theory owes its origin to notions of the 'industrial reserve army'. According to contemporary Marxism–Leninism, Malthusianism has the following features (Smulevich, 1978: 390).

    1. Population growth is the determining factor in socio-economic development, and creates overpopulation, and hence poverty, hunger, unemployment, wars, etc.

    2. It is a biological, unhistorical interpretation of population growth.

    3. Birth control is the main condition for eliminating the socio-economic backwardness of developing countries.

Setting aside the fact that Malthus himself did not espouse the cause of birth control, we can see fom these attributed features not only how entrenched ideologies have become, but also how the initial theories have been modified for reasons which are as much political as scientific. The influence of works derived from those of Malthus and Marx has thus been considerable, although they have not always been Malthusian or Marxist in the strictest sense.

# 2
# Stationary and stable populations

Since all knowledge is theory-impregnated it is all built on sand; but it can be improved by critically digging deeper, and by not taking any alleged 'data' for granted.

Karl Popper, *Objective Knowledge*

The terms 'stationary' and 'stable' are used by demographers in specific senses in their discussions of population theory. A stationary population is one which is static. The number of births is constant from year to year, as is the number of deaths, and the number of births is equal to the number of deaths in a period. The age structure and the fertility and mortality schedules of such a population do not change over time. Obviously stationary population models are extremely simple and in many ways they are also unrealistic, but they provide means of representation and approximation which are valuable because they hold constant a set of complex interacting variables. In a stable population, although both mortality and fertility schedules are defined as constant they are not necessarily assumed to cancel out one another. The number of births in a year need not equal the number of deaths so that a stable population can grow, or decline, but it does so at a constant rate. Further, the relative age structure of a stable population is constant.

The theory of stationary and stable populations will be used here, firstly, to describe the development of age and sex structures; secondly, as a means of reconstructing or estimating demographic measures of populations for which there are inadequate data; and, thirdly, as an example of pure demographic theory which has, nonetheless, important practical applications for the study of population geography. Stationary and stable theories will therefore be used to answer the question, 'How are populations structured in terms of age and sex?' They also offer the possibility of identifying spatial and temporal demographic patterns which would otherwise go unobserved.

## Age and sex structures

### Stationary population models

A stationary population model can be developed by making the following assumptions.

1. The population under consideration is closed; there is no immigration or emigration; net migration is zero.

2. The number of births per year ($l_0$) is constant and equal to the number of deaths per year ($_\infty d_0$) and therefore age-specific mortality ($_n M_x$) together with the probability of dying between ages $x$ and $x + n$ ($_n q_x$) is also constant.

Once $_n M_x$ has been found, which it can be quite simply from

$$_n M_x = \frac{_n D_x}{_n P_x} \tag{2.1}$$

where $_n M_x$ = the age-specific mortality rate between ages $x$ and $x + n$,

$\quad\ _n D_x$ = the actual number of deaths to persons aged $x$ to $x + n$,

$\quad\ _n P_x$ = the average number of persons alive aged $x$ to $x + n$,

then $_n q_x$ can be derived

$$_n q_x = \frac{2[n(_n M_x)]}{2 + [n(_n M_x)]} \tag{2.2}$$

where $_n q_x$ = the probability of dying between ages $x$ and $x + n$,

$\quad\ n$ = the number of years in an age group (usually $n = 5$).

From assumption 2, above, it follows that $_n q_x$ is constant and that there will be $l_0$ births per year, therefore

$$d_0 = l_0 \bullet q_0 \tag{2.3}$$

$$l_1 = l_0 \bullet d_0 \tag{2.4}$$

and in general

$$_n d_x = l_x \bullet _n q_x \tag{2.5}$$

$$l_{x+n} = l_x - _n d_x \tag{2.6}$$

where $l_x$ = the number of persons aged exactly $x$ ($l_0$ is the number aged 0, i.e. the number of births),

$\quad\ _n d_x$ = the number of deaths to persons aged $x$ to $x + n$ in the model structure ($d_0$ is the number of deaths to infants during their first year of life).

The number of persons in an age group is given by

$$_nL_x = \frac{n}{2}(l_x + l_{x+n}) \qquad [2.7]$$

where $_nL_x$ = the average number of persons alive and aged $x$ to $x + n$ in completed years (i.e. $L_0$ is the number of infants who have not yet reached their first birthday and $_5L_{20}$ is the number of persons aged 20 to 24 in completed years).

By using the sequence of stages represented in [2.1] to [2.7] together with assumptions 1 and 2 one can construct a stationary model of a particular population. However, there are a number of specific exceptions to the above equations. For infant mortality

$$q_0 = \frac{D_0}{B} \qquad [2.8]$$

where $q_0$ = the probability of an infant dying during the first year of life,

$D_0$ = the number of deaths to infants in a period,

$B$ = the number of live births in that same period.

Similarly, the number of infants in their first year of life is given by

$$L_0 = 0 \cdot 3 l_0 + 0 \cdot 7 l_1 \qquad [2.9]$$

where $L_0$ = the number of infants aged 0 in completed years (i.e. in their first year of life),

$0 \cdot 3$ and $0 \cdot 7$ = separation factors which are included to resolve the problem created by the fact that deaths during the first year of life are highly concentrated within the first days and weeks.

Special allowance also has to be made for the oldest age group employed in the model. This is usually 70+, 80+, or 85+ so that $_\infty L_{80}$, for example, can be found by

$$_\infty L_{80} = \frac{_\infty d_{80}}{_\infty M_{80}} . \qquad [2.10]$$

A particular example will serve to illustrate the development of a stationary population model. Table 2.1 shows the case of the female population of Italy in the early 1970s. In this instance it is assumed that there will be a constant number of female births each year and that the number of births is equal to 100,000 ($l_0 = 100,000$). It is also assumed that the probability of dying between ages $x$ and $x$

+ $n$ is constant and equal to the $_nq_x$ values in column (5). On the basis of these assumptions a model stationary population structure can be created by using [2.1] to [2.10]. The resulting values of $_nL_x$ are shown in column (8). They demonstrate what the age structure of the Italian female population would be were the mortality conditions operating in 1970–72 to prevail for a very long time, say 100 years; were fertility to remain constant for a similar period; and were international migration to have no net influence.

One of the important contributions of stationary models is that they remove random fluctuation in mortality, fertility and migration and therefore enable one to examine the impact of particular mortality levels on a population's age structure. In the Italian case, life expectancy at birth ($e_0$; $e_x$ is life expectancy at age $x$) was high in the early 1970s ($e_0$ was 74·80 for females and 68·68 for males) so that 90 per cent of females survived to their early 50s and the same percentage of males reached their late 40s. These percentages are clearly demonstrated by the values for $l_x$ (see Table 2.1 column (6)).

The $l_x$ values from stationary models can also be used to provide a general and standardised means of comparing population structures. Population biologists have employed $l_x$ curves to classify the population structures and life chances of a variety of organisms (Hutchinson, 1978). The three most commonly identified patterns are shown in Fig. 2.1. Curve (a) shows a population with extremely high mortality during the first few hours or days of life after which time mortality is relatively unchanged with age, up to some maximum life span. Curve (b) applies to populations with lower infant mortality and with fairly uniform increases in $_nq_x$ with age, whilst curve (c) represents populations with even lower infant mortality together with a slow rate of change of mortality until $_nq_x$ increases rapidly in old age. Curve (a) is typical of the experience of most fish populations, whilst curve (b) applies to birds and curve (c) to higher mammals and *Homo sapiens*. Clearly $l_x$ from Table 2.1 would correspond well with curve (c) in Fig. 2.1. Populations whose $l_x$ values match curves (a) and (c) also tend to have different genetic strategies. The former produce many hundreds or thousands of offspring although only a very small proportion survives to the reproductive stage, whilst the latter have only a small number of offspring but a high proportion survive to reproduce. The geneticists term these strategies **r** and **K**, respectively.

By no means all stationary models for human populations conform to the curve (c) pattern. In countries where mortality is

**Table 2.1** Stationary population model for Italy, 1970–72 (female population)

| Age x (1) | Female population* $_nP_x$ (2) | Female deaths† $_nD_x$ (3) | $_nM_x$ (4) | $_nq_x$ (5) | $l_x$ (6) | $_nd_x$ (7) | $_nL_x$ (8) |
|---|---|---|---|---|---|---|---|
| 0 | 433,814 | 10,971 | 0·02529 | 0·02518 | 100,000 | 2,518 | 98,237 |
| 1 | 1,801,596 | 1,476 | 0·00082 | 0·00327 | 97,482 | 319 | 389,290 |
| 5 | 2,220,579 | 736 | 0·00033 | 0·00165 | 97,163 | 160 | 485,415 |
| 10 | 1,984,684 | 589 | 0·00030 | 0·00150 | 97,003 | 146 | 484,650 |
| 15 | 1,920,433 | 807 | 0·00042 | 0·00210 | 96,857 | 203 | 483,778 |
| 20 | 2,029,531 | 1,011 | 0·00050 | 0·00250 | 96,654 | 242 | 482,665 |
| 25 | 1,821,621 | 1,074 | 0·00059 | 0·00295 | 96,412 | 284 | 481,350 |
| 30 | 1,975,749 | 1,510 | 0·00076 | 0·00379 | 96,128 | 364 | 479,730 |
| 35 | 1,884,089 | 2,195 | 0·00117 | 0·00583 | 95,764 | 558 | 477,425 |
| 40 | 1,889,549 | 3,321 | 0·00176 | 0·00876 | 95,206 | 834 | 473,945 |
| 45 | 1,888,286 | 5,385 | 0·00285 | 0·01415 | 94,372 | 1,335 | 468,523 |
| 50 | 1,255,835 | 6,045 | 0·00481 | 0·02376 | 93,037 | 2,211 | 459,658 |
| 55 | 1,651,700 | 10,884 | 0·00659 | 0·03242 | 90,826 | 2,945 | 446,768 |
| 60 | 1,450,022 | 16,744 | 0·01155 | 0·05613 | 87,881 | 4,933 | 427,073 |
| 65 | 1,170,537 | 22,715 | 0·01941 | 0·09256 | 82,948 | 7,678 | 395,545 |
| 70 | 939,413 | 32,570 | 0·03467 | 0·15952 | 75,270 | 12,007 | 346,333 |
| 75 | 654,292 | 41,615 | 0·06360 | 0·27437 | 63,263 | 17,357 | 272,923 |
| 80+ | 605,056 | 84,895 | 0·14031 | 1·00000 | 45,906 | 45,906 | 327,176 |

\* *De jure* female population recorded in the 1971 census
† Average annual female deaths, 1970–72
*Data sources: Population Census of Italy, 1971; United Nations Demographic Yearbooks*

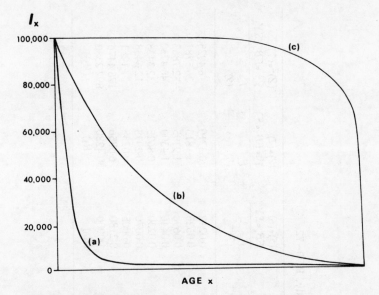

**Fig. 2.1** Standard $l_x$ curves

high, and therefore $e_0$ is relatively low, curve (b) is more likely to provide an accurate description. The underdeveloped countries offer many examples, as do populations from the pre-industrial and indus-trialising periods of economically developed countries. Figure 2.2 gives six examples of $l_x$ curves for a variety of periods. The lowest $e_0$ value is for the male slave population of St James Parish, Jamaica, in 1817–20 and in this instance, at least, the curve for $l_x$ is relatively closer to (b) in Fig. 2.1 than to (c). The slave population was not only subject to paricularly high infant mortality, but also to excep-tional mortality during the working ages. The curves for Swedish males, 1788–92, and English and Welsh males, 1861, represent sta-tionary models for the population of pre-industrial and industrialis-ing Western countries, respectively. Although infant mortality was still very high in these cases $e_0$ was substantially increased to levels in the 30s and low 40s. Contemporary underdeveloped countries, as represented by India and Peru in Fig. 2.2, show $e_0$ levels in the upper 40s and 50s. In comparison with Fig. 2.1 the cases of India and parti-cularly Peru do begin to exhibit clear indications of the curve (c) pattern with relatively low mortality during childhood and early adulthood. Curve (c) is only fully matched by the case of the Italian female population, a representative of an advanced Western society,

**Table 2.2** Estimation of $R_0$, $R_1$ and $R_2$ for the population of Italy, 1970–72

| Age groups Z (1) | Mid-point $Y_z$ (2) | Female population $F_z$ (3) | Female births $FB_z$ (4) | Survival factors* $SY_z$ (5) | $\dfrac{(4)/(3)}{FB_z}$ $F_z$ (6) | $\dfrac{(5)\bullet(6)}{FB_z \bullet SY_z}$ $F_z$ (7) | $\dfrac{(2)\bullet(7)}{Y_z \bullet FB_z \bullet SY_z}$ $F_z$ (8) | $\dfrac{(2)^2\bullet(7)}{Y_z^2 \bullet FB_z \bullet SY_z}$ $F_z$ (9) |
|---|---|---|---|---|---|---|---|---|
| 1 15–19 | 17·5 | 1,920,433 | 42,030 | 0·9676 | 0·0219 | 0·0212 | 0·3710 | 6·4925 |
| 2 20–24 | 22·5 | 2,029,531 | 110,385 | 0·9653 | 0·0544 | 0·0525 | 1·1813 | 26·5781 |
| 3 25–29 | 27·5 | 1,821,621 | 132,102 | 0·9627 | 0·0725 | 0·0698 | 1·9195 | 52·7863 |
| 4 30–34 | 32·5 | 1,975,749 | 90,669 | 0·9595 | 0·0459 | 0·0440 | 1·4300 | 46·4750 |
| 5 35–39 | 37·5 | 1,884,089 | 45,405 | 0·9549 | 0·0241 | 0·0230 | 0·8625 | 32·3438 |
| 6 40–44 | 42·5 | 1,889,549 | 13,995 | 0·9479 | 0·0074 | 0·0070 | 0·2975 | 12·6438 |
| 7 45–49 | 47·5 | 1,888,286 | 1,023 | 0·9370 | 0·0005 | 0·0005 | 0·0238 | 1·1281 |
| Total | | | | | 0·2265 | 0·2180 | 6·0856 | 178·4476 |
| Total × 5 | | | | | 1·1335 | 1·0900 ($R_0$) | 30·4280 ($R_1$) | 892·2380 ($R_2$) |

* $SY_z$ is derived from column (8), Table 2.1
*Data source:* Table 2.1

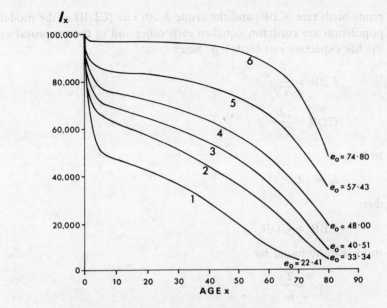

Fig. 2.2 Examples of $l_x$ curves for human populations
*Data sources*: Jamaica from Higman (1976); Sweden, England and Wales, Peru from Keyfitz and Flieger (1968); India from Cassen (1978a); Italy from Table 2.1

1 Male slaves, St. James Parish, Jamaica, 1817–20

2 Swedish males, 1788–92

3 English and Welsh males, 1861

4 Indian males, 1966–70

5 Peruvian males, 1961

6 Italian females, 1970–72

in which life expectancy has nearly reached its biological maximum. The patterns illustrated in Fig. 2.1 therefore enable one to classify particular population structures within the range of possible alternatives.

Stationary population models have a number of more formal properties which should not be overlooked in an assessment of their theoretical value. For example, the annual number of births ($l_0$) is constant and equal to the annual number of deaths ($_\infty d_0$)

$$l_0 = {}_\infty d_0.$$

The total population in the model ($T_0$) is constant; the number in each age group ($_n L_x$) is constant so that the age structure is static; the crude birth rate (CBR) and the crude death rate (CDR) of the model population are constant, equal to each other and to the reciprocal of the life expectancy at birth ($e_0$). Since

$$\text{CBR} = \frac{l_0}{T_0}$$

$$\text{CDR} = \frac{_\infty d_0}{T_0}$$

and

$$l_0 = {_\infty d_0}$$

then

$$\text{CBR} = \text{CDR}$$

and $e_0$ can be found by

$$e_0 = \frac{T_0}{l_0}$$

and

$$\frac{l_0}{T_0} = \frac{_\infty d_0}{T_0}$$

then

$$\text{CBR} = \text{CDR} = \frac{1}{e_0}.$$

To return to the example of the Italian female population, $e_0$ was 74·80 which means that CBR = CDR = 13·37 per thousand and $T_0$ was 7,480,484, so that an annual number of female births equal to 100,000 coupled with constant age-specific mortality, as summarised by the $_n q_x$ column in Table 2.1, would result in a total female population of nearly 7·5 millions. The stationary model can also be used to estimate the annual number of births required to maintain a population at a certain level given a particular schedule of age-specific mortality. For instance, to maintain the female Italian population at a constant 25 millions with the schedule of $_n q_x$ mentioned above would require an annual number of female births equal to 334,203.

To summarise, stationary population models provide a means of examining the influence of mortality on age structure in the absence of distortions due to fluctuation in fertility and migration.

They enable one to summarise and classify population structures in terms of both life expectancy and curves expressing the number of persons alive and aged *x*. Lastly, they provide an internally coherent demographic system in which birth and death rates are equal, that is they represent the most simple demographic conditions imaginable where the population is static, and because of this they offer a basis for the more complex stable and quasi-stable models.

## Stable population models

Although it should be possible to identify a very small number of populations that do meet the assumption for stationary models, that is where CBR = CDR, most populations do show changes in mortality and fertility over time and are unlikely to have equal birth and death rates. The theory of stable populations partially takes account of this observation by employing the following assumptions.

1.  The population's age-specific mortality and fertility schedules are assumed to be constant over time, but it is not assumed that CBR = CDR, although the possibility is not excluded.

2.  The population is assumed to be closed; there is no immigration or emigration.

The implications of making assumption 1 are that a stable population can grow, remain static or decline over time, but that it does so at a constant rate. Further, any closed population with constant age-specific mortality and fertility will, over a period of time, change such that the relative age structure also becomes constant and the absolute number of persons in each age group changes at the same constant rate as that of the total population.

The theory of stable population was outlined and elaborated by Alfred James Lotka (1880–1949), mainly during the 1920s and 1930s (Lotka, 1907, 1922, 1937, 1939; Dublin and Lotka, 1925; Sharpe and Lotka, 1911; see also Spengler, 1976) and has subsequently been summarised, refined and extensively applied (Coale, 1972). Lotka was able to provide a proof for the theorem that in a closed population constant age-specific mortality and fertility ultimately create an age structure with a fixed relative distribution, whilst the total population and the absolute number in each age group change by a constant rate. He termed that constant rate the *intrinsic rate of natural increase, r*. Lotka found that *r* could be approximated from the following integration over the reproductive ages, 15 to 49

$$\int_{15}^{49} e^{-rx} FB(x) S(x) \delta x = 1 \qquad [2.11]$$

where $FB(x)$ = the number of female births per year to females
aged $x$,

$S(x)$ = the probability of a female child surviving from
birth to age $x$,

$\delta x$ = the rate of change of age,

$e$ = the base of natural logarithms,

$r$ = the intrinsic rate of natural increase per year.

Using age groups instead of single year ages, $r$ can be estimated from

$$\frac{r^2}{2}\left[\frac{R_2}{R_0} - \left(\frac{R_1}{R_0}\right)^2\right] - r\frac{R_1}{R_0} + \log_e R_0 = 0 \qquad [2.12]$$

where $R_0$ = the net reproduction rate (NRR) of a population, that
is the average number of female children a woman
would have during her reproductive years and who
might be expected to survive to the age she was when
they were born. (If NRR > 1 then a population will
grow, if NRR = 1 it will be static and if NRR < 1 it
will decline.)

$R_1$ = the first moment under the curve expressed in [2.11],

$R_2$ = the second moment.

Dividing the reproductive ages 15 to 49 into seven five-year
age groups, 15–19 to 45–49, enables one to solve [2.12] using discrete data.
Therefore

$$R_0 = n \cdot \left(\sum_{z=1}^{7} \frac{FB_z \cdot SY_z}{F_z}\right) = \text{NRR} \qquad [2.13]$$

$$R_1 = n \cdot \left(\sum_{z=1}^{7} \frac{Y_z \cdot FB_z \cdot SY_z}{F_z}\right) \qquad [2.14]$$

$$R_2 = n \cdot \left(\sum_{z=1}^{7} \frac{Y_z^2 \cdot FB_z \cdot SY_z}{F_z}\right) \qquad [2.15]$$

where $FB_z$ = female births to females in age group $z$ (here there are
seven five-year age groups 15–19 to 45–49),

$SY_z$ = the probability of a female child surviving from birth
to the mid-point of age group $z$ (i.e. 0–17·5, 0–22·5, .
. .,0–47·5),

$F_z$ = the number of females in age group $z$,
$Y_z$ = the mid-point of age group $z$,
$n$ = the number of years in an age group.

Once $R_0$, $R_1$ and $R_2$ have been found they can be substituted into [2.12], which is a form of quadratic equation where

$$ar^2 - br + c = 0 \qquad [2.16)$$

and has the general solution

$$r = \frac{-b \pm \sqrt{b^2 - 4ac}}{2a} \qquad [2.17]$$

The steps outlined in [2.12] to [2.15] for the estimation of $R_0$, $R_1$ and $R_2$ are illustrated in Table 2.2 for the Italian population, 1970–72. When $R_0$, $R_1$ and $R_2$ have been found then $r$ can be calculated by substitution into [2.12] and solution of [2.17]. As Table 2.2 shows, $R_0$ = 1·0900, $R_1$ = 30·4280 and $R_2$ = 892·2380, therefore
$$19·6433r^2 - 27·9156r + 0·0862 = 0$$
and

$$r = \frac{27·9156 - \sqrt{779·2807 - 6·7730}}{39·2866}$$

$r$ = 0·0030952.

The intrinsic rate of natural increase for the Italian population, 1970–72, was therefore 0·3095 per cent *per annum*.

Once $r$ has been found it can be used to increase each age group in the stationary model population, so that ultimately a stable structure is created whose total population will also grow at a constant $r \times 100$ per cent *per annum*. A stable population model can therefore be obtained by making the following adjustment

$$L_z(1 + r)^{-Y_z} \qquad [2.18]$$

where $L_z$ = the average number of persons alive in age group $z$ and is equivalent to $_nL_x$ from the stationary population model (e.g. $_5L_{20} = L_{20-24}$, $n$ = 5, $x$ = 20 and $z$ is the 20–24 age group),
$Y_z$ = the mid-point of age group $z$ (e.g. if $L_{20-24}$ is the age group then $Y_z$ = 22·5),
$r$ = the intrinsic rate of natural increase.

The multiplier can also be written as follows

$$(1 + r)^{-Y_z} = \frac{1}{\text{antilog } [Y_z \log(1 + r)]} \qquad [2.19]$$

**Table 2.3** Derivation of a stable population structure for Italy, 1970–72 ($r = 0.003095$)

| Age groups Z (1) | Mid-point $Y_z$ (2) | Female population† $L_z$ (3) | Multiplier $(1+r)^{-Y_z}$ (4) | (3)•(4) (5) | Male population‡ $L_z$ (6) | (4)•(6)•SRB§ (7) | Stable population‖ Males (8) | Females (9) |
|---|---|---|---|---|---|---|---|---|
| 1  0–4   | 2.5   | 487,527 | 0.992305 | 483,775 | 484,420 | 506,758 | 3,867 | 3,692 |
| 2  5–9   | 7.5   | 485,415 | 0.977088 | 474,293 | 481,745 | 496,231 | 3,787 | 3,619 |
| 3  10–14 | 12.5  | 484,650 | 0.962106 | 466,285 | 480,518 | 487,378 | 3,719 | 3,558 |
| 4  15–19 | 17.5  | 483,778 | 0.947354 | 458,309 | 478,623 | 478,012 | 3,648 | 3,498 |
| 5  20–24 | 22.5  | 482,665 | 0.932829 | 450,244 | 475,973 | 468,077 | 3,572 | 3,436 |
| 6  25–29 | 27.5  | 481,350 | 0.918525 | 442,132 | 473,280 | 458,292 | 3,497 | 3,374 |
| 7  30–34 | 32.5  | 479,730 | 0.904440 | 433,887 | 470,378 | 448,498 | 3,423 | 3,311 |
| 8  35–39 | 37.5  | 477,425 | 0.890573 | 425,182 | 466,740 | 438,206 | 3,344 | 3,245 |
| 9  40–44 | 42.5  | 473,945 | 0.876917 | 415,610 | 460,393 | 425,619 | 3,248 | 3,172 |
| 10 45–49 | 47.5  | 468,523 | 0.863471 | 404,556 | 450,583 | 410,162 | 3,130 | 3,087 |
| 11 50–54 | 52.5  | 459,658 | 0.850231 | 390,815 | 434,608 | 389,554 | 2,973 | 2,982 |
| 12 55–59 | 57.5  | 446,768 | 0.837193 | 374,031 | 410,950 | 362,700 | 2,768 | 2,854 |
| 13 60–64 | 62.5  | 427,073 | 0.824356 | 352,060 | 375,283 | 326,142 | 2,489 | 2,687 |
| 14 65–69 | 67.5  | 395,545 | 0.811718 | 321,071 | 322,785 | 276,218 | 2,108 | 2,450 |
| 15 70–74 | 72.5  | 346,333 | 0.799271 | 276,814 | 254,663 | 214,582 | 1,637 | 2,112 |
| 16 75–79 | 77.5  | 272,923 | 0.787016 | 214,795 | 177,875 | 147,581 | 1,126 | 1,639 |
| 17 80+   | 87.1* | 327,176 | 0.764009 | 249,965 | 169,240 | 136,312 | 1,040 | 1,908 |

\* The mid-point of age group 80+ is put at 87.1 because $e_{80} = 7.1$
† From column (8), Table 2.1
‡ The male equivalent of column (8), Table 2.1
§ SRB = 1.054225
‖ The total population is set at 100,000
Data source: Table 2.1

which enables $(1 + r)^{-Y_z}$ to be evaluated and the stable age structure estimated.

Table 2.3 gives an example of the use of the multiplier on the stationary population of Italian females shown in Table 2.1. The resulting age structure after multiplying $L_z$ by $(1 + r)^{-Y_z}$ is given in column (5). Although $r$ is estimated from data for the female population only, it can also be used to find the stable age structure for the male population. For males one calculates

$$L_z \bullet SRB(1 + r)^{-Y_z} \qquad [2.20]$$

where SRB = the sex ratio at birth, males : females.

The SRB adjustment is necessary because stationary population models are based on the assumption that the number of male and female births per year is constant and equal, but since in practice it is usual for there to be 105 or 106 : 100, male : female births, some allowance must be made in a model that considers the structure of the total population. Column (7) in Table 2.3 shows the result of using [2.20]. The stable population model for Italy, 1970–72, is given in columns (8) and (9). The total population, males plus females, is set equal to 100,000 so that the relative contribution of each age group of males and females can be recognised. Any population with a constant rate of growth of $r$ *per annum*; constant $_nq_x$ and which is not affected by migration will ultimately reach a stable structure which in relative terms remains constant over time. In the case of Italy in the period 1970–72, $r$ was 0·3095 per cent *per annum* and $_nq_x$ could be assumed to be constant with a female $e_0$ of 74·80 and a male $e_0$ of 68·68. Such conditions, if allowed to operate over a period of time, would generate a stable population of the form shown in columns (8) and (9) of Table 2.3.

Figure 2.3 gives the relative age structures of the actual population of Italy, 1970–72, the stationary model and the stable model. It clearly demonstrates the characteristics of the two model structures, for whilst both model curves display a regular decrease in numbers with age, the stable model provides a better fit to the actual distribution. It allows for the population to grow absolutely whereas the stationary model represents the less realistic static situation. Neither model can fully cxhibit the outcome of the fluctuations in mortality and fertility which have affected the Italian population over the last 100 years, but the stable model in particular gives a suitably smoothed version of the actual age and sex structure. It is this property that is of critical importance for it enables one to examine the

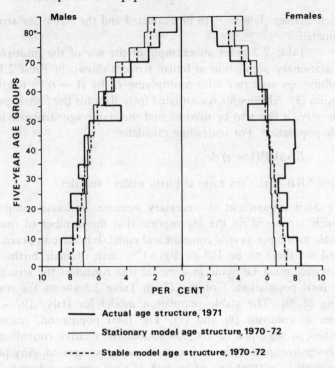

Fig. 2.3 Actual, stationary and stable model age structures for Italy, 1970–72
*Data source*: Table 2.1

effects on age and sex structure of variations in mortality and fertility conditions.

Stationary and stable populations are true models – they are simplified representations of reality – but they do possess a number of extremely practical uses because they can be generalised. It is possible to combine a variety of age-specific mortality and fertility schedules and thus create series of age structures. For example, high mortality would be combined with high fertility; and low mortality with low fertility to create distinctive model age structures. Various attempts have been made to establish a series of general stationary and stable population models, but only two will be discussed at any length here.

Demographers working for the United Nations organisation have developed a set of tables of generalised model stationary populations from an analysis of 158 national life tables (United Nations, 1955). These models have been arranged into a series of 'levels' which express the values of $_nq_x$ given a particular life expectancy at birth, $e_0$. The levels range from 0 to 115, that is from an $e_0$ for males and females combined of 20 to an $e_0$ of 73·9. The importance of these generalised stationary models is twofold. Firstly, they specify the relationships between $e_x$, $_nq_x$ and $l_x$ so that given information on one it is possible to select an appropriate level and read off what the corresponding values of the others should be. Secondly, given information on a population's age structure at two points in time it is possible using the *United Nations Models* to select a representative level from the tables which will give an indication of the mortality experience of the intervening period. This latter property can be extremely valuable in cases where no vital statistics are available but where there are data on age structure, as is the case in many underdeveloped countries and as was the case in Europe and North America before the nineteenth century.

Although the *United Nations Models* (United Nations, 1955) have proved useful they have now been superseded by a set of generalised stationary models which have been derived by Coale and Demeny (1966). Coale and Demeny have based their work on the observation that populations with the same level of life expectancy need not necessarily have the same age-specific mortality; that is, the same $e_0$ can be generated by different series of $_nq_x$. Coale and Demeny (1966) identify four distinctive patterns of $_nq_x$ functions which they call North, South, East and West largely because the patterns would be observed in the life tables for populations in northern, southern, eastern and central, and western Europe plus Europe overseas. To take a specific example, the South pattern displays consistently higher infant mortality and lower mortality in middle age than the other three patterns.

These four 'families' of generalised stationary population models are also divided into levels. These range from level 1 ($e_0$ for females = 20) to level 24 ($e_0$ = 77·5), so that for each family – North, South, East, West – there are twenty-four levels based on $e_x$. Coale and Demeny have used these stationary populations to create ninety six sets of stable population models by allowing the intrinsic rate of natural increase ($r$) to take on the thirteen values $-0·10$, $-0·05$, $0·00$, $0·05$, $0·10$, ..., $0·50$. The resulting network of 1,248 stable populations should be sufficient to summarise the structure of any closed population with constant age-specific mortality and fertility. (Coale and Demeny (1966) have also constructed an alternative network of 1,248 stable populations by using thirteen values for the gross reproduction rate, GRR (i.e. 0·80, 1·00, 1·25, 1·50, 1·75, 2·00, 2·25, 2·50, 3·00, 3·50, 4·00, 5·00, 6·00).)

Table 2.4 gives examples of stable population structures from the West and South families. Levels 9 and 21 ($e_0$ for females = 40·0 and 70·0) are used with three values for $r$. When $r = 0·00$ the population structure is stationary, but $r$ values of 0·15 and 0·30 reflect moderate and rapid growth respectively. The 12 structures shown in

**Table 2.4** Examples of stable female populations with differing mortality levels and growth rates

Level 9 $e_0 = 40$

| Age groups (1) | West | | | South | | |
|---|---|---|---|---|---|---|
| | $r = 0·00$ (2) | $r = 0·15$ (3) | $r = 0·30$ (4) | $r = 0·00$ (5) | $r = 0·15$ (6) | $r = 0·30$ (7) |
| 0–9 | 18·70 | 26·68 | 35·07 | 18·01 | 26·07 | 34·65 |
| 10–19 | 17·02 | 20·86 | 23·55 | 16·18 | 20·12 | 22·94 |
| 20–29 | 15·72 | 16·59 | 16·13 | 15·11 | 16·18 | 15·89 |
| 30–39 | 14·11 | 12·82 | 10·73 | 13·86 | 12·77 | 10·79 |
| 40–49 | 12·35 | 9·66 | 6·96 | 12·56 | 9·96 | 7·25 |
| 50–59 | 10·28 | 6·92 | 4·29 | 10·98 | 7·51 | 4·70 |
| 60–69 | 7·34 | 4·26 | 2·28 | 8·30 | 4·90 | 2·65 |
| 70–79 | 3·68 | 1·85 | 0·85 | 4·17 | 2·12 | 0·99 |
| 80+ | 0·80 | 0·35 | 0·14 | 0·84 | 0·37 | 0·15 |

Level 21 $e_0 = 70$

| Age groups (8) | West | | | South | | |
|---|---|---|---|---|---|---|
| | $r = 0·00$ (9) | $r = 0·15$ (10) | $r = 0·30$ (11) | $r = 0·00$ (12) | $r = 0·15$ (13) | $r = 0·30$ (14) |
| 0–9 | 13·76 | 21·31 | 29·78 | 13·28 | 20·87 | 29·46 |
| 10–19 | 13·65 | 18·20 | 21·88 | 13·14 | 17·78 | 21·58 |
| 20–29 | 13·51 | 15·50 | 16·04 | 13·04 | 15·19 | 15·87 |
| 30–39 | 13·27 | 13·12 | 11·68 | 12·88 | 12·91 | 11·61 |
| 40–49 | 12·90 | 10·97 | 8·41 | 12·63 | 10·90 | 8·43 |
| 50–59 | 12·16 | 8·90 | 5·88 | 12·14 | 9·02 | 6·01 |
| 60–69 | 10·56 | 6·67 | 3·79 | 11·02 | 7·06 | 4·05 |
| 70–79 | 7·26 | 3·96 | 1·95 | 8·17 | 4·51 | 2·24 |
| 80+ | 2·94 | 1·38 | 0·58 | 3·69 | 1·75 | 0·75 |

*Data source*: Coale and Demeny (1966)

Table 2.4 vary quite markedly. When mortality is relatively high and the growth rate is high – columns (4) and (7) – one would expect to find more than a third of the population aged less than 10. When mortality is low and the growth rate zero – columns (9) and (12) – one would expect to find a population whose age–sex pyramid has straight parallel sides. If mortality is relatively high and the growth rate low – columns (2) and (5) – or mortality is low and the growth rate high – columns (11) and (14) – then the resulting age–sex pyramid would be expected to have sloping sides, although the gradients would be steeper in the latter case. The differences between West and South are also identifiable. Populations with the same $e_0$ and $r$ will tend to have a lower proportion in the younger ages in the South structure than in the West and in consequence they will also tend to have higher proportions in the older age groups.

The generalised stable population models tabulated by Coale and Demeny (1966) enable one to proceed a stage further than did the United Nations stationary models because they make possible the reconstruction of the age structure, the mortality and the fertility patterns for populations that lack vital statistics. This important property of stable population models will now be described in detail.

## Demographic reconstruction

To the geographer the theory of stationary and stable populations is of particular value if it enables him to identify the regional or local patterns of population structure. Many countries in Latin America, Asia and Africa still do not have organisations for the registration of vital statistics and many that do only take sample counts which are often biased towards the urban areas and the most developed regions. In these circumstances demographic theories and techniques that enable the geographer to estimate mortality and fertility levels for sub-national units offer a means of first approximation for the analysis of regional population structures. However, there are dangers in relying too heavily upon the results of such estimation since they are no real substitute for studies based on data from regular censuses; accurate and continuously recorded vital statistics; and migration counts and surveys. Such estimates also depend upon a number of assumptions: that the population being reconstructed is not affected by migration; that there is reliable information on age structure for at least two points in time; and that the generalised stationary and stable population models to be used in the estimation exercise are capable of truly reflecting the underlying characteristics of the population to be reconstructed.

Each of these assumptions raises its own particular problems. Few inhabited areas of the globe are not subject to in-migration and out-migration, but the balance of migration need not always have a significant net impact on the structure of an area's population, particularly if that population is a large one (White and Woods, 1980: 24–8). In order to use model stationary and stable populations for reconstruction it is necessary to have two age structures, but in many underdeveloped countries such census-derived structures are subject to both under-enumeration and age misreporting. However, it is often possible to adjust the data on reported ages, although such adjustments are obviously liable to distort the final results. The use of the Coale and Demeny models as opposed to the United Nations ones should reduce the problems associated with the third assumption, but it is possible that the characteristics of the population under analysis do not conform precisely to one of the levels-families. The work of Brass (1971, 1975) on two-parameter and Zaba (1979) on four-parameter logit models has made it possible to develop standard stationary population models, the parameters of which can be adjusted to fit most mortality patterns. While that of Ledermann (1969) on the construction of a set of variable model life tables side-steps the need for precise levels and families. In the examples that follow, however, the Coale and Demeny (1966) system of reconstruction has been utilised and thus the results so obtained may differ from those which would have been found using either Brass's (1975) or Ledermann's (1969) methods.

The importance of the assumptions outlined above, the associated problems and the overall value of generalised stationary and stable population models for demographic reconstruction will be illustrated by reference to the examples of Sri Lanka and India. Sri Lanka will be used to show the theory of reconstruction and India to show the possibilities for the analysis of regional population structures.

## The population of Sri Lanka

The 1953 *Population Census of Sri Lanka* (Ceylon became independent in 1948 and changed its name to Sri Lanka in 1972) gave the population as 8,162,126 whilst the total in 1963 was given as 10,582,064; figures which were subsequently raised to 8,290,000 and 10,646,000, respectively, to allow for under-enumeration. The age structures of these populations are shown in Table 2.5 and the relative female age structures are graphed in Fig. 2.4. It is clear from this figure that there is both age-selective under-enumeration and age-clumping in the Ceylonese population. The under-enumeration of females in their late teens and early twenties is a common feature of many Third World populations, but one which is gradually being removed as a comparison of the curves for 1953 and 1963 will indicate. (Brass *et al.*, 1968, have discussed this problem in the African context.) Figure 2.4 also shows attempts to adjust for under-enumeration and age-misreporting by a simple *ad hoc* method of graphical interpolation. The results of these adjustments are shown in Table 2.5, columns (6) and (7), for the female population.

After such adjustments have been made it is possible to proceed to the selection of a mortality level which summarises the experience of the population in the inter-census period. Female population structures are normally used to make this selection because they

**Table 2.5** Population of Sri Lanka, 1953 and 1963

| Age groups | Females | | Males | | Females (adjusted) | |
|---|---|---|---|---|---|---|
| | 1953 | 1963 | 1953 | 1963 | 1953 | 1963 |
| (1) | (2) | (3) | (4) | (5) | (6) | (7) |
| 0–4 | 604,738 | 800,921 | 613,694 | 821,291 | 651,690 | 843,827 |
| 5–9 | 540,296 | 721,339 | 554,244 | 735,481 | 543,467 | 725,180 |
| 10–14 | 449,108 | 654,496 | 478,383 | 685,075 | 476,024 | 618,806 |
| 15–19 | 342,201 | 506,910 | 367,229 | 521,179 | 403,091 | 516,524 |
| 20–24 | 375,366 | 444,388 | 398,198 | 447,314 | 345,058 | 450,041 |
| 25–29 | 340,441 | 370,912 | 374,054 | 378,208 | 298,005 | 373,330 |
| 30–34 | 237,417 | 316,693 | 287,493 | 355,627 | 250,951 | 318,609 |
| 35–39 | 245,453 | 312,198 | 294,380 | 345,656 | 211,348 | 286,390 |
| 40–44 | 162,802 | 214,059 | 212,181 | 260,414 | 176,450 | 235,249 |
| 45–49 | 160,265 | 198,287 | 212,979 | 248,463 | 145,866 | 199,450 |
| 50–54 | 119,464 | 153,118 | 160,890 | 195,146 | 122,131 | 153,935 |
| 55–59 | 80,336 | 113,838 | 109,780 | 156,030 | 91,362 | 114,556 |
| 60–64 | 70,061 | 103,554 | 84,602 | 139,611 | 71,364 | 104,327 |
| 65–69 | 51,019 | 65,842 | 62,571 | 85,014 | 50,975 | 66,483 |
| 70–74 | 35,701 | 47,194 | 40,808 | 56,628 | 36,074 | 47,561 |
| 75–79 | 21,886 | 26,568 | 22,995 | 30,695 | 22,350 | 26,593 |
| 80–84 | 13,565 | 18,462 | 15,686 | 21,401 | 13,724 | 18,411 |
| 85+ | 10,514 | 14,611 | 11,326 | 15,441 | 10,587 | 14,831 |
| | 3,860,633 | 5,083,390 | 4,301,493 | 5,498,674 | 3,921,117 | 5,114,103 |

*Data sources: Population Censuses of Sri Lanka, 1953 and 1963*; Fig. 2.4

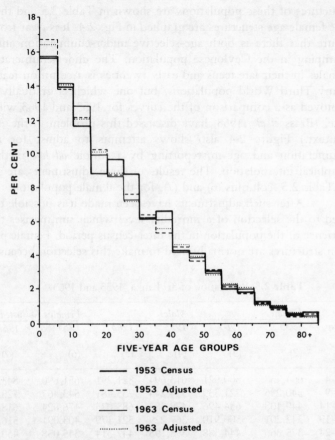

**Fig. 2.4** Relative age structures for the female population of Sri Lanka, 1953 and 1963 (census and adjusted)
*Data source*: Table 2.5

tend not to display as many irregularities due to war losses and migration as the male structures. This convention and others outlined by Coale and Demeny (United Nations, 1967) will be followed here. The use of Coale and Demeny's (1966) model stationary populations enables one to choose the most appropriate mortality level by surviving forward the initial age structure such that the level with the best fit projection to the second age structure will be the one that most closely approximates the average mortality conditions of the intervening period.

In the case of Sri Lanka, 1953–63, the five-year age groups in 1953 can be survived 10 years on to match those in 1963, so that the probability of surviving from age group 0–4 in 1953 to 10–14 in 1963, for instance, would be $_5L_{10}/_5L_0$. In this case the West and South families were used for illustrative purposes and a range of possible mortality levels was tried. Table 2.6 shows the final stage of this selection procedure. It gives the comparison of cumulated population 10 and over, 15 and over, etc. and cumulated projected population for a variety of mortality levels from the West and South models. Cumulations are compared in order to avoid the distorting influence of minor oscillations that can occur from one age group to another. Columns (7) and (13) give the interpolated mortality levels appropriate for each age cumulation. For example, the number of females in the adjusted actual population in 1963 aged 10 and over was 3,545,096 which lies between the projections obtained with West levels 13 and 14 (3,521,507 and 3,551,027). In fact it lies 0·80 of the way between them so the interpolated level can be estimated at 13·80. The West models give a range of levels from 13·41 to 15·37 (variance = 0·42), but the South models show a narrower range from 11·76 to 12·89 (variance = 0·13). The South models therefore provide a more consistent representation of the mortality experience of the Ceylonese female population in the ten-year period 1953–63. The precise selection of an individual level can be made by taking averages of the interpolated levels. The mean is South level 12·43 and the median is 12·53. Therefore it would seem justified to select South level 12·50 ($e_0$ = 48·75) as a summary of mortality conditions.

The crude birth rate (CBR) can be found by substitution in the equation

$$R = \text{CBR} - \text{CDR}$$

once $R$ and the crude death rate (CDR) have been estimated. The natural growth rate ($R$) is found from

$$\frac{P_t}{P_0} = e^{Rt}$$

and

$$R = \frac{\log_e \dfrac{P_t}{P_0}}{t}$$

where $P_t$ = the population at time $t$,
$\quad P_0$ = the population at time 0,
$\quad\ t$ = the number of time units between time 0 and time $t$,
$\quad e$ = the base of natural logarithms.

**Table 2.6** The selection of a mortality level for the female population of Sri Lanka, 1953–63

| Age groups (1) | Adjusted actual, 1963 (2) | West level 13 (3) | level 14 (4) | level 15 (5) | level 16 (6) | Interpolated level (7) |
|---|---|---|---|---|---|---|
| 10 and over | 3,545,096 | 3,521,507 | 3,551,027 | 3,580,968 | 3,609,737 | 13·80 |
| 15 and over | 2,926,290 | 2,917,195 | 2,939,611 | 2,963,296 | 2,986,200 | 13·41 |
| 20 and over | 2,409,766 | 2,394,488 | 2,414,187 | 2,435,318 | 2,455,885 | 13·78 |
| 25 and over | 1,959,725 | 1,939,790 | 1,957,109 | 1,975,717 | 1,993,904 | 14·14 |
| 30 and over | 1,586,395 | 1,559,111 | 1,574,293 | 1,590,282 | 1,606,010 | 14·75 |
| 35 and over | 1,267,786 | 1,236,309 | 1,249,421 | 1,262,891 | 1,276,273 | 15·37 |
| 40 and over | 981,396 | 959,969 | 971,055 | 982,200 | 993,377 | 14·93 |
| 45 and over | 746,147 | 729,445 | 738,674 | 747,812 | 757,056 | 14·85 |
| 50 and over | 546,697 | 537,478 | 545,079 | 552,548 | 560,164 | 14·22 |

| Age groups (8) | Adjusted actual, 1963 (9) | South level 11 (10) | level 12 (11) | level 13 (12) | Interpolated level (13) |
|---|---|---|---|---|---|
| 10 and over | 3,545,096 | 3,496,722 | 3,517,466 | 3,562,476 | 12·61 |
| 15 and over | 2,926,290 | 2,917,304 | 2,929,185 | 2,965,984 | 11·76 |
| 20 and over | 2,409,766 | 2,397,750 | 2,406,587 | 2,440,614 | 12·09 |
| 25 and over | 1,959,725 | 1,944,461 | 1,950,604 | 1,982,108 | 12·29 |
| 30 and over | 1,586,395 | 1,565,112 | 1,568,554 | 1,597,519 | 12·89 |
| 35 and over | 1,267,786 | 1,242,724 | 1,251,549 | 1,270,300 | 12·87 |
| 40 and over | 981,396 | 965,579 | 972,229 | 988,894 | 12·55 |
| 45 and over | 746,147 | 733,449 | 738,267 | 753,176 | 12·53 |
| 50 and over | 546,697 | 539,326 | 542,643 | 556,115 | 12·30 |

*Data sources:* Table 2.5; Coale and Demeny (1966)

Thus for Ceylonese females, 1953–63,

$$R = \frac{\log_e 1{\cdot}30425}{10}$$

$$R = \frac{0{\cdot}26563}{10}$$

$$R = 0{\cdot}02656 \text{ per year.}$$

The above calculation is made with the assumptions that net migration is negligible and that the rate of natural increase is the same as the rate of actual increase.

The crude death rate can be found by summing the product of the average population 1953–63 and the age-specific model death rates ($_5M_x$) taken from South level 12·50 of Coale and Demeny's tables. This sum of the expected number of deaths can then be rationed over the average total population ($P_t/P_0$) to give the crude death rate. By such a process the CDR was found to equal 0·01734 or 17·34 per thousand.

Solution of

$$R = \text{CBR} - \text{CDR}$$

gives

$$0{\cdot}02656 = \text{CBR} - 0{\cdot}01737$$

$$\text{CBR} = 0{\cdot}04393.$$

To summarise, the female population of Sri Lanka in the period 1953–63 probably had a crude birth rate of 43·93 and a crude death rate of 17·37 per thousand, whilst $e_0$ was between 47·50 and 50·00. Comparison of these figures with those quoted by Wright (1968: 750) from official Ceylonese publications suggests that the overall CBR might have been even higher than 39·4 in 1953 and 34·6 in 1963 or even 43·3 per thousand in 1953, assuming a 10 per cent under-registration of births. If the average CBR was between 42 and 44 per thousand during 1953–63, then the recent decline in Ceylonese fertility to give CBR levels of 29 to 31 per thousand in the late 1960s and early 1970s stands out as a remarkable instance of demographic change for a Third World country.

The above estimates can be corroborated by using the various stable populations which are associated with South level 12·50. Assuming that $r = 0{\cdot}02656$ then the corresponding model stable population is as shown in Table 2.7. Interpolations are made between levels 12 and 13 to derive level 12·50 and between values of

**Table 2.7** Characteristics of a model stable population for the female population of Sri Lanka, 1953–63

| Age groups | Average female population, 1953–63 | Average adjusted female population, 1953–63 | Model stable population, South level 12·50 $r = 0·02656$ |
|---|---|---|---|
| (1) | (2) | (3) | (4) |
| 0–4 | 15·72 | 16·55 | 16·97 |
| 5–9 | 14·11 | 14·02 | 13·74 |
| 10–14 | 12·34 | 12·12 | 11·80 |
| 15–19 | 9·49 | 10·18 | 10·15 |
| 20–24 | 9·17 | 8·80 | 8·68 |
| 25–29 | 7·95 | 7·43 | 7·40 |
| 30–34 | 6·19 | 6·30 | 6·29 |
| 35–39 | 6·23 | 5·52 | 5·35 |
| 40–44 | 4·21 | 4·56 | 4·52 |
| 45–49 | 4·01 | 3·83 | 3·81 |
| 50–54 | 3·05 | 3·06 | 3·18 |
| 55–59 | 2·17 | 2·28 | 2·61 |
| 60–64 | 1·94 | 1·94 | 2·06 |
| 65–69 | 1·31 | 1·30 | 1·53 |
| 70–74 | 0·92 | 0·93 | 1·03 |
| 75–79 | 0·55 | 0·54 | 0·57 |
| 80+ | 0·64 | 0·64 | 0·31 |
|  | 100·00 | 100·00 | 100·00 |

*Characteristics of the model stable population:*

| | |
|---|---|
| $e_0$ = 48·75 | Average age = 23·39 |
| CBR = 44·05 | Average age at death = 22·19 |
| CDR = 17·49 | |
| GRR = 2·87 | |

*Data sources*: Table 2.5; Coale and Demeny (1966: 702–5)

0·025 and 0·030 to derive $r = 0·02656$. Columns (2) and (3) show the relative age structure of the average female population of Sri Lanka, 1953–63, based on the two censuses (col. (2)) and adjusted by interpolation (col. (3) is from Table 2.5, cols. (6) and (7)). Column (4) gives the structure of the stable model from South level 12·50 with $r = 0·02656$. The fit between columns (3) and (4) can be seen to be close.

Table 2.7 also gives the demographic characteristics appropriate to a population with the structure of column (4). The crude birth rate is 44·05 and the crude death rate is 17·49 per thousand, which compare well with previous estimates of 43·93 and 17·37 per thousand. The gross reproduction rate (GRR) is 2·87, the average age of the female population is 23·39 and the average age at death is 22·19. The estimated TFR would probably be about 5·85, which is higher than the officially reported figures for 1953 and 1963, which were 5·32 and 5·04 respectively (Wright, 1968: 746). The differences are probably mainly due to the under-registration of births, although TFRs of 4·50 and less for the 1960s and 1970s do demonstrate a real and substantial fertility decline (see Fernando, 1972, 1974, 1975, 1976). The mortality experience of the Ceylonese population has certainly changed radically since the Second World War. Although the above calculations suggest a CDR value of 17 per thousand, estimates for the late 1960s and the 1970s range from 9 to 7 per thousand. Arguments over the causes of this decline have been fierce. Although it now seems that the eradication of malaria in the dry zone of Sri Lanka accounted for some 23 per cent of the initial reduction, other improvements, such as the provision of medical facilities and the rise in the standard of living, have helped to reinforce the process (Meegama, 1967; Gray, 1974; Palloni, 1975).

The example discussed above illustrates the value of model stationary and stable populations for the reconstruction of the demographic characteristics of populations with poor or non-existent vital statistics. However, it must be emphasised that the whole exercise is founded on specific assumptions. The migration history of Sri Lanka indicates the existence of substantial emigration and immigration flows. For example, some 9,000 Ceylonese were recorded as living in England and Wales in the 1961 *Population Census* and the estimate for 1966 was 12,900. The movement of Tamils from southern India to and from Sri Lanka has also been considerable. In these circumstances the assumption that net migration is not affecting age structure is questionable although the precise nature of any such influence cannot be assessed. Further, the enumerated age structures of populations in many Third World countries tend to display abnormalities which it is often desirable to remove before the reconstruction proceduce begins. However, such adjustments may influence the final results of the reconstruction especially when the number of young children has been seriously under-enumerated. Table 2.7 illustrated this particular problem in the case of Sri Lanka.

Apart from the migration and age structure assumptions other problems are likely to be encountered which are specific to the population under analysis. For example, most populations have different $e_0$ values for males and females, but normally $e_0$ is 2 to 4 years higher for females than males. However, in South Asian populations the reverse is usually the case. The evidence of Table 2.5 confirms the pattern for Sri Lanka since it shows the excess of males over females in all but the youngest age group. Although the mortality experience of females can be summarised by South level 12·50, it is probable that level 15 with an $e_0$ of nearly 52 would be more appropriate for males. Since all Coale and Demeny's (1966) models are based on the assumption that $e_0$ for females is higher than that for males the atypical characteristics of South Asian populations do raise important problems when they are the object of reconstruction.

Despite these drawbacks the method of demographic reconstruction outlined above can be used quite effectively when at least two age structures are available. It provides a set of reasonable estimates of the characteristics of the population in question which would not otherwise be available.

Although the population geographer is concerned with international demographic patterns he is also interested in regional differences within particular countries. For this reason the regional population structure of India in the 1960s will now be discussed as a means of elaborating the theory of demographic reconstruction based on stationary and stable models.

## The regional population structure of India

The study of the regional population structure of India provides stable theory with one of its greatest challenges. Although censuses have been carried out in India since the late nineteenth century a continuous system of vital registration has not been initiated, largely because of the expense and the daunting scale of the administrative organisation that would be involved. The recently implemented Sample Registration Scheme, which is based on household interviews in a random selection of rural and urban districts, provides one means of estimating vital rates, but of necessity it utilises only a very small sample size. Demographic estimates for the 1950s and 1960s must therefore be founded on census data or upon the numerous surveys carried out at the village level (Wyon and Gordon, 1971). National and regional estimates are entirely limited to census data. If the methods of reconstruction founded on stable population theory can be employed in this context to derive realistic demographic variables then they will be of great practical utility whilst the underlying theory will itself be validated. Although this analysis deals specifically with regional variations demographic estimation for India as a whole has already been well developed (see for example Coale and Hoover, 1958; Visaria, 1969; Das Gupta, 1971; Adlakha and Kirk, 1974).

Both the 1961 and 1971 *Population Censuses of India* give data on age structures by single years and by five-year age groups, but in the period between censuses several state boundaries were adjusted and the new states of Haryana and Himachal Pradesh were created. For comparative purposes the Punjab, Haryana and Himachal Pradesh have been combined in the following example while Jammu and Kashmir, and Assam have been excluded from consideration because of frontier or boundary changes. Demographic reconstruction was therefore performed on twelve separate states and one combination of three states. (The state boundaries are shown in Fig. 2.5.)

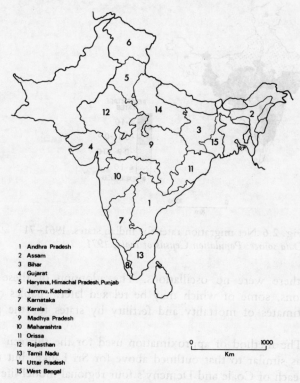

1 Andhra Pradesh
2 Assam
3 Bihar
4 Gujarat
5 Haryana, Himachal Pradesh, Punjab
6 Jammu, Kashmir
7 Karnataka
8 Kerala
9 Madhya Pradesh
10 Maharashtra
11 Orissa
12 Rajasthan
13 Tamil Nadu
14 Uttar Pradesh
15 West Bengal

0 _____ 1000
Km

**Fig. 2.5** Indian state boundaries

As usual one is bound to begin estimation by making a number of assumptions which are open to criticism. Firstly, it is assumed that over the decade mortality was at a constant level. For India as a whole this would not be entirely unreasonable for it seems that $e_0$ rose by between three and eight years from the 1950s to 1960s (Cassen, 1978a, Table 2.11, p. 116), but it is unlikely that this change was followed uniformly in all states. Secondly, it is assumed that the age-specific net impact of inter-state migration and emigration was zero. Here again there is reason to believe that the relative magnitude of the numerical impact varied from state to state, but because the states have such large populations the absolute impact is likely to be negligible (see Gosal and Krishan, 1975). Figure 2.6 shows the inter-census net migration rates in per cent, all of which are comparatively low. The third assumption is that age- and sex-specific fertility changed in an orderly progression over the

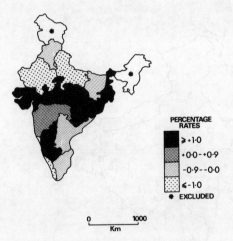

**Fig. 2.6** Net migration rates for Indian states, 1961–71
*Data source: Population Census of India, 1971*

decade; there were no oscillations. The adoption of these three assumptions, some of which may be relaxed later, enables one to make estimates of mortality and fertility by states for the period 1961–71.

The method of approximation used for the thirteen Indian states was similar to that outlined above for Sri Lanka, but in this instance each of Coale and Demeny's four regional model life tables was used as a source for survival factors and males and females were treated independently. These ten-year survival factors were applied to the 1961 populations in five-year age groups and the resulting projections compared with the 1971 populations in their cumulated forms (see Table 2.6). One illustration is shown in Table 2.8 for Andhra Pradesh. The four families of model life tables yield different approximations of the mortality experience of the state's population in the 1960s. However, the model with the lowest variance is the logical choice as the best representation. In this respect the pattern of model life table levels shown in Table 2.8 is typical. The variance of levels is lower for females than males and the North, West and South families are, in that order, generally superior to the East family. The best representation of the mortality experience of the male population is given by the North family whilst the West family provides the best estimate for the female population. By convention the median is used to approximate the average level, which after rounding gives North level 12 for males and West level 9 for females (see United Nations, 1967; Shryock and Siegel, 1976: 491–96).

The method shown in Table 2.8 was reproduced for the other twelve states and the same criteria were used to select the most suitable model life table level. The results of this operation are shown in Table 2.9. The next stage in the sequence is to estimate $R$, the annual rate of natural increase, for each state's male and female population separately. Once this has been done from the census figures it can be corrected using estimated inter-census migration rates (see Fig. 2.6), thus relaxing the second assumption made above. Corrected for net migration, the annual growth rates of the male and female populations of Andhra Pradesh, for example, were 0·01979 and 0·01844, respectively. Values of $R$ estimated in this way can then be used as approximations of $r$, the intrinsic rate of natural increase, in order to locate stable population models within the network presented by Coale and Demeny (1966). For instance, using North level 12 and $r = 0·01979$ (R = 19·79 in Coale and Demeny's usage) CBR and CDR for Andhra Pradesh males can be found by interpolation to be 39·65 and 19·86, which when combined with values of 41·76 and 23·32 for females found in similar fashion give overall crude birth and death rates of 40·65 and 21·57 in parts per thousand. The gross reproduction rate of 2·80 can also be found from West level 9 with $r = 0·01844$ for the female population, assuming that the average age at maternity is 29.

The final results of this reconstruction exercise are shown in Table 2.10 which gives $e_0$ and $e_5$ for males and females, CBR, CDR and GRR. These key mortality and fertility measures are also shown

**Table 2.8** Model life table levels used to estimate the mortality experience of Andhra Pradesh, 1961–71

| Age groups (1) | North Males (2) | North Females (3) | South Males (4) | South Females (5) | East Males (6) | East Females (7) | West Males (8) | West Females (9) |
|---|---|---|---|---|---|---|---|---|
| 10 and over | 12·30 | 7·99 | 10·42 | 7·52 | 10·40 | 7·32 | 12·20 | 8·81 |
| 15 and over | 8·99 | 6·30 | 6·53 | 4·81 | 6·69 | 4·91 | 9·43 | 6·81 |
| 20 and over | 12·49 | 10·28 | 10·81 | 8·94 | 11·52 | 9·65 | 13·37 | 11·07 |
| 25 and over | 16·45 | 11·17 | 15·13 | 9·86 | 16·69 | 10·86 | 17·43 | 11·39 |
| 30 and over | 14·58 | 7·89 | 13·24 | 6·46 | 14·71 | 7·35 | 15·85 | 8·86 |
| 35 and over | 12·95 | 7·42 | 11·67 | 5·86 | 13·15 | 6·89 | 14·55 | 8·34 |
| 40 and over | 13·22 | 7·99 | 12·19 | 6·46 | 13·98 | 7·67 | 15·11 | 8·93 |
| 45 and over | 10·89 | 7·58 | 9·43 | 6·21 | 11·00 | 7·49 | 12·70 | 8·55 |
| 50 and over | 10·02 | 8·97 | 8·56 | 7·92 | 10·06 | 9·41 | 11·87 | 10·13 |
| Mean | 12·43 | 8·40 | 10·89 | 7·12 | 12·02 | 7·95 | 13·61 | 9·21 |
| Median | 12·49 | 7·99 | 10·81 | 6·46 | 11·52 | 7·49 | 13·37 | 8·86 |
| Variance | 5·02 | 2·25 | 5·86 | 2·86 | 9·12 | 3·35 | 6·05 | 1·69 |

*Data sources: Population Censuses of India, 1961 and 1971; Coale and Demeny (1966)*

**Table 2.9** Best-fit model life table levels for Indian states, 1961–71

| States (1) | Males (2) | Females (3) |
|---|---|---|
| 1 Andhra Pradesh | North level 12 | West level 9 |
| 2 Bihar | North level 12 | North level 8 |
| 3 Gujarat | West level 16 | South level 12 |
| 4 Haryana, Himachal Pradesh and Punjab | North level 16 | South level 11 |
| 5 Karnataka | North level 13 | West level 12 |
| 6 Kerala | North level 17 | West level 13 |
| 7 Madhya Pradesh | North level 13 | North level 11 |
| 8 Maharashtra | West level 15 | North level 12 |
| 9 Orissa | North level 12 | North level 9 |
| 10 Rajasthan | North level 13 | North level 12 |
| 11 Tamil Nadu | North level 14 | West level 9 |
| 12 Uttar Pradesh | North level 14 | North level 7 |
| 13 West Bengal | West level 11 | North level 9 |

in Fig. 2.7 ($e_0$ for males and females), Fig. 2.8 (CBR and CDR for 1951–61 and 1961–71) and Fig. 2.9 (GRR) for the thirteen Indian states in 1961–71.

It is clear from these figures and Tables 2.10 that there are wide inter-state variations in both mortality and fertility. For males, $e_0$ ranges from 56·3 (Kerala) to 42·1 (West Bengal) and for females the range is similar from 50·0 (Kerala) to 35·0 (Uttar Pradesh). In all but one instance $e_0$ for males exceeds that for females. Figure 2.7 reveals a distinctive east–west trend for female $e_0$ with the lowest levels occurring in Uttar Pradesh and Bihar. However, for male $e_0$ spatial patterns are less easily recognisable. The crude birth rate (Fig. 2.8) and the gross reproduction rate (Fig. 2.9) give impressions of the inter-state variation in fertility which, apart from Bihar and Gujarat, seems to have a north–east to south–west gradation, high to low.

Explanation of these spatial variations may prove troublesome not only because of the small number of areas which will affect ecological correlations, but also because the controlling factors are inter-linked in a highly complex fashion. To take one example, variations in fertility may be associated with levels of information about and willingness to adopt methods of family limitation which will themselves be connected to levels of literacy, especially amongst females (see, for example, Mamdani, 1972; Chandrasekhar, 1972; Mandelbaum, 1974). Figure 2.10 shows the percentage of married

**Table 2.10** Estimated mortality and fertility measures for Indian states, 1961–71

| States (1) | Males | | Females | | CBR (6) | CDR (7) | GRR* (8) |
|---|---|---|---|---|---|---|---|
| | $e_0$ (2) | $e_5$ (3) | $e_0$ (4) | $e_5$ (5) | | | |
| 1 Andhra Pradesh | 44·3 | 51·9 | 40·0 | 49·7 | 40·65 | 21·57 | 2·80 |
| 2 Bihar | 46·7 | 53·3 | 37·5 | 47·8 | 39·15 | 21·88 | 2·76 |
| 3 Gujarat | 54·1 | 57·6 | 47·5 | 57·1 | 41·07 | 15·49 | 3·03 |
| 4 Haryana, Himachal Pradesh and Punjab | 53·9 | 57·5 | 45·0 | 55·5 | 39·23 | 16·67 | 2·96 |
| 5 Karnataka | 46·7 | 53·3 | 47·5 | 54·4 | 40·47 | 17·77 | 2·82 |
| 6 Kerala | 56·3 | 59·0 | 50·0 | 55·5 | 37·99 | 14·01 | 2·68 |
| 7 Madhya Pradesh | 46·7 | 53·3 | 45·0 | 52·7 | 43·15 | 18·71 | 2·99 |
| 8 Maharashtra | 51·8 | 56·3 | 47·5 | 54·3 | 38·76 | 16·06 | 2·80 |
| 9 Orissa | 44·3 | 51·9 | 40·0 | 49·5 | 43·31 | 21·72 | 3·03 |
| 10 Rajasthan | 46·7 | 53·3 | 47·5 | 54·3 | 43·57 | 17·84 | 3·01 |
| 11 Tamil Nadu | 49·1 | 54·6 | 40·0 | 49·8 | 39·65 | 19·84 | 2·81 |
| 12 Uttar Pradesh | 49·1 | 54·7 | 35·0 | 46·2 | 41·46 | 22·14 | 3·08 |
| 13 West Bengal | 42·1 | 50·8 | 40·0 | 49·5 | 46·88 | 22·62 | 3·58 |

* GRR has an underlying maternity schedule with a mean age of 29
*Data sources: Population Censuses of India, 1961 and 1971; Coal and Demeny (1966)*

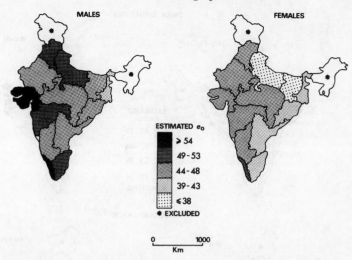

**Fig. 2.7** Estimated life expectancy at birth ($e_0$) for Indian states, 1961–71
*Data source*: Table 2.10

couples effectively protected by birth control methods in 1974–75 (Visaria and Jain, 1976: 38). Punjab, Haryana, Gujarat, Maharashtra, Kerala and Tamil Nadu were those states with the highest levels of birth control adoption in the mid-1970s and some of them also had relatively lower levels of fertility in the 1960s (Blaikie, 1975; see especially Narayan, 1977). In terms of literacy, Fig. 2.11 shows the percentages literate amongst males and females in 1961. The differences between rates for males and females is quite substantial as is the inter-state variation. Kerala, in particular, stands out as having a relatively high literacy rate, just as it stood out having a low GRR. Similarly those states with lower literacy also tend to have higher fertility. The effect of differences in education and literacy is fully brought out in Fig. 2.12 which related to the age-specific fertility of married women during the year prior to the 1971 *Population Census*. The total fertility rates for the illiterate females and the graduate females, were, respectively, 5·32 and 3·71 largely because of the higher number of high parity births to the less educated or illiterate females. (Fernando, 1977, 1979 has observed similar patterns in Sri Lanka.)

The estimates presented in Table 2.10 must, however, be treated with some caution. Firstly, there are difficulties associated with the assumptions required for the practical application of stationary and stable models. An attempt has been made in this

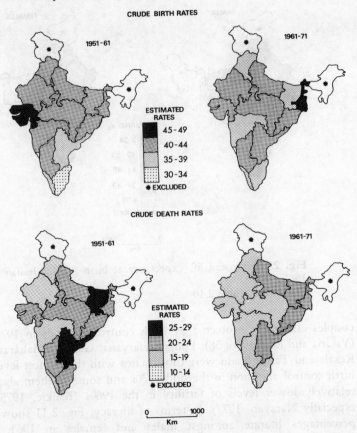

**Fig. 2.8** Estimated crude birth and death rates (CBR and CDR) for Indian states 1951–61 and 1961–71
*Data sources*: 1951–61 from Bose (1967); 1961–71 from Table 2.10

reconstruction to take account of net migration differentials, but this was done only after the life table-stationary model had been selected. Only the use of age-specific net migration rates for each state to adjust the observed cumulative age structure for 1971 would have allowed for the full effects of migration. Perhaps more seriously it has been assumed that age-specific mortality and fertility have remained constant. While these assumptions are not completely unreasonable they may lead to distortions in the final estimates which can be partially alleviated by the use of quasi-stable models in which corrections are made for mortality decline (see Coale, 1971: Mari Bhat, 1977).

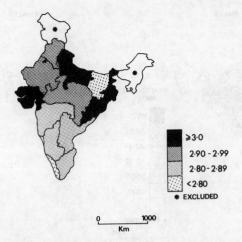

**Fig. 2.9** Estimated gross reproduction rates (GRR) for Indian states, 1961–71
*Data source*: Table 2.10

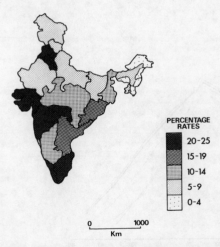

**Fig. 2.10** Percentage of married couples effectively protected by birth control methods, Indian states, 1974–75
*Data source*: Visaria and Jain (1976, Table 14, p. 38)

Secondly, although reconstructions via stable population theory are capable of partially overcoming the problems associated with differential age under-enumeration and misreporting because they compare cumulative observed and expected populations (see

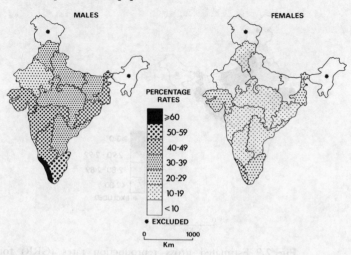

**Fig. 2.11** Percentage of males and females aged five and over who were literate, Indian states, 1961
*Data source*: Bose (1967)

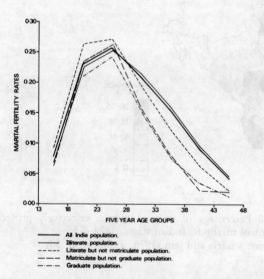

**Fig. 2.12** Age-specific marital fertility rates by education and literacy, India, 1971
*Data source: Population Census of India, 1971* (Paper 2 of 1977, Fertility Tables, 1971 (1 per cent sample))

Coale and Demeny's discussion in United Nations, 1967), they are not able to combat the problems raised when under-enumeration or age misreporting change radically from one census to the next. Although it is virtually impossible to gain an impression of the inter-state variation in under-enumeration the question of age mis-reporting can be tackled. The Myers index of age-clumping mea-sures the degree to which respondents report their ages as having parti-cular terminal digits; for example, 30 rather than 29 or 31, 35 rather than 34 or 36 (Myers, 1940; see also Woods, 1979: 30). Calcula-tion of the Myers index using the age ranges 10–69 and 20–79 for the populations of the Indian states as reported by single years of age in the 1961 and 1971 censuses reveals both considerable spatial variation and a certain amount of change between censuses. Figure 2.13 shows the discrepancy between age-clumping for males and females, the range of indices observed and the increase or decrease between 1961 and 1971; while Fig. 2.14 shows the spatial variation in index levels in 1961 and 1971. The change in age-clumping between 1961 and 1971 is the most crucial aspect for the above reconstruction

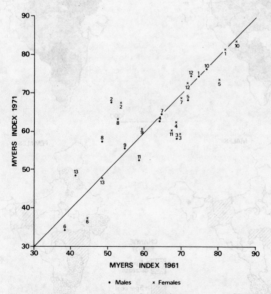

**Fig. 2.13** Myers indices for Indian states, 1971 against 1961 (num-bers refer to those used in Table 2.10)
*Data sources: Population Censuses of India, 1961* (Paper 2 of 1963, Age Tables) and *1971* (Series 1, Part II-c (ii), Social and Cultural Tables)

because in states like Bihar, Maharashtra and, for males at least, West Bengal age–clumping was substantially worse in 1971 than 1961. The

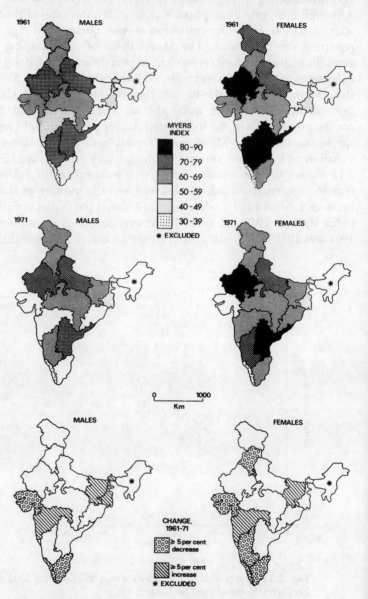

**Fig. 2.14** Myers indices for Indian states, 1961 and 1971
*Data sources*: see Fig. 2.13

suspicion must arise, therefore, that the overall quality of the census age structure data deteriorated in 1971. Perhaps under-enumeration also became worse, which means that age structure based estimates are bound to be affected by apparent changes which, in the case of the three states named above, would over-estimate life expectancy and under-estimate fertility meeasures. The gross reproduction rate for Bihar is probably an under-estimate of the true level of fertility. These two considerations – the nature of assumptions and under-estimate fertility measures. The gross reproduction rate use of stable population theory as a basis for demographic reconstruction, but their importance should not be over-dramatised in relation to the general practical value of the theory as a device for making first approximations. The application of this pure demographic theory does after all make possible the identification of geographical patterns which would not otherwise have been revealed.

# 3
# Over time and through space

Over the land freckled with snow half-thawed
The speculating rooks at their nests cawed
And saw from elm-tops, delicate as flower of grass,
What we below could not see, Winter pass.
Edward Thomas, *Thaw* from *Collected Poems*

One aspect of geography which has traditionally received close attention and which has recently taken on a new sophistication is the analysis of spatio-temporal patterns and the processes that form them. In population geography there has been a long-standing concern to study the changing distribution of population and especially spatial and temporal variations in its density per unit area; a concern which has usually been put into effect by the comparison of census results on a cross-sectional basis. A series of mosaics is created, with each individual mosaic offering prospects for pattern recognition and the illusion of a kaleidoscope when viewed consecutively. Similarly, the study of the magnitude, length and direction of migration flows has taken on a temporal as well as a specifically spatial form with the use of methods derived from network and matrix analysis. Population geographers have, however, been less occupied with the analysis of changing mortality and fertility patterns which has represented a serious lacuna in their overall contribution to the study of population. This omission is made all the more regrettable because the study of variations in mortality and fertility patterns over time and through space poses several interesting problems, both from the point of view of modelling and the construction of causal theory, on which geographers may reasonably be expected to shed some light.

The central questions are these. How do geographical areas which may have their own particular economic, social and political structures respond to external stimuli? How are those stimuli communicated? Are changes endogenously or exogenously induced? Can the endemic and chronic effects be separated from the epidemic and acute? How do technical and ideological innovations diffuse and why are they adopted? And more generally, can processes be identified from patterns? Some of these issues have already been touched on in passing in Chapters 1 and 2, but while Chapter 1 was specifically concerned with the temporal aspects of population growth and Chapter 2 was largely occupied in the identification of spatial patterns at a particular point in time, which would otherwise have remained obscure, here we are explicitly concerned with all of these issues and particularly with their implications for theory construction.

Two concrete examples will be used as testing grounds for two groups of theories. The first group deals with the spatial and temporal manifestations of an acute event, namely demographic crises in pre-industrial societies, whilst the second group tackles the voluntary control of human fertility during the nineteenth century. Particular empirical examples are drawn upon, respectively, seventeenth-century Yorkshire and England and Wales, 1861–91.

## Demographic crises

One of the characteristic features of pre-industrial, pre-capitalist societies is their recurrent exposure to demographic crises. Although these can be defined in various ways (Schofield, 1972) the essential point is that the number of deaths exceeds the number of births by a substantial amount over a relatively short period of time. A population is therefore likely to decline absolutely during that period and is certainly unable to replace itself naturally. Such crises can occur for four main groups of reasons. Firstly, but of least quantitative importance, is the natural disaster, such as the flood, earthquake or volcanic eruption. Although these events can have catastrophic consequences their range is normally localised and their occurrence, apart perhaps for the first-mentioned, is extremely intermittent. The second group is associated with the outbreak of diseases which, particularly when they are of the airborne, or water- or food-borne varieties, exhibit distinctive patterns of spatial incidence although actual case fatality rates can vary considerably between particular diseases.

The third group of reasons is traditionally placed under the heading of 'subsistence crises', but the Malthusian connotations of the phrase can be misleading. Subsistence crises are food shortage crises, but the causes of the shortages are various. Malthus's explicit assumption is that the shortage is created by population pressure, that numbers rise beyond the level supportable by the resource base, and that the 'positive check' must therefore exact its regulatory toll. There are other possibilities, of course, most of which are related to the supply of food. Harvest failures can result from climatological vicissitudes, or oscillations, but they are more likely to be found where the agricultural methods employed are relatively simple and where the land is marginally productive. What is more important for the food supply in general is the manner in which food is distributed; whether there is an active market, whether it can be easily transported between surplus and deficit regions, but, perhaps above all, who is ultimately in control of its production and use. Is it the cultivator, the landowner, the merchant or the State?

The fourth group of reasons is associated with military activity which can have influences both via its disruptive effects on food production and distribution, and because it is liable to aid the communication of epidemic diseases.

The importance of demographic crises can easily be over-emphasised not only because of the indelible mark they left on contemporaries (see Clarkson, 1975), but also because of the dramatic form in which they appear in modern studies which use parish registers or probate records. The Essex village of Terling, for instance, had only one disastrous year (1625) in the whole period from 1540 to 1725 (Wrightson and Levine, 1979: 45–6). However, Helleiner (1957) has argued that one of the first signs of the onset of the demographic transition in western Europe was the reduction in severity and the increasing infrequency of demographic crises and thus they had a peculiarly important role in keeping pre-transition mortality especially high. Likewise, Flinn (1974) has characterised the demography of pre-industrial Europe as being one of instability where the notion of a normal death or birth rate had little value. In fifteenth-century East Anglia, Gottfried (1976, 1978), using a sample of 20,000 probated wills, has demonstrated that of the 50 years from 1430 to 1480 some twenty seven had clearly identifiable demographic crises although there were also distinctive areas of endemic mortality, particularly near the coast and in the Fenland–Breckland region. Gottfried (1978: 225) concludes, however, that, 'The most important factor of mortality was epidemic disease, especially plague, and the most important feature of plague was not the virulence of any given epidemic, but rather the frequency of continual epidemics. From 1430 to 1470, and perhaps 1480, infectious disease was the primary factor in controlling population growth.'

This observation leads us to an issue which has been debated even more intensely than that of the impact of demographic crises as a whole, namely the relative balance between the influence of 'disease crises' and 'food shortage crises'. One of the most intriguing aspects of this debate is concerned with the fourteenth century. Postan (1950, 1972), on the one hand, has argued that the population of England had stabilised or begun to decline even before the Black Death of 1348, that a position of relative over-population had been reached which brought into effect positive checks and pushed death rates to a 'punishing height', and that there was the possibility of lower birth rates as constraints were imposed on marriage by the limitation of access to land. Certainly there is strong corroborating evidence for severe 'agrarian crises' in the period 1315–22 (Platt, 1978: 96). On the other hand, Hilton *et al.* (1976: 28) and Bridbury (1973, 1975: vii–xxiv, 1977) argue from an opposing point of view, whilst Russell (1948: 280, 1966a, b; see also Chambers, 1972: 19; Hatcher, 1977: 71; and Fig. 1.7) presents a different image of reality. They emphasise the significance of the distribution of power, both economic and political, in society and the way it affects the ownership of, access to and use of land. In this particular context the issue is fundamental for reasons which are purely technical: patterns of population change over time must be inferred from price or wage series which may be artificaly inflated by landholders without that necessarily signifying the existence of population pressure. What has been challenged less often is the severity of the impact which bubonic or pneumonic plague had on population numbers in 1348. Nearly all commentators would agree that the Black Death of the mid-fourteenth century represents the classic instance of a disease-based demographic crisis; that to its direct demographic influence can be attributed a population reduction of about a third in western Europe; and that its recurrence had important consequences for the late Medieval economy and society which made them distinct from those of the early Medieval period.

The causes of demographic crises are more easily identifiable when parish registers become available, which in England means the period after 1538, although there are still problems of interpretation and difficulties inherent in the sources themselves. Again, the central issue concerns the relative importance of food shortages and outbreaks of epidemic disease. There are occasions when it is obvious which one is the main causal agent. Goubert's (1960) studies of the Beauvaisis, for instance, have provided a clear example of famine conditions holding sway in 1694 in the grain lands of northern France. Similarly, Schofield (1977), using family reconstitution data for Colyton, Devon, is able to isolate the influence of an outbreak of bubonic plague in 1645–46. In many instances, however, it has proved difficult to specify exactly what was the major cause of a demographic crisis. Famine conditions provide a background for the outbreak of infectious disease. The link between such food shortages and, for instance, typhus, or famine fever, has often been observed as has the association between famine and amenorrhea (reduced fecundity) (see Le Roy Ladurie, 1969). This particular link means that during food shortage crises the number of conceptions declines and hence that a trough in the birth rate will lag by 9 to 12 months the peak in the death rate.

The most commonly employed method of distinguishing between the two main forms of demographic crises has been to correlate time series of burials, derived from parish registers, with those of prices, usually for cereals. The belief is that where there are coincidences then these will show the relationship between high grain prices, food shortages and peaks in mortality, but where peaks exist which are unrelated to sharp rises in grain prices then there will be indirect evidence for the influence of disease.

For England, at least, there are technical difficulties in employing this particular method because of the scarcity of local price series. Hoskins (1964, 1968; see also Harrison, 1971) has relied heavily on the combination of local series of grain prices compiled by William Beveridge in the 1930s, which have been used to classify harvests into six categories (dearth, bad, deficient, average, good and abundant). Much of our knowledge of these series is in fact derived from the work of J. E. Thorold Rogers in the second half of the nineteenth century (see Bowden, 1967: 865–70). Those scholars who have actually tried to match up vital and grain price series have, however, found that there are not only problems which relate to the sources and quality of the time series, but also that there are difficulties to be encountered in drawing conclusions.

The case study presented by Appleby (1975) and the debate on the proof necessary to establish death by starvation provide useful examples. Using the Bills of Mortality for London, which purport to record the numbers and causes of deaths per week, together with a series for maximum permissible bread prices, Appleby (1975) is unable to demonstrate any statistical association between cause of death and what he takes to be a surrogate for nutrition, apart from the case of typhus which does give a slightly better positive fit. The rather tentative conclusion is that such evidence, for what it is worth, tends to support Chambers's (1972: 77–106) concept of the 'autonomous death rate'; that there were recurrent disease-based demographic crises whose incidence and frequency were largely unrelated to economic conditions, or if related then only by chance, and that these particular forms of crisis were responsible in large measure for controlling population growth. In this scheme it is the biological factor which dominates the environmental.

Discussion on the criteria necessary to define the cause of a crisis has focused on the work of Laslett (1965: 113–34) and Appleby (1973, 1978). Appleby (1973: 421) develops a new methodology for the elaboration of such criteria. Definitional characteristics for famine ought to include the following: burials should exceed twice the annual mean; similar conditions should be observable in adjacent parishes; a positive association should exist between the number of burials and the level of prices; corroborative evidence should exist in contemporary accounts; the 'economically marginal' (wanderers, beggars, children, widows) should be most affected; and a reduction in the number of conceptions should indicate the existence of famine amenorrhea. Using these criteria Appleby (1973) is able to distinguish two famine years, 1597 and 1623, in the period 1560 to 1640, but he also claims one plague year, 1598, and 'one year of typhus probably aggravated by famine, 1587' (p. 429). Apart from 1623 there seem to have been periods of demographic crises with multiple causes in the 1580s and 1590s in the villages of Cumbria. This only serves to illustrate the point that although Appleby's criteria represent an improvement on those outlined by Laslett (1965), they are in certain senses more sophisticated than the data available for pre-census England are able to support. Demographic crises were commonly of a multiple origin; plague followed conditions of food shortage, typhus combined with them, and only rarely was there a pure famine or a single dramatic outbreak of bubonic plague. (Useful tables of the characteristics of infectious diseases appear in Rogers, 1975: 32–33; or Schofield, 1977: 121.)

An important factor which also needs to be taken into account is the degree to which a population was engaged in agricultural production, that is the extent to which a local society was a landed community. Drake (1962) and Appleby (1973, 1978) have both emphasised the potential significance of that section of the population which was not engaged, or only partially engaged, in agriculture. In the West Riding of Yorkshire and Cumbria most of this landless or partly landless group was active in weaving, which implies that entire communities could be susceptible to trade cycles and depressions as well as the vicissitudes of the harvest and the chance attacks of epidemic disease. Drake (1962: 436) has sketched one sequence of events: 'A bad harvest causes food prices to rise and possibly curtails expenditure on manufactured goods, e.g. woollen cloth. This produces a depression in the industrial sector of the economy, cuts incomes and increases the distress already caused by higher food prices. The number of people who need to seek relief from the parish authorities rises, and this makes the parish officials eager to reduce their burden by getting rid of vagrants, and others who might not have been in the parish for very long. The circulation of those people most likely to be disease carriers is thereby increased.' It is, of course, possible for depressions in the manufacturing sector to occur in ways other than as an indirect effect of poor harvests. Inter-regional and international trade also exhibited signs of fluctuations in the economy of sixteenth- and seventeenth-century Europe (see Coleman, 1977).

Any theory of the temporal and spatial incidence of demographic crises will, therefore, have to incorporate at least three major elements. The first will comprise a series of shocks which are normally random in the time dimension, but which are biased towards compounding the effects of a food-shortage crisis in that same dimension and towards the urban environment in the spatial dimension. This series shows the occurrence of epidemic diseases. The second element also comprises a random series, but in this instance there is some temporal clumping of extreme events (the 'seven good and seven bad years' phenomenon). This series, which reflects variations in the harvest, is related to climatic factors, but it is affected in the spatial dimension by the marginality, level of technical development and organisation of agriculture, and in the longer term by the demand for agricultural products. The third element can be thought of as a group of cyclical series with each individual series responding to fluctuations in the demand for manufactured goods or traded commodities. (Lipsey, 1966: 618–30, provides a simple introduction to the concept of economic cycles.) The importance of these particular series is biased towards those areas having high proportions of their populations engaged in non-agricultural activities, but particularly to the manufacturing sector.

The nature of these three series is shown in abstract form in Fig. 3.1. The disease series consists of sharp peaks which rise from a low and relatively constant level representing the disease's endemic residual. If a particular disease is not endemic then there will be no

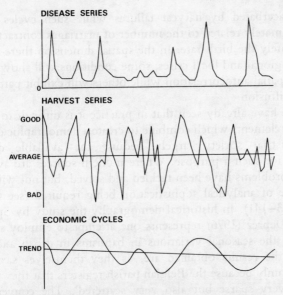

**Fig. 3.1** Epidemic, harvest and economic series

fatalities between major outbreaks and peaks will spring directly
from the zero base line. The harvest series exhibits the pattern
which has often been identified empirically (see Hoskins, 1964: 39,
1968: 24) of fluctuations between good and bad years, but with the
possibility of short series of above or below average years. Figure 3.1
also shows a series with four economic cycles which has a trend line
passing through them. These economic cycles are likely to have
varying wavelengths and amplitudes and to affect different sectors of
the economy by varying amounts at different times. There will be
short-run cycles in long-run waves. Although these cycles do not
reach their full significance until the period of industrial capitalism
(Mandel, 1975: 108–46 and 438–73) their operation can still be
observed, at least in their long-wave form, in pre-industrial societies
with a strong mercantile element or where small-scale commodity
production is increasing (Frank, 1978a: 260–62).

In reality these three forms of time series combine to
influence the two series of vital events: births and deaths or, from the
point of view of the data available, baptisms and burials. The final
form that the vital series take is highly complex because the initial
series are not entirely independent either in time or space. Epidemics
affect the number of deaths as do harvest fluctuations, but the latter
may also influence the number of births. Troughs in economic cycles

can be exacerbated by harvest failures while such cycles are in general intimately related to the number of marriages contracted and thus ultimately the birth rate. In the spatial dimension there will be national, regional and local crises; some conditions will show a high degree of spatial autocorrelation while others will exhibit patterns of spread or diffusion.

We have already seen that in practice it is difficult to isolate the various elements which combine to create a demographic crisis in a pre-industrial society largely because the available data is inadequate for such a purpose. Where modern sources are available analagous problems have been tackled and solved, but not without a high degree of analytical sophistication being required (see Cliff *et al.*, 1975: 83–141). In historical demography the study by Spencer, Hum and Deprez (1976) represents one attempt to employ spectral analysis on the seasonal variations in baptisms in urban and rural areas, but the results obtained are, as they themselves say, very tentative mainly because the Belgian parish registers that they use are 'not only very sparse but also very scattered'. The conventional method of comparing time series of vital events can be illustrated by the work of Palliser (1974), on sixteenth- and seventeenth-century Staffordshire; Slack (1979), on Devon and Essex in the sixteenth century; Imhof and Lindskog (1974) on Sweden and Finland in the eighteenth century; and Del Panta and Livi-Bacci (1977), on Italy in the seventeenth, eighteenth and early nineteenth centuries. Little attention is normally given to the spatial dimension although there is often some attempt to compare towns and village communities. The last mentioned study represents something of an exception because its explicit aim is to contrast the experiences of some fourteen Italian towns (18 series) ranging from Turin to Palermo. It shows, for instance, that there were three major periods of crisis in the seventeenth century: 1629–31, 1648–49 and 1656–57 which can be attributed, respectively, to plague, typhus and plague. But its drawback is that it only deals with mortality and is therefore likely to miss evidence which might reduce the importance attached to epidemic disease. The approach adopted by Del Panta and Livi-Bacci (1977) can be extended to include time series for baptisms and may be employed more effectively at the regional scale. These points will be illustrated by reference to a particular example, namely the case of seventeenth-century Yorkshire.

For the period after 1538, Anglican parish registers provide a valuable, yet by no means perfect, source of data for the analysis of both the temporal and the spatial patterns of vital events (see

Wrigley, 1966b; Wrigley and Schofield, 1981). They record information on burials, baptisms and marriages; the names of those persons involved in each particular religious ceremony together with the names of parents or close relatives where these provide additional means of identification. Here they will merely be used to construct time series of vital events although their potential uses extend to family reconstitution and total or community reconstitution (Macfarlane *et al.*, 1977). It must be assumed, however, that burials and baptisms provide a reasonable approximation for deaths and births. Clearly the degree to which this is valid will change from time to time and place to place in a manner which is itself unknowable (Wrigley, 1975, 1977). It must also be borne in mind that such a source of data is liable to contain frequent breaks of up to several years and that when utilised in its aggregate form it is incapable of providing estimates of total population size, and hence the facility for calculating rates, unless additional and even more dubious assumptions are to be made.

The location of twenty nine Yorkshire parishes is shown in Fig. 3.2. They provide a reasonable spatial coverage (although by no means representative in the statistical sense) as well as including both urban and rural parishes, within the constraints imposed by register survival and availability for the period of the seventeenth

**Fig. 3.2** Location of sample Yorkshire parishes (those named appear in Fig. 3.5)

century. The average aggregate series for burials and baptisms
derived from the sample of twenty nine are shown in Fig. 3.3

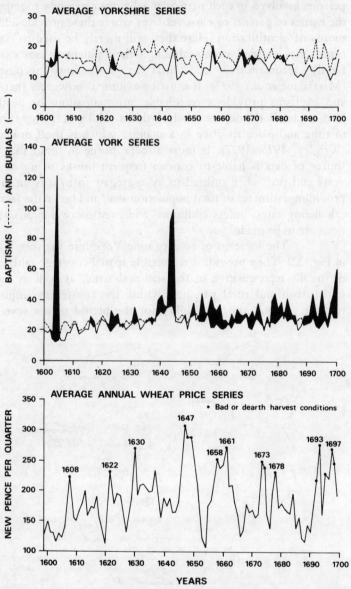

**Fig. 3.3** Average aggregate vital series for sample of twenty nine
Yorkshire parishes and five York parishes together with national
wheat price series for the seventeenth century
*Data sources*: Yorkshire Parish Registers; Hoskins (1964, 1968)

together with the comparable series for five York parishes. (Only one York parish, St Michael-le-Belfrey, is included in the twenty nine.) It seems clear that as far as the region as a whole is concerned there was only a small number of years in which burials exceeded baptisms, and that these years when they did occur tended to be isolated. Only the years 1665–72 and 1678–82 give any indication of short-run periods when the population was in natural decline. By way of contrast, the series for York reveal an example of an urban area whose population could not have increased without the aid of massive immigration (see Tillott, 1961; Cowgill, 1967; Palliser, 1973). This pattern has also been found in Leeds (Drake, 1962: 438–41) and has been generalised in the notion of the city as the 'demographic sink' of pre-industrial societies. (Sharlin, 1978, provides a contradictory view.) In 1604 and 1643–44 York experienced demographic crises which were by all standards dramatic. Their effects can be seen in Fig. 3.4 where the annual difference between baptisms and burials is added to a common standard population for both Yorkshire and York of 1,000 in January 1600. The two curves reflect natural change in the populations

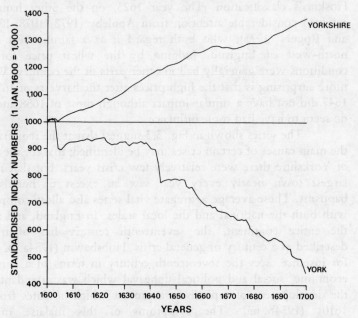

**Fig. 3.4** Standardised natural change series for twenty nine York-shire parishes and five York parishes in the seventeenth century (1 January 1600 (new style) = 1,000)
*Data source:* Yorkshire Parish Registers

during the seventeenth century. In Yorkshire only the 1660s and 1670s were decades with stationary populations, but in York the crises of 1604 and 1643–44 created breaks in the curve from which there was no natural recovery whilst after 1653 a new pattern of decline was initiated. While it is unlikely that the population of York did actually decline it is probable that its growth was only gradual and as a result of net immigration. Clark and Slack (1976: 83), for example, suggest that its population was, respectively, 8,000, 11,000 and 12,000 *c.* 1520, 1603 and 1670. Figure 3.4 also makes clear with what apparent ease it was possible for a region to brush off the effects of an isolated crisis, while a sequence of crises provided a more substantial problem.

Returning to the theoretical scheme outlined above and represented in Fig. 3.1, there is strong evidence to suggest that 1604 was a plague year in York, with some 56 per cent of burials occurring in the third quarter of the year, and that the crisis of 1644 may have had a similar origin (45 per cent in the third quarter). Beveridge's national series of wheat prices shown in Fig. 3.3 gives little indication that these should be described as bad or dearth years on Hoskins's classification. The year 1623, on the other hand, has received considerable attention from Appleby (1973, 1978: 133–54) and Rogers (1975), who both regard it as a famine year in the north-west of England. Judging by the wheat price for 1622 conditions were generally bad in other parts of the country. What is more surprising is that the high prices after the harvests of 1630 and 1647 did not have a similar impact although those of 1658 and 1678 do seem to have had some influence.

The series shown in Fig. 3.3 suggest that at the regional level the main causes of certain crises may be identified; that for the whole of Yorkshire there were relatively few crisis years, but that for the largest town nearly every year saw an excess of burials over baptisms. These average aggregate vital series also allow comparison with both the national and the local scales. In England, and indeed the entire continent, the seventeenth century has often been described as a century of general crisis. Hobsbawm (1954a, b, 1960), for instance, sees the seventeenth century in terms of a period of economic, social and political upheaval which was attendant upon the development of capitalism, a process which he dates from the 1610s (1954b: 63). The symptoms of this malaise manifest themselves in social revolt, war, European overseas expansion and the stagnation of population growth. The underlying cause is to be found in the emergence of a new mode of production and hence the creation of a new social formation. Although this interpretation has not gone unchallenged (see Aston, 1965) it provides an overall perspective on a period of radical social change, but relative economic depression (Frank, 1978a: 65–102).

The case of English population growth suggests that the second half of the century experienced long periods in which natural increase was impossible whilst in the years prior to 1650 there were relatively short periods in which deaths exceeded births. The work of the Cambridge Group for the History of Population and Social Structure (using a sample of 404 English parishes) has revealed that the period from 1560 to the late 1580s was one of rapid population growth; that the late 1580s and 1590s experienced several years of national crisis; that expansion continued into the seventeenth century, but at a reduced rate; that it was interrupted in 1623 and 1630, and effectively stopped in the 1650s only to begin again in a halting way at the end of the century (Coleman, 1977: 16; Wrigley and Schofield, 1981). The experience of the Yorkshire parishes shown in Fig. 3.3 largely conforms to this national pattern, although there are minor differences which can be attributed to the relative strengths of peaks in mortality. There seems little reason to argue that the experience of Yorkshire as a whole was unrepresentative of the national vital series, but there is some evidence to suggest that the rate of natural growth was positive for longer and remained higher than it did in the south (see Fig. 3.4).

When one turns to compare the regional aggregate series with those for local areas then a high degree of variation becomes readily apparent. Baptism and burial time series for eleven individual parishes are given in Fig. 3.5. (Their location is shown in Fig. 3.2.) This selection of parishes provides a broad cross-section of those in the sample of twenty nine (apart from St Crux and St Mary Castlegate, York, which are not included in the general sample), but again they cannot be regarded as statistically representative. It must also be remembered that the data are liable to under-registration and thus that short-term fluctuations may be more apparent than real.

Two common features are observable, however. Firstly, it is clear that throughout the region the 1670s and 1680s were the years most susceptible to significant excesses of burials over baptisms. This applies as much to the upland parishes of Wensley and Danby as it does to the large villages in the south (Kippax and Wragby) and the agricultural parishes in the east (Wintringham and Burton Fleming). It is certainly evident in the three York parishes shown in Fig. 3.5. Secondly, one can identify relatively long periods in which

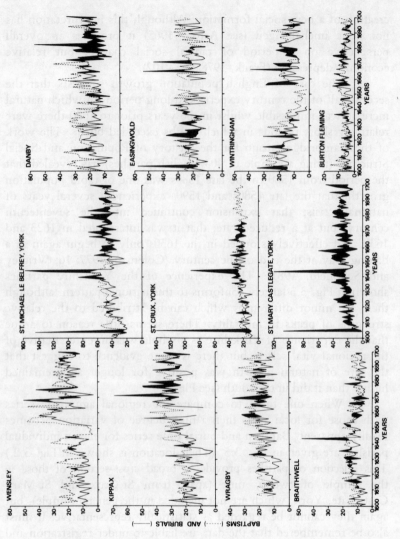

**Fig. 3.5** Vital series for eleven Yorkshire parishes in the seventeenth century
*Data source*: Yorkshire Parish Registers

local populations must have been growing naturally especially during the 1610s and 1620s (Wensley, Wragby, Danby).

What is perhaps more significant is the tremendous variation that exists between parishes which are only a matter of 40 or 50 kilometres apart. The 1604 and 1643–44 disease crises provide a useful illustration of this point. Both are evident in the three York parishes, but in Easingwold and Kippax the crisis year is 1603, and in Wintringham and Burton Fleming it is 1602. In neither 1602 nor 1603 is it clear from the seasonality of burials that these should be counted as plague years, as 1604 can in York. Wensley, Danby and Braithwell seem to have escaped these particular events. There is little to suggest that plague was spread into the surrounding countryside from York after 1604; it might even be argued that it was the city that was the recipient. Signs of the 1643–44 crisis are also to be found in Easingwold and Braithwell, as well as Halifax, Leeds and the Wapentake of Morley (Drake, 1974:99 and 109). It seems likely that most of the region and certainly the most populous central area was affected, albeit to varying degrees, by disease based crises in those years. Even the effects of what is normally taken to be a famine year in the north, 1623, are by no means uniform. In Easingwold, Wintringham and Burton Fleming there are signs of an excess of burials, but in Danby, Wensley, Kippax, Wragby and Braithwell the evidence is not quite as pronounced, even though the data presented by Drake (1962, 1974) is conclusive.

All of the vital series shown in Fig. 3.5 provide evidence for outbreaks of epidemic disease at some point during the seventeenth century even if it is only of a circumstantial nature. They indicate that acute food shortages could also have been responsible for certain crises and it may be speculated that chronic shortages, especially among the landless classes, were probably the source of general population stagnation in the 1670s and 1680s. It is almost impossible to see any direct signs of economic fluctuations, but one can surmise that they were nonetheless in evidence generally and might even have been responsible for the sustained natural increase of Yorkshire's population. The series for Kippax are suggestive of absolute growth in an area which was developing its specialisation on coal mining while the pastoral economy of Danby, in the Cleveland Hills, might have suffered a collapse in the 1670s.

The spatial comparison of time series derived from parish register data is fraught with problems. But it nonetheless offers a means of examining local variations in the pattern of changing births and deaths; of tentatively identifying the magnitude and frequency of mortality peaks as well as their relative impact; and thus of elaborating a theory which will account for both the causes and the incidence of demographic crises. Two lines of advance are now necessary. The one involves the quantitative analysis of larger samples so that trends and cycles can be isolated and local, regional and national scales compared by using the methods of the epidemiologists and the economic geographers in their respective studies of contagious diseases and regional economic structures. (These general issues are discussed by Bennett, 1979.) The second means of developing a spatio-temporal theory of demographic crises is concerned more with the process of verification than the making of theoretical statements. Only detailed local studies can provide information which will allow the precise cause of a crisis to be specified and without a set of systematic impact studies the inference problem remains a substantial one.

## The decline of fertility

Just as the theoretical treatment of demographic crises has to cope with a mixture of exogenous and endogenous factors so theories of the voluntary control of human fertility are bound to deal not only with the diffusion and adoption of new social norms or new techniques of family limitation, but also with a population's economic, cultural and political environment which will condition its response to external stimuli. The geographer can make particular contributions by analysing spatial variations in the levels of fertility and their ecological correlates; by modelling the diffusion of contraceptive knowledge as though it were analagous to that of any technical innovation; and by studying the changing spatio–temporal pattern of fertility decline in order to identify leading and lagging regions. But as a social scientist one can also make a general contribution to the construction of a comprehensive theory of change in human fertility by stressing the spatial perspective.

Theories of fertility decline have taken on a disciplinary and thus a partial form. Economists stress the costs and returns of having children as though they are consumer durables or part of the stock of human capital. Sociologists emphasise non-financial aspects and point to the symbolic importance that is attached to child-bearing, together with the social pressure on couples to have children, that exists in all cultures. The human biologists and demographers stress the role of family limitation methods and the necessity to balance births and deaths in order to ensure group survival. There is, however, a growing awareness that these disciplinary approaches are not capable individually of providing a theory of fertility decline without trivialising what is a most complex, if not the most complex, problem in the study of population. This dissatisfaction with simple theorising has stimulated social scientists to develop socio-economic models and theories and to reconsider the pre-conditions which are necessary for fertility to decline. Three products of this initiative will be discussed here together with their implications for an explanation of temporal and spatial changes in fertility in nineteenth-century Europe, but especially those changes which took place in England and Wales.

The recent theoretical work of Harvey Leibenstein (1974a, b, 1975, 1978: 123–35) represents a substantial modification to the classical economic theory of fertility which is to be found in the writings of Gary Becker (1960, 1965, 1973, 1974; Becker and Lewis, 1973; see also the contributions to T. W. Schultz, 1974). Becker (1960) views a couple's desire for children in terms of their purchasing power, income and fertility being positively associated. But with higher income also comes the desire for higher quality children; children who will be more expensive as a result of the income that will be absorbed during their education, for example. Leibenstein suggests a socio-economic theory of fertility which, although it is still based on notions of a trade-off between goods and children, emphasises the role of rural–urban migration; rising average income levels and consumption standards; 'social copying' together with 'felt competition'; all within the overall process of economic development. In short, 'as a steadily rising proportion of the population shifts into higher socio-economic groups, the competition between maintaining a higher consumption standard and rearing a certain number of children becomes more severe' (Leibenstein, 1974a: 454). This competition may affect the decision to have high parity children, but it will not influence the desire for one or two children whose utility, '*for their own sake* may be so very high as to overcome any disutility attributed to the costs of children' (Leibenstein, 1974a: 450–51). Leibenstein (1975, 1978: 123–35) has proceeded to elaborate these notions by considering the links between economic development and the creation of economic status groups, and their effects via the competition between households for the esteem which is founded on material possessions. His theory of the 'relative status income compression phenomenon', in which, 'status expenditures increase in absolute amount to a greater degree than the increase in income', suggests that there will normally be a greater pressure on the higher status households to avoid having even medium parity children whilst there are likely to be constraints on all households to avoid high parities. Leibenstein (1978: 142) also emphasises the utility value of children and the decline of that value both with rising status and the increase of *per capita* income. Children's utility value is connected with their contribution to the family labour pool; their performance of duties in the context of the extended family; and their ability to provide security for their parents' old age. The potential of each of these contibutions will be assessed differently by members of the various status groups who will make adjustments according to their existing family size.

To oversimplify, Leibenstein's theory of fertility is firmly grounded in the principles of economic decision making and the trade-off between costs and values, but it also emphasises the significance of status acquisition which comes with economic development (a term which is used to imply economic growth coupled with improvements in material well-being) and increasing *per capita* income. It stresses that at certain low parities children will have a social value that outweighs any economic costs which they may necessitate; and that their economic value at higher parities will vary with the importance attached to the acquisition of status, which will itself be affected by rising living standards and the urban division of labour. The theory can be used to provide interesting empirical statements which have direct bearing on the changing temporal and spatial patterning of fertility decline. For example, one would expect to find an inverse relationship between the level of economic development, or *per capita* income, and fertility as well as a progression of decreasing fertility on moving up the status hierarchy. Over time status acquisition and 'relative status income compression' should lead to absolute fertility decline in urban society and with it the break-up of the last vestiges of the extended family system amongst rural populations.

Richard A. Easterlin (1969, 1975, 1978; Easterlin, Pollak and Wachter, 1980) has also taken as his starting point the economic theory of Becker (1960) in which 'demand for children is based on the household's balancing of its subjective tastes against externally determined constraints of price and income in a way that maximizes its satisfaction' (Easterlin, 1978: 61). But the importance of his work lies in its attempt to combine both economic and sociological theories of fertility. The latter, which are outlined by Hawthorn (1970) and Andorka (1978: 11–38 and 363–84), owe their origin to a scheme devised by Davis and Blake (1956). Easterlin's theory emphasises the role of norms, values and attitudes in the parental decision-making process together with the importance of motivation and access to means of birth control in their effect on a couple's ability to realise their desired family size. Easterlin attempts to combine economics-based demand determinants with supply factors that have their origins in sociological theory (Easterlin, 1978: 99). He argues that in pre-modern societies the demand for surviving children exceeds supply; that this is partly a function of fluctuations in mortality, and hence survivorship; and that the resulting pattern will be that of 'natural fertility' (Henry, 1961; see Knodel, 1979, for an empirical study using this framework). Income level will therefore be directly related to fertility because of its positive influence on the ability to conceive and the absence of any desire to regulate fertility. In a modern society the supply of surviving children is likely to exceed the demand for them. Normally this will be the result of a rise in supply together with a fall in demand. This leads to the creation of a number of unwanted children, but it also encourages voluntary fertility regulation. The number of unwanted children will be directly related to the costs of fertility control and thus as costs decline the actual number of surviving children will tend towards the desired number. Fertility regulation will probably also pass from 'social control' to 'individual control' (Bourgeois-Pichat, 1967) as the costs of regulation begin to decline. (Easterlin, 1978: 106, shows the operation of these mechanisms in diagrammatic form.)

The rise in supply of and fall in demand for children is to be linked to the process of modernisation, which is also associated with changes in the cost of fertility regulation. Easterlin uses the term modernisation conventionally to refer to positive changes in, for example, public health, education, urbanisation, material well-being and *per capita* income. Each of these will affect natural fertility and survivorship (supply of surviving children); tastes, incomes and prices (demand for children); the subjective and financial costs of fertility control; and thus ultimately the level of fertility obtaining in a population. Easterlin (1978: 132–3) summarises his argument in the following way: 'In modernized societies, then, fertility is governed by the interaction of the factors shaping family size desires, the potential output of children, and the costs of fertility regulation. Modernization thus alters the essential nature of fertility regulation. Child-bearing in premodern societies, though "regulated" by a variety of social and biological mechanisms working through natural fertility, is not yet viewed by the household as involving a potential problem of unwanted children. In contrast, in modern societies, fertility poses difficult problems of individual choice regarding the limitation of family size.'

The importance of Easterlin's (1978) theoretical framework is threefold. Firstly, it attempts a long overdue integration of the sociological and economic perspectives by balancing their interpretations of supply and demand factors. Secondly, it has a strong historical emphasis and is therefore capable of recognising that the balance between the social, economic and biological variables which cause observable differences in fertility patterns can change radically from one period to another. Thirdly, it provides a flexible theory of fertility which can be developed to include more complex notions on, for instance, the cultural and biological influences on natural fertility. Its major drawback is that it relies for its motive force on the concept of modernisation which not only presumes a distinction between traditional and modern societies, but which also requires its own highly complex set of causal theories before it can itself be explained. Why does urbanisation occur? How do *per capita* incomes grow? What causes industrialisation? (These issues, which stem from the definition and use of the term modernisation, are discussed more fully in Chapter 5.)

Easterlin has also attempted to develop a theory of short-term changes in the level of fertility which are associated with economic cycles (Easterlin, 1968: 77–138, 1973; Easterlin and Condran, 1976; see also D. Freedman, 1976; Ermisch, 1979). And elsewhere he has posed the question, 'does human fertility adjust to the environment?' (Easterlin, 1971). In theory it should because, Esterlin argues, the optimum number of births is determined by prevailing infant and child mortality in combination with the optimum number of children, itself a function of tastes, prices and income. The discrepancy between optimum and actual births being a function of, 'attitudes toward and extent of information about fertility control practices' (Easterlin, 1971: 400). Tastes for children are particularly affected by the extent of education and the availability of consumer goods. Both the outlay on and returns from children will influence the costs incurred by parents in childbearing while access to methods of family limitation will vary with education and income. Easterlin also argues that tastes, costs and fertility control practices will vary with location; that in the context of nineteenth-century America the populations of old urban areas, new urban areas, settled agricultural areas and the frontier will experience different levels of education; access to consumer goods and birth control methods; and for which children will represent varying costs and returns. Fertility will be highest on the frontier and will reach its lowest level in the old urban areas as tastes for children decline, costs increase and fertility control methods become more available. Further, as new urban areas become old ones and as the frontier is transformed into a settled agricultural area so there will be an overall reduction in fertility. (For a detailed test of this theory and discussion of its implications see Easterlin, Alter and Condran, 1978, and Lindert, 1978.)

The importance of Easterlin's socio-economic theories for an explanation of spatial variations in fertility is quite clear. Tastes for and costs of children, and the balance of supply and demand, change over time and through space in a fashion which is intimately linked with the economic and social conditions in which populations live. With urbanisation, greater access to formal education and the supply of consumer goods, will come a radical change in tastes and costs that will alter the demand side of the equation while better material standards will move the supply side in the opposite direction. The role of family limitation methods is also important, but it is knowledge about them, their costs and access to them that affect their use once supply is regarded as exceeding demand.

Both Leibenstein and Easterlin begin their theories of fertility from the standpoint of economists, although for the former economic man is no longer a perfectly rational optimiser and for the latter sociological theory is an indispensable adjunct. Their theoretical statements are deductive in origin; they are logically derived from first principles and assumptions which are gradually relaxed so that

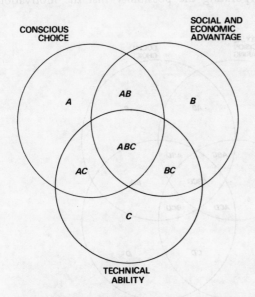

**Fig. 3.6** Representation of Coale's model of the pre-conditions for fertility decline
*Source*: based on Coale (1973: 65)

the resulting empirical statements may appear more realistic. The demographer Ansley J. Coale, on the other hand, has taken a more inductive line in his analysis of the pre-conditions for fertility decline. Coale (1973: 65) distinguishes 'three general prerequisites for a major fall in marital fertility'. They are that decision making on fertility should be a matter of conscious choice; that reduced fertility should be seen as a social and economic advantage; and that the technical ability to reduce fertility must be present. These three pre-conditions are brought together in model form in Fig. 3.6. Only population *ABC* will possess all the pre-conditions and only under those circumstances will fertility be reduced. It is possible, however, that the 'social and economic advantage' condition represents too broad a category for practical use. A modification would involve the use of such terms as 'social choice' and 'economic necessity'. In Fig. 3.7 populations *ABC* and *ACD*, as well as *ABCD*, would have the necessary prerequisites because 'social choice' and 'economic necessity' would act as alternative pre-conditions that must be combined with *A* and *C*. The advantage of this model is that it allows the motivation for fertility regulation amongst middle-class couples to stem from a social choice (high parity children become unfashionable), whilst incorporating the possibility that the motivation for

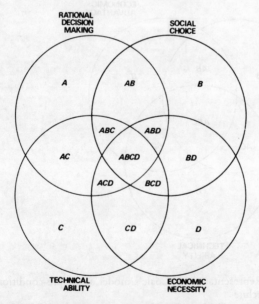

**Fig. 3.7** Modified model of the pre-conditions for fertility decline

regulation amongst working-class parents is the potential economic cost of high parity births once child survivorship has begun to rise.

Coale's perspective has been particularly influenced by studies of the secular decline in European fertility which took place in the nineteenth and early part of the twentieth centuries (Coale, 1969). During this period there is evidence to suggest that both social choice and economic necessity impelled certain groups to decide to control fertility within marriage; that traditional contraceptive methods were being deployed not only to space births, but also to directly restrict completed family size; and that as new techniques were developed control over marital fertility became even more effective. The distinctions between overall fertility, marital fertility, illegitimate fertility and nuptiality are important in this particular context, because it seems that at least in north-west Europe overall fertility was being kept well below its biological maximum by the practice of delaying marriage to the late 20s or early 30s (Hajnal, 1965). Malthus's preventive check was in fact being used quite effectively. A reduction in marital fertility was, therefore, the main way in which overall fertility could have declined.

Coale's (1973) pre-conditions model does, nonetheless, have more general value for the construction of a fertility theory. It stresses the complexity of the processes involved and the necessity for a multivariate approach. Decision-making procedures, motivations and the actual technical ability to directly limit fertility can all be thought of in the temporal and spatial dimensions. Knowledge about and availability of new appliance methods of birth control can diffuse spatially and through a network of social groups thus enabling fertility to be reduced where and when rational decision makers are already so motivated. Social fashions and economic conditions can alter, so stimulating the conscious decision to avoid high parity births and the practical means to translate that decision into reality.

The theories and models of Leibenstein, Easterlin and Coale should provide a means of explaining the decline of fertility in nineteenth-century Europe. Leibenstein suggests that we should be able to observe variations between status groups as *per capita* incomes rise, consumer goods become more available and relative income compression begins to operate. Easterlin's theory tells us that spatial variations should occur between urban and rural environments and that with modernisation will come changes in demand for and supply of children which will ultimately transform the traditional pattern of natural fertility. Coale shows us that the coincidence in time and space of a small number of determining pre-conditions must obtain before fertility decline will occur.

Reality is, of course, far more complex. In France, for example, fertility began to decline early in the nineteenth century, or even in the late eighteenth century (Flandrin, 1979: 212–42), and proceeded in step with the fall in mortality (Bourgeois-Pichat, 1965). Van de Walle (1974, 1978, 1979) has been able to trace the changing spatio-temporal pattern of fertility using the measures of overall fertility ($I_f$), marital fertility ($I_g$), illegitimate fertility ($I_h$) and proportion married ($I_m$) which were first devised by Coale (1967; see also Woods, 1979: 118–21). ($I_f$, $I_g$, $I_h$ and $I_m$ are measures indirectly

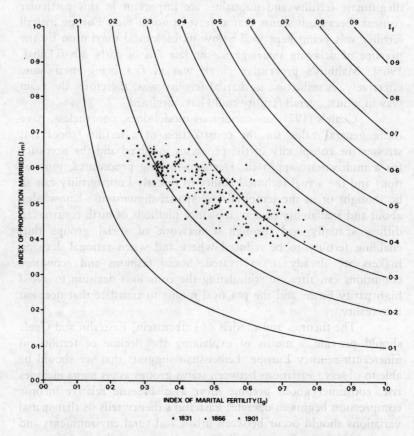

**Fig. 3.8** Index of proportion married ($I_m$) against index of marital fertility ($I_g$) for French rural *départements*, 1831, 1866 and 1901
*Data source*: van de Walle (1974)

standardised on the age-specific marital fertility of a population with natural fertility, namely the American Hutterites, so that the maximum value for $I_g$ and $I_m$ is 1 and the indices are related in the following way: $I_f = I_g \bullet I_m + I_h (1 - I_m)$.) Van de Walle has shown, firstly, that the earliest decline in marital fertility in rural France occurred in those *départements* in Normandy and the south west where standards of material well-being were relatively high and, secondly, that the poorest, most remote and traditional populations in the Massif Central, Savoy and Brittany were the last to limit their marital fertility below the level appropriate to natural fertility ($I_g$ less than 0·6). By plotting the index of proportion married ($I_m$) against the index of marital fertility ($I_g$) Fig. 3.8 reveals the changing pattern of fertility in the French rural *départements* in 1831, 1866 and 1901. Assuming that illegitimate fertility ($I_h$) is negligible then $I_m$ and $I_g$ combine to express overall fertility ($I_f$) (i.e. $I_f = I_g \bullet I_m$ when $I_h = 0$), which is shown by the isolines in Fig. 3.8. $I_f$ began to decline because of the effect of reduced $I_g$, and only when $I_g$ was already under control was $I_m$ able to rise without having an adverse effect on $I_f$. It is also clear that at any one time in the nineteenth century there was a considerable range of fertility levels between French *départements*, particularly in respect to $I_g$.

A comparable illustration using data for the Republic of Ireland (Eire) in 1926 and 1971 (Fig.· 3.9) also suggests that nuptiality ($I_m$) is weighed against marital fertility so that when the latter falls the former can rise. But in the case of Ireland this has meant a rise in overall fertility and the abandonment of a traditional means of checking population growth by delaying marriage and encouraging a high level of celibacy. Figure 3.9 also shows that in the Irish case there was little difference between the urban boroughs and the rural counties, although in both 1926 and 1971 the lowest $I_g$ value was to be found in that suburban part of County Dublin outside Dublin itself (Coward, 1978).

The French and Irish examples cited above serve to illustrate some of the complex problems that have to be faced in attempts to explain temporal and spatial variations in the pattern of European fertility decline. What happened in France, where effective family limitation was employed so early, and in Ireland, where low nuptiality was so importantt after the 'Great Irish Famine', was not typical of the rest of western Europe where fertility began its secular decline in the 1870s, or slightly later, and where nuptiality, although an important demographic regulator, was not as effectively used as in Ireland (see Matras, 1965a; van de Walle, 1972). (For the cases of

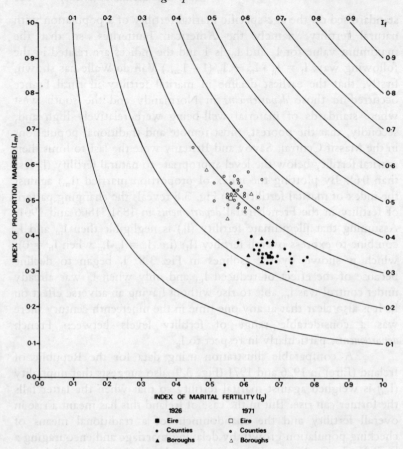

**Fig. 3.9** Index of proportion married ($I_m$) against index of marital fertility ($I_g$) for Republic of Ireland counties and boroughs, 1926 and 1971
*Data source*: Coward (1978)

Germany, Belgium and Italy, and the exceptional case of Russia see, respectively, Knodel, 1974; Lesthaeghe, 1977; Livi-Bacci, 1977; Coale, Anderson and Härm, 1979.)

The population of England and Wales in the nineteenth century provides a more typical illustration of the experience of urban–industrial Europe. There the national secular decline in fertility began in the 1870s and proceeded in a regular downward course until it reached its nadir in the 1930s (Glass, 1938; Innes, 1938). It is now also conventional to assert that whatever were the underlying processes causing fertility to change they did not create substantial differences in the spatial pattern of decline (Teitelbaum, forthcoming), as they did in France (Fig. 3.8) or Italy, and that, 'Fertility among married people first fell among the middle classes, in the last part of the nineteenth century [reference to Banks (1954)], and little fall is observable in the rest of the population before the end of the century' (Anderson, 1980: 55)). These interpretations can

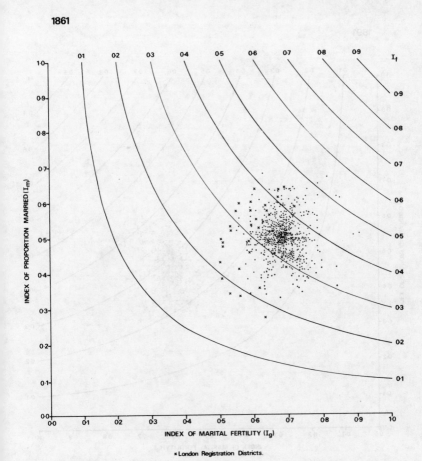

**Fig. 3.10** Index of proportion married (I_m) against index of marital fertility (I_g) for registration districts in England and Wales, 1861
*Data sources*: Registrar General's *Twenty-fourth, Twenty-fifth* and *Twenty-sixth Annual Reports for 1861, 1862* and *1863; Population Census of England and Wales, 1861*

be challenged quite successfully, however. Figures 3.10 and 3.11 show the relationship between $I_m$ and $I_g$, and thus the level of $I_f$, in 1861 and 1891. Their construction is based on data for a common set of 590 provincial registration districts together with thirty six and twenty nine for London in 1861 and 1891, respectively. (The boundaries of these 590 registration districts, which were the basic units used for the recording of vital statistics, are shown in Fig. 3.12.)

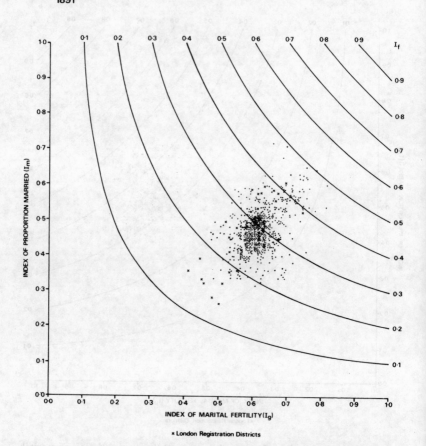

**Fig. 3.11** Index of proportion married ($I_m$) against index of marital fertility ($I_g$) for registration districts in England and Wales, 1891
*Data Sources*: Registrar General's *Fifty-fourth, Fifty-fifth* and *Fifty-sixth Annual Reports for 1891, 1892* and *1893; Population Census of England and Wales, 1891*

Comparison of Figs. 3.10 and 3.11 reveals that overall fertility declined in England and Wales between 1861 and 1891 because both the proportion married ($I_m$) and marital fertility ($I_g$) were reduced. It shows that in 1861 few of the registration districts

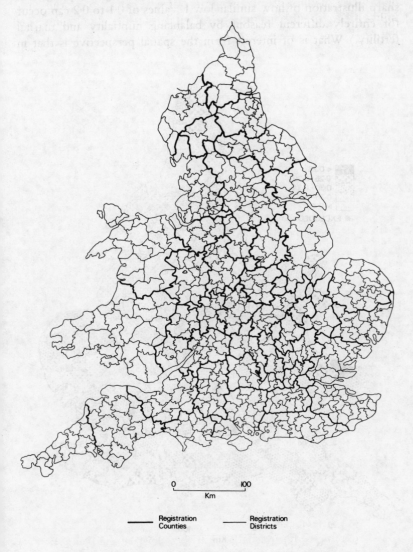

**Fig. 3.12** Boundaries of common registration counties and districts in England and Wales, 1861–91
*Data sources: Population Censuses of England and Wales, 1861 and 1891*

had $I_g$ values below 0·6 and were thus unlikely to be effectively limiting fertility within marriage. Of those districts with $I_g$ levels below 0·6 most were in London. By 1891 a substantial number of districts had $I_g$ values less than 0·6, although again the lowest $I_g$, $I_m$ and thus $I_f$ were in London. (Comparison with Fig. 3.8 provides a sharp illustration of how similar low $I_f$ values of 0·1 to 0·2 can occur for entirely different reasons by balancing nuptiality and marital fertility.) What is of interest from the spatial perspective is that in

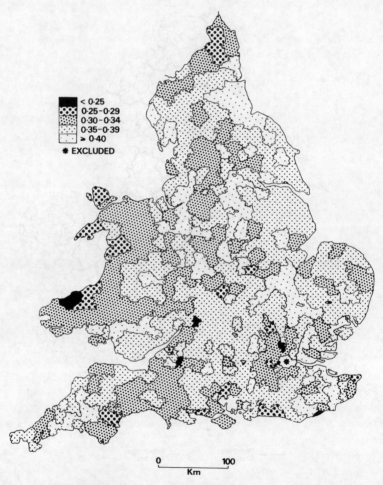

**Fig. 3.13** Index of overall fertility ($I_f$) by registration districts, England and Wales, 1861
*Data sources*: see Fig. 3.10

both Fig. 3.10 and Fig. 3.11 the populations of registration districts are likely to experience very different levels of fertility; that there is a pattern to the decline of fertility both over time and through space.

Those districts with the highest overall fertility tend to fall into one of two categories. They are usually either the remoter rural, and thus most agricultural areas, or they are the most highly industrialised ones (Figs. 3.13 and 3.14). These urban–industrial districts tended to be the ones with populations who retained their high fertility levels longest. There are, however, very important distinctions that must be made between districts within the urban–industrial category. Those areas in which coal mining was an important occupation – South Wales, Staffordshire, Nottingham-shire, Derbyshire, Yorkshire, Lancashire and County Durham – not only had high $I_m$ levels, but fertility within marriage was also high so that in combination fertility also tended to reach its highest overall levels there. In the textile towns of Lancashire and Yorkshire nuptiality was lower than the national average and it was particularly in those districts that decline in $I_g$ between 1861 and 1891 induced a reduction in $I_f$ (compare Figs. 3.15 and 3.16, and Figs. 3.17 and 3.18). Those districts in which marital fertility was at its lowest prior to 1861 tended either to be in the West End of London or to comprise small coastal or market towns in southern England. By 1891 many more agricultural districts in the south, together with North Wales and the textile areas of Lancashire and Yorkshire, could be added to the list. The changing pattern is picked out clearly in Fig. 3.19 which shows those provincial districts with $I_g$ levels below 0·6 in 1861 and 1891.

The sequence of images presented in Figs. 3.13 to 3.19 is a highly complex one. There are no clear divisions between northern and southern, urban and rural districts, although low fertility-early decline and high fertility-late decline populations can be characterised with some precision. There are patterns to be identified in these changes in fertility, but they are by no means straightforward ones. Thus any theory constructed to account for them will have to handle a considerable number of causal factors with differing effects depending upon the particular social and economic environment in which they are operating. How do the theories of Leibenstein, Easterlin and Coale measure up to this task?

Leibenstein's theory stresses the role of status groups and their response to rising consumption standards through 'felt competition' and the 'relative status income compression phe-nomenon'. Leibenstein's is a theory to explain why fertility tends to

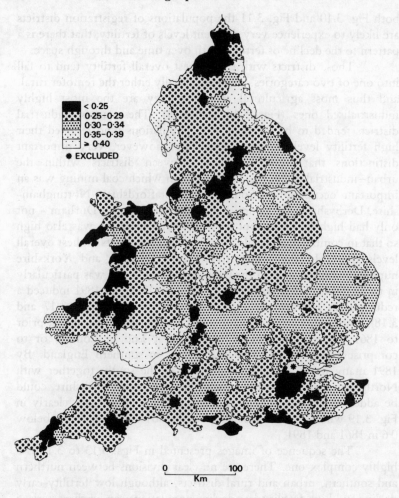

**Fig. 3.14** Index of overall fertility ($I_f$) by registration districts, England and Wales, 1891
*Data sources*: see Fig. 3.11

Legend:
- < 0·25
- 0·25–0·29
- 0·30–0·34
- 0·35–0·39
- ≥ 0·40
- ✳ EXCLUDED

0    100
Km

become inversely related to *per capita* income with economic development. It should tell us why the higher economic status groups begin to control their marital fertility, as well as their nuptiality, and why such control becomes the norm if there is a high volume of structural social mobility associated with growth in the secondary and tertiary sectors of an economy. There is strong evidence from Innes (1938), who uses the 1911 *Census of Fertility*, and

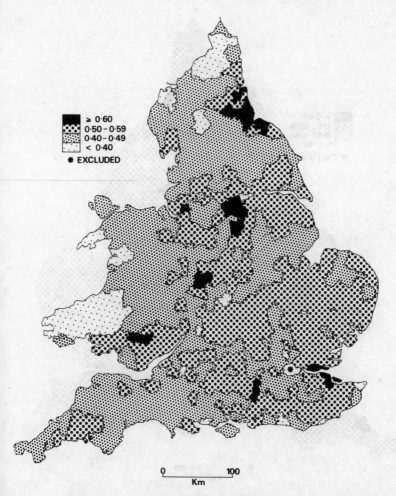

**Fig. 3.15** Index of proportion married ($I_m$) by registration districts, England and Wales, 1861
*Data sources*: see Fig. 3.10

Matras (1965b) that middle-class couples were restricting their fertility within marriage even in the 1850s, and perhaps before that. This evidence is supported by data for some of the London registration districts shown in Fig. 3.10. Banks (1954) has argued that in the 1870s the middle class was suffering from what would now be called 'relative deprivation' or the effects of 'relative income compression' which were partly reflected in its substitution of

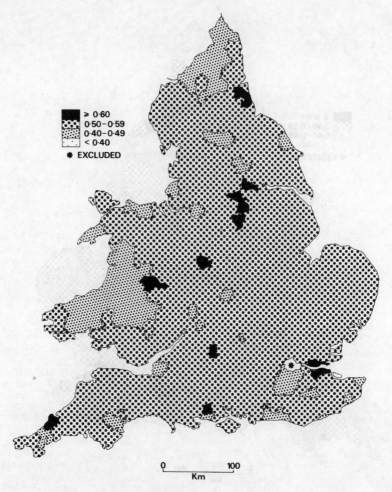

**Fig. 3.16** Index of proportion married ($I_m$) by registration districts, England and Wales, 1891
*Data sources*: see Fig. 3.11

consumer goods for high parity children and greater expenditure on its remaining offspring.

What of the working classes? Did their greater absolute prosperity influence their parenthood? Was practice of family limitation spread down the social hierarchy to them? Liebenstein's theory suggests that the urban proletariat would eventually be affected in a fashion similar to that of the middle class, but as

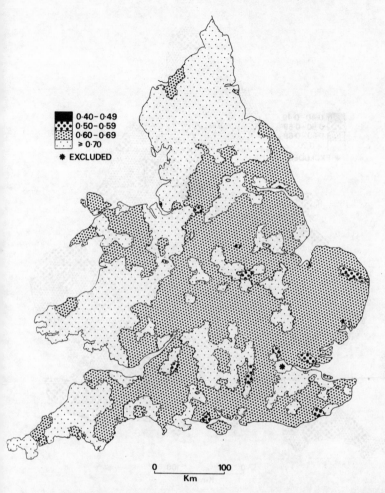

**Fig. 3.17** Index of marital fertility ($I_g$) by registration districts, England and Wales, 1861
*Data sources*: see Fig. 3.10

Figs. 3.17 and 3.18 show, marital fertility in many urban–industrial areas of South Wales, the Midlands and the North of England remained high longer than one would expect were the balance of costs and returns to be unfavourably tipped against childbearing by the spirit of urbanism. The fertility of coal mining families provides an interesting, albeit extreme, example. Haines (1977, 1979; see also Friedlander, 1973) has outlined a socio-economic theory of fertility

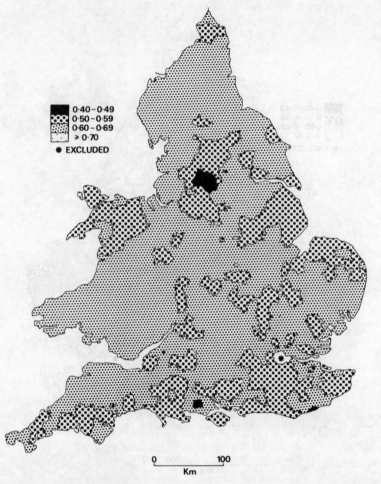

**Fig. 3.18** Index of marital fertility ($I_g$) by registration districts, England and Wales, 1891
*Data sources*: see Fig. 3.11

specific to a mining population. It states that, 'The conditions of work and the relative geographic and social isolation of mining and some industrial populations acted to preserve relatively high fertility norms characteristic of the semirural environment itself or at least to retard changes in tastes resulting from generalized "modernization" of attitudes towards reproduction. Given tastes and norms as relatively constant or changing more slowly than for the overall

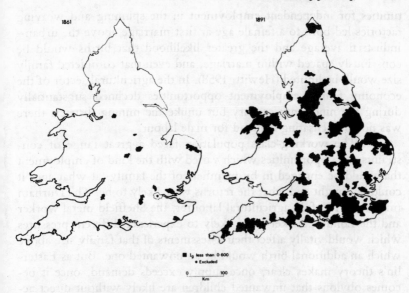

**Fig. 3.19** Registration districts with $I_g$ values less than 0·6, England and Wales, 1861 and 1891
*Data sources*: Figs. 3.17 and 3.18

population, early income potential, relatively high wages, restricted female employment outside the home, possible secondary employment in agriculture or handicrafts, possible child labour and higher mortality and debility would all have favored higher fertility and, in part, earlier marriage' (Haines, 1979: 52). The process of modernisation, which is so important in Easterlin's theory, is thought to be retarded in such populations so that natural fertility remains intact. Nuptiality is kept high because new households may be established relatively easily with the early peak in male earning capacity; the need to check marital fertility does not arise because there are few opportunities for female employment outside the home and the demand for child or young adult labour remains buoyant.

Where there were opportunities for females to enter the work-force, which was generally the case in nineteenth-century Britain (Pinchbeck, 1930; Scott and Tilly, 1975), very different patterns of fertility might emerge. Anderson (1976), for example, has revealed the negative association that existed between $I_m$ and the proportion of the female population who were 'in service' in 1861. In the northern textile districts there is reason to believe that the opportunities for independent employment in the spinning and weaving factories led both to a female age at first marriage above the urban–industrial average and the greater likelihood that births would be consciously spaced within marriage, and even that completed family size would be limited (Hewitt, 1958). In the agricultural sector of the economy female employment opportunities declined substantially during the nineteenth century but unlike the mining districts there was no compensating demand for male labour.

The working-class population faced a great range of constraints and opportunities which varied with the kind of employment that could be engaged in by members of the family, at what ages it could be sought and what the returns were likely to be. The Durham miner, the Norfolk agricultural labourer, the Sheffield metal worker and the London docker were likely to experience different pressures which would vitally affect their assessments of that family size above which an additional birth would be an unwanted one. But as Easterlin's theory makes clear, once supply exceeds demand, once it becomes obvious that unwanted children are likely without direct action, then it is the cost of fertility control that will affect the decision to limit completed family size. This technical ability to control fertility is also part of Coale's scheme of necessary pre-conditions for fertility decline (see Fig. 3.6).

The matter of establishing what means of birth control were known about and used effectively by whom and when is an exceedingly troublesome one. It is usual to argue from the sort of evidence shown in Fig. 3.20 that British marriage cohorts were not using appliance methods of birth control until well into the twentieth century and certainly this view would be consistent with evidence on the wide-scale manufacture and distribution of male contraceptives, intra-uterine devices and female oral contraceptives (Himes, 1936; Peel, 1963). But it is also the case, as McLaren (1977, 1978) and Branca (1975: 114–42) have argued, that traditional methods of birth control were widely known and used by middle-class women at least, and that abortion was employed by working-class women (Potts, Diggory and Peel, 1977: 154–77). The availability of such methods would clearly have changed over time and would have varied from place to place, as would the cost. Little is known about the former, but one may surmise that the adoption curves for the use of individual methods would show forms similar to those in Fig. 3.21 for the contemporary American experience, but with the rider that all less effective methods would show a decline in use during competition with newer, more effective or cheaper means. It is

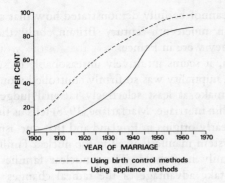

**Fig. 3.20** Use of birth control methods by British marriage cohorts
*Data sources*: generalised from Lewis-Faning (1949); Rowntree and Pierce (1961); Pierce and Rowntree (1961); Langford (1976)

also probable, as Easterlin (1971) assumed, that those birth control methods which could be retailed were more likely to be available in the larger cities. With respect to costs, Peel (1963: 110) gives some examples for pessaries and sponges in the 1880s, all of which would seem to be out of general reach of working-class women.

While it is clear that Coale's 'technical ability' pre-condition is met in the population of nineteenth-century England and Wales, it is also obvious that such methods that were available to the majority, like induced abortion and *coitus interruptus*, were less than ideal means of limiting family size; that many of the other methods were restricted by cost to the middle or upper classes, and that their availability would vary in time and space. Whilst it can be shown that marital

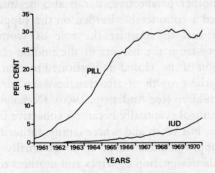

**Fig. 3.21** Percentage of ever-married female respondents under thirty five reporting using Pill or IUD, USA, 1961–70
*Source*: Westoff and Ryder (1977: 31)

fertility did decline it cannot be fully demonstrated how that change was brought about in nineteenth-century Britain, only that the means were there as they were in France.

In similar vein, it seems intuitively unreasonable to suggest that a society in which nuptiality was so firmly controlled would not have the capacity to make at least selectively rational judgements about childbearing within marriage. Macfarlane (1978) tells us that 'individualism' has very early origins in England and that one aspect of that particular value system manifests itself in the nuclear family, the independent single family household. These nuclear families were able to adapt to and take advantage of the radical changes which occurred during the industrial revolution. They could be geographically mobile, and potentially socially mobile too, in a way which would be limited in the setting of the extended family system (see, for instance, Anderson, 1971). An implication to be drawn from this point of view is that high marital fertility was not regarded as unbeneficial by large numbers of the working population; if the demand for children had been far exceeded by supply then action would have been taken to check supply given that the size of the nuclear family was a matter for rational decision making.

In broad terms this is probably a valid interpretation of the demography of a society experiencing rapid economic growth via industrialisation and social change through urbanisation. Marital fertility remained high in England and Wales during the first three-quarters of the nineteenth century because there was a strong, demand for labour – the economy's demand for new workers did not exceed supply in the long term. In Coale's phrase, children remained socially and economically advantageous.

Viewed from another perspective, it can also be imagined that this demand imposed a considerable burden on the supply side of the equation. It is usual to consider the role of women in nineteenth-century society from the heights of the middle class; to observe the social diffusion of the 'closed domesticated nuclear family' (Stone, 1977: 8) and the growth of affection between husbands and wives, parents and children (see Anderson, 1980). Decision making on matters of birth control eventually became a collective one, or one for the woman alone, but when and where family authority was male dominated then supply could be kept up to externally established demand through the resignation of wives and mothers to their conjugal duties. In this sense rational decision making takes on a variety of forms. Decisions will vary in terms of whether the objective is to satisfy the society as a whole, the family, living children, the husband or the wife. The balance became tipped towards living children and the wife earlier in the middle class than it did in the working class, where the demands of society and the new family wage economy were felt more strongly and for longer (see Tilly, Scott and Cohen, 1976; Tilly and Scott, 1978). In the coal mining districts, for example, emphasis was on male employment and the family economy, whilst in the textile areas women could become economically independent in their own right, both areas being quite distinct from the middle-class districts of London, the spas, resorts and country towns where women early on became the makers of rational decisions for the benefit of their children and themselves.

Each of the theories and models proposed by Leibenstein, Easterlin and Coale provides useful insights when applied to the spatial and temporal patterning of fertility in nineteenth-century England and Wales, but they all have serious drawbacks. In Leibenstein's theory the role of the goods-children trade-off and the urbanisation effect give cause for concern. In Easterlin's theory while the supply and demand mechanism provides an important analytical framework, together with the influence of family limitation costs, the attribution of prime mover status to modernisation avoids the issue of distinguishing between the relative influences of structural economic changes and changes in the value system of a society. It is not enough to say that the two are inextricably linked. Coale's model of pre-conditions for the decline of fertility also raises problems. Firstly, it avoids the matter of degree of technical ability to control fertility, all populations have some ability if only in indirect forms, and as the example of France so dramatically shows even traditional means can be most effective if generally applied. Secondly, the conscious choice or rational decision-making condition implies that there is likely to be a universal concensus on what fertility goals should be aimed for. This may not be the case, especially when decisions over high parity children are concerned. It also implies that there are societies in which no choice is possible or where irrationality reigns. Thirdly, the balance of motives that stimulates a decision to be made and put into effect is only poorly specified.

What new or reconstructed theory should be put in the place of those suggested by Leibenstein, Easterlin and Coale? Should it aim to patch up or demolish their contributions? What key elements must it contain?

This last question can be approached obliquely by considering, by way of example, the families of Robert Malthus and Karl Marx. Fig. 3.22 shows for the two familes the age of the mothers at the birth of their children. Both Malthus and Marx married women who were in their late twenties, as was typical for their time and class, and who conceived shortly after marriage. In each case three children were born in quick succession, but while there were more additions to Marx's family, two of whom died in infancy, the completed family size of the Mathuses remained at three. Any theory of fertility ought to be able to explain the differential use and effect of delaying marriage, of child mortality, of spacing out births and of limiting completed family size. It should also tell us how and why Jenny Marx's six births stopped being the general rule and the three confinements of Harriet Malthus became typical. Further, it should make clear why the urban–industrial working-class pattern represented by the Marx family persisted in certain areas when in other

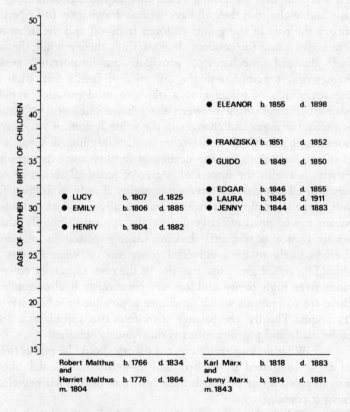

**Fig. 3.22** Age of Harriet Malthus and Jenny Marx at the birth of their children
*Data sources*: James (1979); McLellan (1973)

places the middle-class pattern of the Malthus family was firmly established.

We may begin to approach the construction of an appropriate theory, although we can be quite certain that no one theory will ever be entirely successful in either the general sense or in its ability to explain the behaviour of individuals, by stressing two points which Marx himself would doubtless have made. Firstly, it is necessary to devise theories which are specifically historical in form; they should not have pretensions to the universal. Secondly, the dominant mode of production and the social formation that rests on it provide the context in which theory is to operate by establishing the patterns of employment together with their associated class relationships. It is these employment and class relationships working within a particular historical period that establish the determining economic and social costs and returns which in turn affect the supply of and demand for children. The demographic régime linked with nineteenth-century industrial capitalism contained elements, such as the nuclear family and the high mean age at first marriage, which had their origins in the society of pre-industrial Europe, but it also contained elements peculiar to the new mode of production. The interests of the external economy's demand for labour and the family wage economy's needs will be paramount among the working-class population largely because of the necessities of survival and the rigours of poverty. This can change if the overall demand for male and child labour falls; if female labour is in demand; if decision making shifts towards the interests of the children or the mother; or if the female gains access to a cheap and effective means of birth control. During the nineteenth century the overall demand for labour fell in the agricultural districts while in the textile districts females became closely involved in the factory system. The bourgeoisie, on the other hand, faced a shift in the balance of decision making within the family towards the wife whilst simultaneously gaining access to newfound absolute and relative prosperity. Not only would the choice be made to avoid high parity births, but consumer goods could be substituted for children and the tenets of human capitalism employed within the home. When more effective appliance methods of birth control became available, they would therefore be utilised by middle-class women and when they became cheap and plentiful they would be used by working-class women, in circumstances where either labour demand or the balance of decision making permitted. By the 1930s that applied to the entire population. Bounded or selective rationality was always present, it was the aims and objectives that changed.

Technical ability was always present, but it became more effective, more female orientated, cheaper and more accessible by degrees.

A theory of this form suggests that there are elements of the schemes put forward by Leibenstein, Easterlin and Coale which need to be retained, but that different emphases are required. Firstly, the implication, stemming from the notion of modernisation, that there are traditional, in some ways backward, societies that go through a process of change which makes them modern, needs to be treated with caution especially where changes are endogenously induced and not externally imposed. The tradition of late age at marriage, of which the Malthuses and Marxes are examples, was an important one for demographic regulation. As Figs. 3.10 and 3.11 show, this practice was quite capable of depressing overall fertility. Secondly, it is most important to stress the aspect of constrained choice in decision making on childbearing and to show how constraints will vary between classes, types of employment and, therefore, socio-economic environments. In terms of Easterlin's framework, one needs to specify who is responsible for making the decisions on supply and demand, and what range of alternatives they have open to them. The ladies of Mayfair made their own social choices while the women of the Rhondda were constrained to act for the good of the family wage economy. Thirdly, the essential pre-conditions for the secular decline in fertility in the urban–industrial society of nineteenth-century England and Wales were that women should be able to exert control over their own reproductive powers; and that they should have safe, cheap and effective means of doing so. The former came with rising real incomes, or embourgeoisement, or entry into the labour force, or a general fall in the demand for labour; and the latter through the limitlessness of science. In these specific instances Marx's pessimism over pauperisation proved unfounded and Engels's trust in the wonders of science was justified.

# 4
# Migration theories

What is your aim in philosophy?–
To shew the fly the way out of the fly-bottle.

Ludwig Wittgenstein, *Philosophical Investigations*

Theories of migration are clearly divisible into two groups. The first comprises those that take as their starting point the questions 'Why' and 'How'. They ask, for example, 'Who migrates and why?', 'What forms do migrations take?', 'Why do migration streams take on particular patterns in time and space?'. Such theories are concerned with the causation and structuring of migrations, they search for motivations and constraints, and generally attempt to account for the forms and processes of migration. The second group of theories take a different line of approach, their objective being to explain the effects which migration has on varying physical, social, economic and political environments. These impact theories deal with the influences on origins and destinations together with those on the migrants themselves. Obviously these two major groupings can be further subdivided. For instance, one could develop theories of the demographic impact of migration, its effect on fertility patterns and its possible distortion of mortality rates; or one could focus on migration and the process of social change, the manner in which the act of changing place of residence alters a migrant's attitudes and his role in society.

Although this distinction is convenient – it appeared in more generalised form in Fig. 1.1 – it is by no means easy to make in practice. By tradition migration has been viewed as a demographic regulator with beneficial effects (see Ch. 5). It relieves population pressure in the Old World and in rural–agrarian societies. It keeps the marriage rate low and thus reduces the birth rate. It helps in the process of economic growth by transferring workers to the modern industrial sector and out of the less productive agricultural sector (Lewis, 1954; Ranis and Fei, 1961; Fei and Ranis, 1964). Finally, it provides a mechanism for social modernisation by spreading innovations, changing attitudes and raising expectations. Viewed from another perspective, however, migration also assists in the development of capitalism and the decay of the pre-capitalist mode of production by translating a rural agrarian peasantry, or proletariat, into an urban industrial proletariat (Dobb, 1946; see also Hilton *et al.*, 1976) and helping to create a permanent industrial reserve army by filling vacancies during periods of labour demand boom (see p. 42; Jerome, 1926; Todaro, 1976).

In all its functional forms migration is both a cause and an effect of spatial and temporal variations and changes in the organisation of society. In the following discussion pride of place will be given to theories which treat the causes of migration rather than the consequences, in the belief that it is in this particular area that the most substantial advances can now be made. What causes human beings to migrate? Answers to this question are largely conditioned by scale. Since definition of the term *migration* involves the specification of both a time scale and a set of boundaries within which and across which movement takes place the elements of time and space are built into the concept from the outset. The terms mobility and migration can be distinguished by these dual properties, for whilst the latter implies the crossing of a definitional boundary and remaining over that boundary for a specified length of time, mobility implies that either the boundary has not been crossed, even though movement has taken place, or that the boundary has been re-crossed (see White and Woods, 1980: 3–7). Scale is also of relevance because it points to the important distinction that must be made between the individual and the group. The aggregation of individuals into age, sex, class, ethnic, racial and cultural groups, for example, helps in making generalisations about both the pattern and the causes of migration. It also facilitates the forecasting of future migrations merely because it reduces the random element which is considerable when the prediction of individual behaviour is attempted.

Figure 4.1 provides a very general illustration of the relationship between individual and group within the context of a particular chain of argument. Attitudes lead to behaviour – or as Boulding (1956: 6) puts it, action is dependent upon image – which in turn gives rise to observable patterns that may have spatial as well as social, economic and political manifestations. The 'attitudes' and 'behaviour' boxes show the reciprocal relationship between the individual and the group. The individual's attitudes are affected by group norms which are some function of the combination of like-minded individuals or the dominance of a single person. The links between

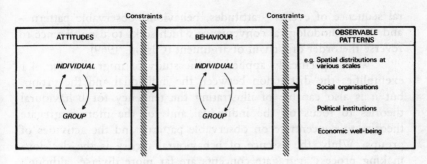

**Fig. 4.1** The associations between attitudes, behaviour and observable patterns

the boxes are not straightforward causal associations, attitudes are not always directly translated into behaviour, thoughts do not turn to deeds, and, in a more memorable phraseology, 'people make their own history, but they do not make it exactly as they please' (see Gouldner, 1980: 68). Similarly, behaviour is constrained by pre-existing socio-economic patterns, by the physical environment, by the level of technology attained and so on. Although it is reasonable to suppose that attitudes condition behaviour and that certain modes of behaviour create observable patterns, the construction of theories on the inter-linkage between these three boxes has tended to work against the direction of flow in Fig. 4.1. Geographers particularly have analysed form in the guise of spatial pattern and have then proceeded to infer the nature of the causal processes responsible for its creation. For example, social geographers have looked at the problem of segregation, in the sense of spatial separation, which they have inferred is caused by discriminatory behaviour which is itself linked to prejudiced attitudes. Blalock (1967) has even suggested that the level of segregation can be used to assess the degree of discrimination in a society. This reversal of the chain of argument brings to light major difficulties which are generally lumped together under the heading of the equifinality problem, that is the inference of process from form (see Cox and Golledge, 1969).

The inter-linked boxes shown in Fig. 4.1 only deal with the most simple of systems, since in reality behaviour is likely to affect subsequent attitudes and existing patterns will influence both behaviour and the formation of attitudes. In this sense it is a gross oversimplification of the real world, but it nonetheless serves to spell out the importance of distinguishing between the individual and the group together with the contradiction that exists between the natural sequence of events – attitudes, behaviour, observable pattern – and the methodological convenience which seeks to use inference to reverse the order of a chain of argument (Olsson, 1969).

When specifically applied to the study of migration Fig. 4.1 exemplifies the distinction between the individual and the group, but it is also capable of illustrating the tendency for behavioural theories to focus on the individual and for the more aggregate theories to concentrate on observable patterns and the activities of groups. Whilst the essence of behavioural theory is the decision-making process aggregate concepts are far more diverse, although many seek to use changing spatial structures or social organisations as causal mechanisms to which migration is seemingly an automatic response. The contrast between theories of individual and group migration will be used here as a device for introducing the behavioural and aggregate perspectives.

## Individuals

The behavioural approach focuses on the way in which an individual forms a set of attitudes which are then translated into action. As Lowenthal (1961: 260) has remarked, 'Every image and idea about the world is compounded . . . of personal experience, learning, imagination and memory'. Individuals possess 'private geographies', they live in 'individual and consensual worlds', but they are obliged to do, to act, as well as to think. It is in the study of how thoughts lead to actions that the key problems of behavioural geography are to be found (see Gold, 1980). In the specific context of migration, the object is to understand the manner in which a person assesses his present environment, together with other possible environments; how he decides whether to remain where he is or to move and, if he decides to move, which of the myriad of potential destinations he is to choose. Expressed simply, this means that explanation must concern itself with the quantity and quality of information an individual receives about different places, including his present area of residence, together with the ability of the individual to assimilate that information and to draw conclusions from it.

If one begins by making the assumptions that individuals are rational; that the level and quality of information available to them is unlimited; and that their actions are unconstrained, then one can investigate the decision-making process at its most straightforward. For instance, the objective of economic man is to optimise his economic and financial returns in a utilitarian fashion. These hypothetical persons will assess the information available to them on the economic benefits of alternative locations and if those benefits, or utilities, exceed those of the current place of residence migration will occur. In this sense the decision-making process is almost mechanical and the range of criteria used to make judgements is both narrow and predetermined. Just as the farmer who, if he is an economic man, will change the combination of crops that he grows in accordance with distance from market, so the potential migrant, who is motivated in a similarly economically optimising fashion, will move once he considers that there are greater benefits to be obtained elsewhere.

Julian Wolpert (1965) has outlined the concept of a 'place utility matrix' as a framework for studying rational decision making in the context of migration. The place utility matrix ($U$) consists of variables x places so that $u_{mn}$ gives the utility of place $n$ on characteristic or variable $m$. The list of variables that is used to assess the utility of places can vary from person to person as may the relative significance which is attached to each variable. For this latter reason it is important to multiply the place utility matrix by a vector of $m$ weights, one for each variable, which will yield a weighted place utility matrix ($W$). The sums of the values in the $n$ columns of $W$ will give scores for each place. The individual will then use these scores both to judge the utility of his current place of residence (which can be taken to be one of the $n$ places in the matrix) *vis à vis* the $n-1$ other places and to decide which of the other places would provide the maximum utility. In the most simple case Wolpert's place utility matrix could apply to economic man who has only a small number of economic or financial variables with which to evaluate alternatives. These would lead him to choose a place with the highest score in terms of economic utility, thus pinpointing his optimum location.

In the hands of economic man the place utility matrix is a very precise decision-making instrument. The list of variables to be used is short since they merely reflect economic well-being; alternatives are assessed rationally with unlimited accurate information; and readjustments are made once sub-optimality becomes evident. If the economic man assumption is removed and replaced by the simple notion of rationality then the place utility matrix becomes rather more realistic. By this means the range of variables to be used is much enlarged, although migration still depends upon evidence from $W$. In addition to economic variables social, political and environmental forces, for example, can now be brought into play. The potential migrant may use such variables as environmental stress, housing quality, recreational and educational facilities, social class affiliation, employment opportunities, land availability and so on which he will weigh according to his assessment of their relative importance. In other respects the place utility matrix (**W**) can be used in a similar fashion to that adopted by economic man, although the resulting decision may differ because social variables have out-weighed economic ones – educational facilities have been weighted higher than employment opportunities.

At this stage in the argument the concept of the place utility matrix still remains a valuable one, in the intellectual sense at least. Rational decisions are made from abundant information and the range of variables used, although potentially long, is not infinite. Even though individuals tend to employ different variables and dif-fering weighting systems there are several elements of conformity. The life cycle, for instance, tends to lead to the use of common sets of variables and similar weights by those in the same stage of family building or career (Speare, 1970). The young married couple seeks a new dwelling away from their parents; the couple with an expanding family looks for a larger house; and the newly retired require less space. In each of these three cases the variables used in the place utility matrix and the weights applied will be quite different although one would expect to find some degree of consensus within each group. However, as the economists and economic geographers have found, human behaviour is by no means always rational, being at best 'boundedly rational' or in Leibenstein's (1976: 71–94, 1978: 77–97) phrase 'selectively rational'. Although the place utility of a location may be exceeded by that of one or a number of other locations, migration is not necessarily a consequence, either because rational decision making is not translated into behaviour, or, alterna-tively, the decision-making process itself may lack logicality. It is constrained within bounds which predetermine a sub-optimal con-clusion. An individual will not always migrate when he should or, if he does migrate, move to the location with the highest place utility.

The final stage in the process of peeling away assumptions requires the consideration of information availability. It is obvious that in reality the quantity and quality of information about alterna-tive locations will be both limited and biased; that decisions, howev-er rational, will have to be founded on imperfect knowledge; and, further, that it is an individual's perception of the attributes of places, as opposed to their objective attributes, that is fundamental to the decision-making process. Research on spatial perception and information flow has advanced rapidly in recent years. The review presented by Gould and White (1974), for instance, shows clearly the simple influence of distance on perception, but it also reveals how distortion can be created by large concentrations of populations, cultural and political boundaries, and by 'regional images' – California and the English Lake District for example. Similarly, the work of Lynch (1960) and Goodey (1971a, b, 1974) depicts the non-random nature of the intra-urban spatial learning process with its neighbourhood, sector and central area biases.

It may prove useful, although artificial, to draw the distinction between information flow and perception, the former being merely a contributory element of the latter. However, the manner in which information is received and the way in which it is translated into an image of reality also require consideration because together they provide raw data for an individual's perception and hence the decision-making process. Information about the characteristics of places and about the possibility of their changing in the near future comes to the individual in a variety of ways: direct experience; verbal or written reports from relatives or friends; communications from an organisation, such as those sponsoring emigration, planning authorities or the mass media. Each of these channels provides the means of gaining either first hand or received knowledge to which can be assigned varying degrees of credibility. Further, the mode of gaining information varies with scale. Direct experience tends to be locally orientated and display a sharp decline with distance whilst reports from friends and organisations cover distant places in a more haphazard fashion. Local and international migrations are therefore likely to be founded on information received in completely different ways. For instance, letters from pioneer migrants often serve to create a rosy image of a relative's new home and this in turn, with the help of remittances, encourages secondary migrants so that eventually an observable pattern of chain migration is established. This point is well illustrated by the work of Tannous (1942), Hvidt (1975: 183–94) and, more generally, Conrad (1980) on, respectively, the migration of members of a Lebanese rural community to America; the nineteenth-century emigration of Danes to America; and the creation of a European image of America. On a local scale Hägerstrand's (1967) classic studies of innovation diffusion have shown how information spreads over time and through space via the neighbourhood effect. Here the mode of communication is by word of mouth so that distance, physical barriers and purely random directional biases can be clearly identified.

The sorting, evaluation, assimilation and storage of information once received comprises the complex psychological process of cognition (see Bennett and Chorley, 1978: 223–49). Here the personality traits of the individual are of particular importance. The cautious and the adventurous will react in different ways to the same information as will the optimist and the pessimist. The identification of such personality traits and the specification of their effects on cognition have proved intractible problems for the psychologist. Although Knox and MacLaran (1978: 239–40) have attempted to formulate a model of perceived well-being which includes objective and perceived characteristics of places; expectation and aspirations; life experiences and personal factors; as well as personal and reference group values the 'cognition problem' has tended to be side-stepped in geography by the use of Pred's behavioural matrix. Here level of information is cross-classified by the catch-all dimension 'ability to use' (Pred, 1967, 1969). Figure 4.2 illustrates the potential of such a concept for studying the decision-making process of the potential

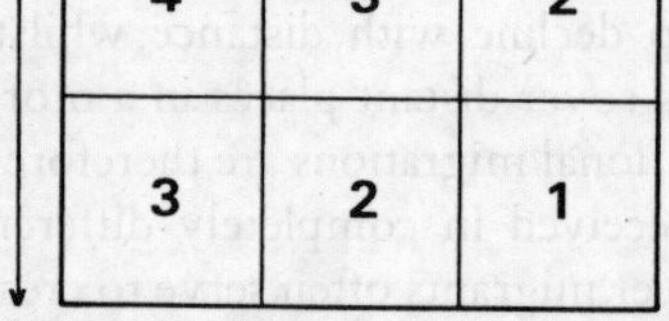

**Fig. 4.2** Pred's behavioural matrix applied to the migration process.

migrant. Those individuals who are the recipients of large amounts of information and have a high ability to use it (square 1) will attempt to employ their own place utility matrices so that an optimum location will be identified. At the other extreme, those in square 5 may hit on an optimum location, but it will be by chance, sub-optimality being more likely. Individuals who receive a high level of information, but have a low ability to use it (square 3'), may be unable to make rational decisions or be boundedly rational or rational in the sense of being satisficers. For such persons the different criteria used to translate information into attitudes are bound to create behaviour patterns which are dissimilar to those of persons in square 1. Alternatively, those persons in square 3 may use some form of the place utility matrix, but because they only have a limited supply of information they may not make optimum decisions in terms of staying or moving.

Although Pred's behavioural matrix was originally designed so that behavioural elements could be introduced into the locational analysis of economic activities, it also serves as a way of considering the sub-optimality that is common in the migration decision-making process. In the context of migration studies Pred's 'ability to use' axis could be relabelled 'ability to use the place utility matrix in a rational manner'.

Any assessment of the behavioural approach to migration studies and particularly the relevance to individuals' movements must focus both on its overall logicality and on the way it can shed light on observable patterns. Wolpert's place utility matrix, to take the most obvious and accessible example, requires specific assumptions to be made before the behaviour of an individual can be predicted. If the potential migrant is irrational in his use of the place utility scores or if he is rational but employs a set of satisficer values (Harvey, 1969) his actions will not simply be determined by the information available to him as they would be were he an economic man. In economic location theory major problems are encountered once the *lex parsimonii* is broken (see Webber, 1972: 88–116; Leibenstein, 1976). Similarly in population geography once the assumption of rational decision making is abandoned any theory which is constructed to account for the migratory behaviour of individuals is bound to lose both rigour and simplicity. The concept of the place utility matrix is therefore liable to become a model of the elements involved in the decision-making mechanism rather than a full theory which will predict the outcome given certain pre-conditions. The model will specify that weights are applied to variables in an assessment of places; that information about places will be quantitatively and qualitatively uneven; and that the ability to interpret, sort and store that which is received will vary from individual to individual.

However, migrations are not random walks but the result of decisions which can be predicted in the probabilistic sense. It is more likely that a potential migrant will move to *A* than *B* if he perceives that *A* will offer him more advantages in terms of his current assessment of benefits than place *B*. Not all potential migrants will behave in the same way although they will all go through the same decision-making procedure. In this sense the place utility matrix provides a model of the migrant's decision-making mechanism which has universal properties and constitutes a theory of any one individual's probable behaviour.

A second means of assessing the behavioural approach is to question the empirical validity of, for example, the place utility matrix. Few have specifically attempted to tackle the measurement problems entailed, problems which are also common to perception studies in general (Downs, 1970). One recent approach has been made by Lieber (1978; see also Gustavus and Brown, 1977). As he remarks, 'The first step is to identify the relevant attributes that contribute to the final value of place utility. A survey of the work by earlier scholars in migration research provides little guidance on how such identification is to be accomplished, nor does it provide a list of variables that have proven to be satisfactory for purposes of constructing the model' (Lieber, 1978: 16). Lieber studied the way in which his sample of 421 final year students at the University of Iowa formulated their preferences for migrating to alternative types of environments. He found that there was a substantial amount of agreement on the sorts of variables to be employed in an individual's place utility matrix: access to a major city, fresh air recreational facilities and close relatives being the most important variable combinations. Lieber also found that he could predict the types of areas to which 63 per cent of his respondents actually migrated upon graduation, even though the specific location could not be forecast. Naturally this study also raises problems. Although Lieber's potential migrants were standardised by age and educational level they were not, as are most potential migrants, assessing the place utility of their present place of residence, *vis a vis* other places. However, Lieber's (1978) study does represent a step towards the exploration of variable combinations and weightings, as specified by individuals themselves, which are used in their process of decision making, and a justification for the belief that individuals with the same characteristics tend to employ similar variables.

The behavioural approach to migration and the notion of place utility have proved valuable to urban social geographers concerned with intra-urban migration. However, it is important to draw a distinction between, on the one hand, inter-urban and rural-urban migration and, on the other hand, intra-urban and urban-rural or suburban movement. Whilst the former pair normally involve the search for new employment as well as residential relocation the latter are usually restricted to residential migration alone. This point needs to be borne in mind because it implies that intra-urban migration is a less complex process since it only involves residential search behaviour and assessment of the utility of a smaller number of places within the same built-up area, whilst inter-urban migration, for instance, involves both this process and the choice of destination urban area (see Clark and Avery, 1978: 136).

Despite this reservation, Brown and Longbrake (1969, 1970), Brown and Moore (1970), Clark (1970), Adams (1969), Johnston (1972), Jackson and Johnston (1974), Huff and Clark (1978) and others have employed the concepts of place utilities, action spaces and mental maps to investigate apparent regularities in the behaviour of intra-urban migrants, although these terms are not always made directly applicable to the individual. Brown and Longbrake (1970: 375), for instance, argue that, 'since the flow of population reflects a subjective place utility evaluation by households, the social scientist studying intra-urban migration behaviour may employ variables which characterise areas of destination and origin to construct a surrogate place utility function'. Process is therefore to be inferred from form via ecological correlation. Further, all of these studies owe a considerable debt to the work of Rossi (1955: 174) since they tend to adopt his compartmentalisation of the residential relocation process (Adams, 1969: 312). In Rossi's scheme the decision to leave the old home is taken first, either from necessity or choice, and only after that decision has been made is residential search begun and the choice between alternatives finally made. This partitioning of the decision-making process provides a further instance of simplification which tends to abstract Rossi-based interpretations of the intra-urban case from migration theories founded on universal principles. It could be argued, therefore, that intra-urban migration represents a relatively simple form of migration; that it has been simplified even further by reducing the decision-making process to three distinct stages; and that individual behaviour has often been studied indirectly by using surrogate variables to measure aggregate relationships.

Urban geographers have also become more interested in the behaviour of shoppers and retailers as a reaction to the tyranny imposed by central place theory. Golledge (1967), Golledge and Brown (1967), Rushton (1969) and Burnett (1973), for example, attempt to examine the geography of retailing by studying the spatial decision-making process of potential purchasers. However, the title of Gerard Rushton's paper – *Analysis of spatial behavior by revealed space preference* – highlights the ever-present problem of causal inference. Rushton argues that it is possible to study the decision-making process via the resulting behavioural outcome, but one of the objectives of the behavioural methodology is to avoid the inferential leap that results from image ← action arguments. The behaviour of individuals must be studied directly: perceptions, images and attitudes need to be causally linked with patterns of behaviour whether that behaviour is in the role of consumer or migrant.

The contribution of behavioural geography to the interpretation of individuals' activities, especially in the field of migration, is very considerable, although fraught with new problems. Wolpert's notion of a place utility matrix provides an essential conceptual framework for the study of the migrant's decision-making process, but it does not enable one to predict whether an individual will be mobile and if he is where he will migrate to and it does tend to overemphasise 'free choice' and minimise the role of constraints. A migrant migrates because he believes that the benefits that will acrue to him in another place will be greater than those he is receiving in his present place of residence; that at least is clear. Future research will need to focus on the factors that affect the selection of variables and weights, together with the distortions that are generated by the differential availability of information; it will be required to operate specifically within the context of bounded or selective rationality; and will need to give due importance to the influence of constraints. Advances will stem from explicitly psychological studies of the cognition process which encompasses both spatial learning and decision making (see Gold, 1980).

## Groups

Explanations of mass migration can be divided into four particular, although not necessarily mutually exclusive, groups. The first, and most traditional, stems from attempts to make law-like generalisations on the characteristics of migration and migrants which are derived from empirical observation. E. G. Ravenstein's 'laws of migration' are the most obvious examples of this genre, but their pattern has been emulated repeatedly (see Grigg, 1977; Lee, 1966; Redford, 1926; Shaw, 1975: 133–6). This entire approach lacks any theoretical grounding. The second group stresses the selective nature of the migration process – that emigrants are not randomly chosen from origin societies and that immigrants are not homogeneous with the population of destinations (see White and Woods, 1980: 12–18). This interpretation is valuable because it can be linked to the concept of place utilities and also provides a framework for the analysis of migration impact. The migration of self-selected groups – pioneers and colonists, innovators and adopters, primary leaders and secondary followers – can thus be seen to respond to levels of socio-economic development in the classic cause and effect relationship (Muth, 1971).

The third group of explanations interprets migration in the context of the development of capitalism, that is, as but one element of the materialist dialectic. Migration is part of the tension which exists between core and peripheral, urban and rural, metropolitan and colonial areas (see Frank, 1969: 145–50). The core uses the periphery as a source of labour supply just as it appropriates the latter's inanimate commodities, a function which it may perform with involuntary labour taken from yet another peripheral area. The migrant enters the class structure of the core area at a particularly disadvantaged level not only because of his position as a newcomer, but also because of the subordinate status which may be ascribed to him if he is a member of a distinctive ethnic or racial group. This form of analysis has proved particularly appropriate for an understanding of migrant labour in Europe (Böhning, 1972: 54–71; Castles and Kosack, 1973a, b) and the system of chattel slavery developed in the western hemisphere and supplied by the Atlantic slave trade (see Finley, 1980: 86 and 132), but it has many implications which are useful at other scales and to enquiries with empirical objectives. One of its more important contributions is the provision of an all-embracing social, economic and political framework for the analysis of human society which deals explicitly with spatial and temporal inequalities in socio-economic development. These inequalities lead to both a positive and a negative response by potential migrants who react to the opportunities, pressures and constraints which they impose.

The fourth group of explanations is also explicitly couched in theoretical terms, but is firmly rooted in the literature of neo-classical economics. Migration is discussed in the vocabulary of costs and returns; of investment in human capital. These notions were developed by T. W. Schultz and Gary Becker in the early 1960s, although they were originally applied to education and retraining in employment (see T. W. Schultz, 1961, 1962, 1974; Becker, 1962, 1964). Sjaastad has made their relevance explicit by treating migration as a problem of resource allocation; as an, *'investment increasing the productivity of human resources,* an investment which has costs and which also renders returns' (Sjaastad, 1962: 83). This theory requires the measurement of financial and non-financial costs and returns.

The non-financial costs involve 'opportunity costs', that is, wages forgone in the move and the search for employment, and 'psychic costs' which, although crucial in any behavioural interpretation, are ignored by Sjaastad (1962: 86) because they involve 'no resource cost'. The concepts developed by T. W. Schultz and L. A. Sjaastad have provided grounding for a large number of more empirical studies which have sought to test and thence extend the tenets of the 'investment in human capital' theory of migration (see Herrick, 1965: 10–22; Sabot, 1979).

The theory itself can be expressed most simply in the following form

$$PV = \left( \frac{I_j - I_i}{rd_i} \right) - C_{ij} \qquad [4.1]$$

where $PV$ = the net present value of a migration investment for the average migrant,

$I_j$ and $I_i$ = the average real incomes in places $j$ and $i$, respectively,

$rd_i$ = the rate of discount applied to future real income in $i$,

$C_{ij}$ = the costs of migrating from $i$ to $j$ including the opportunity costs,

and since one would expect the number of migrants moving from $i$ to $j$ ($M_{ij}$) to be positively related to $PV$, then

$$M_{ij} = f \left[ \left( \frac{I_j - I_i}{rd_i} \right) - C_{ij} \right] \qquad [4.2]$$

Migration from $i$ to $j$ is therefore seen as a function of the income differential between places $i$ and $j$, discounted for future income in $i$, less the costs of migrating from $i$ to $j$. Migrants invest time, effort and money in an attempt to achieve greater returns in the form of economic rewards. They respond to differences in real income between places, but they also deduct the costs that are likely to be incurred in the process of relocation. Behaviour is consciously economic in motivation, costs and returns are evaluated as though on a balance sheet and decisions are made so that the stream of financial gains can be maximised.

Many researchers have used this theory either explicitly or implicitly, on its own or as part of a broader framework. Most have found the general notion valid, when it is applied at the interregional scale to account for the migration streams of the economically active sector of the population, but it has been usual to make amendments so that elements like distance, information flows, age, education, kinship patterns and subjective expectations can also be taken into account. These elements turn the investment in human capital theory into one more akin to the concept of migration as a form of selection process biased towards groups with certain economic and social characteristics. This sequence can be illustrated using a variety of more empirical examples.

Laber and Chase (1971) have argued that $C_{ij}$ in [4.2] is a positive function of $D_{ij}$, distance between $i$ and $j$. So that in linear regression terms they write

$$M_{ij} = \alpha + \beta_1\left(\frac{I_j - I_i}{rd_i}\right) - f(D_{ij}) \qquad [4.3]$$

and by assuming that $rd_i$ is equal in all possible origins and destinations

$$M_{ij} = \alpha + \beta_1(I_j - I_i) - \beta_2 D_{ij} + \varepsilon. \qquad [4.4]$$

The geographer must naturally be wary of such a substitution since he knows that distance itself can be measured in a variety of ways – straight line, hierarchical, in terms of cost or time – that it often stands as a proxy for information flow and that it is responded to in different ways according to a population's age, sex, educational and class characteristics. The work of Olsson (1965) has shown that distance moved can itself depend upon income and unemployment rates in origin and destination together with the social and economic attributes of the migrants. Most geographers have tended to see aggregate migration flows more in terms of gravity model formulations in which

$$M_{ij} = f(P_i, P_j, D_{ij}) \qquad [4.5]$$

or in regression form (Olsson, 1970: 22)

$$\log M_{ij} = \alpha + \beta_1 \log P_i + \beta_2 \log P_j \\ - \beta_3 \log D_{ij} + \varepsilon \qquad [4.6]$$

where migration is simply positively associated with the product of the population of $i$ and $j$ ($P_i \bullet P_j$) and inversely related to the distance between them (see also Olsson, 1967; Olsson and Gale, 1968; Gale, 1973). But as will be argued later this formulation owes more to geography's empirical-modelling approach than to any theory of causality.

The economist Aba Schwartz (1973) has also considered the role of distance and the costs it imposes. His analysis recognises the possibilities that, firstly, the limiting effect of distance could be due purely to psychic cost, which is itself also directly related to age, or that, secondly, it could be primarily due to diminishing information which is in turn affected by length of formal education. In other words, those most prone to respond to the $I_j - I_i$ differential are the well-educated young and those least likely are the less-educated elderly, since for the former group there is a low psychic cost-information barrier but for the latter there is a high barrier which will manifest itself in a strong distance effect. Schwartz (1973) has examined this confounding problem with data for inter-regional migration in the USA. His conclusions generally support these notions for they emphasise the strength of the education–information –distance sequence whilst recognising the existence of one which links age to distance via psychic costs. Similar results have been obtained by Bowles (1970), who found that levels of education improved the effect of income gain on the probability of migrating while increasing age tended to reduce the effect.

Even before the theory of human capital was developed by T. W. Schultz and Becker, the work of Nelson had shown how complex the associations between real income differences, information and what Nelson (1959: 49) calls the 'relatives and friends multiplier' are in influencing the migration of groups. 'Relatives and friends provide a unifying principle for the variables determining migration. The money income hypothesis determines which variables will affect migration, but the relatives and friends multiplier determines the relative importance of these variables' (Nelson, 1959: 62). The role of information is mediated by the distribution of relatives and friends, which is itself the product of past migration, and this in turn has an influence on the distance moved and the possible responses to real income differences. Nelson's empirical findings tended to reduce the effect of this last-mentioned factor although they did stress the significance of income and unemployment levels in potential destinations as important independent variables. Two more empirical studies of migration in India and Venezuela by Greenwood (1973) and Levy and Wadycki (1973), respectively, explored another aspect of the 'family and friends' notion by using multiple regression models which relate contemporary migration streams to past streams, on the grounds that the movement of family and friends will affect subsequent migration in the classic chain-like form mentioned earlier (see Choldin, 1973). However, Mincer, by viewing migration in the light of American experience in the 1970s, has revealed a new perspective which is summarised by the observations that, 'Tied migration ranks next to child rearing as an important dampening influence in the life-cycle wage evolution of women' (Mincer, 1978: 771), which can lead to strain in and break up of marriages and hence more migration.

The original investment in human capital theory of migration still stands, but it has grown by the accretion of detail so that it involves real income disparities, distance associated costs, information flows, age selectivity, and the 'relatives and friends multiplier'. The model presented by Todaro (1969, 1976: 28–46, 1977: 186–203, 1980) strips the theory back down to its bare essentials, but then incorporates the critical concept of expectations. Todaro (1969: 138) argues that, 'when analysing the determinants of urban labour supplies, one must look not at prevailing real income differentials as such, but rather at the rural-urban "expected" income differential, i.e. the income differential adjusted for the probability of finding an urban job'. Such a model finds a first expression in the following form

$$M_{ij} = f(I_j - I_i, PE_j) \tag{4.7}$$

where $PE_j$ = the probability of finding employment in
        $j$. (Todaro deals with the special case
        where $i$ is a rural area and $j$ an urban one.)
It has the following general features (Todaro, 1976: 35–6).

    1. Migration is stimulated primarily by rational economic considerations of relative benefits and costs, mostly financial but also psychological.

    2. The decision to migrate depends on 'expected' rather than actual urban–rural real wage differentials where the 'expected' differential is determined by the interaction of two variables, the actual urban–rural wage differential and the probability of successfully obtaining employment in the urban modern sector.

    3. The probability of obtaining an urban job is inversely related to the urban unemployment rate.

    4. Migration rates in excess of urban job opportunity growth rates are not only possible but also rational and probable in the face of continued positive urban-rural *expected* income differentials.

It is more fully developed in Harris and Todaro (1970) as

$$M_{ij} = f(I_j^e - I_i) \tag{4.8}$$

and

$$I_j^e = \frac{I_j \cdot E_j}{P_j}$$  [4.9]

where  $I_j^e$ = the *expected* real income (wage) in $j$,

$I_j$ = the real minimum income (wage) adjusted for the proportion of the total labour force in $j$ actually employed $(E_j/P_j)$,

$E_j$ = the labour force in employment in $j$,

$P_j$ = the total labour force in $j$. (Again $i$ is rural and $j$ is urban.)

And if

$I_j^e - I_i = 0$ then $M_{ij} = 0$.

Potential rural migrants are therefore assumed to behave as 'maximisers of expected utility' and rural–urban migration will continue just as long as expected urban real income exceeds real agricultural returns.

The Harris–Todaro model has its origins in empirical work carried out on the causes and effects of rural–urban migration in East Africa (Harris and Todaro, 1968, 1969). Why, they ask, does urban in-migration persist when there are high rates of urban unemployment? A question that is appropriate for most of Africa and Latin America. Their answer focuses on the role of migration as a disequilibrating force and the existence of urban minimum wage rates which are maintained at higher levels than would be expected were simple market forces to operate. However, it also highlights the fact that rural–urban migration involves a shift between sectors of the economy and between occupations. As Sjaastad (1962: 87) originally remarked, 'The more relevant alternatives for migrants may be *among* rather than *within* occupations.'

The Todaro (1969) and Harris and Todaro (1970) models are open to a number of criticisms. For example, Godfrey (1973: 67) has argued that the Todaro model is not strictly testable because it deals with migrants' subjective expectations and cannot therefore be refuted. Santos (1979: 168) says that the Harris and Todaro (1968) view 'stems from an overhasty generalisation applied to all Third World countries from situations existent in only some countries'. Santos bases this criticism on his view that the Harris–Todaro model merely requires rural and urban wage rates to be equalised, whereas in fact it requires there to be a reduction in expectations of urban real incomes on the part of potential rural–urban migrants. This point is also brought out by Miyao and Shapiro (1979: 1163) who suggest that the governments of underdeveloped countries should spread 'pessimistic information' to discourage urban immigration. More fundamental criticisms concerning predicted levels of urban unemployment rates have been raised by Bhagwati and Srinivasan (1974) and Fields (1975). At a more practical level, the Todaro and Harris–Todaro theories fail to take into account the degree of 'migratory circulation' that is present in most Third World countries where return migration is a vital aspect of the whole process. They also tend to avoid the problems which stem from the assessment of $I_i$ in monetary terms. Many rural pupulations are not engaged, or only partially engaged, in the wage economy and would therefore find it impossible to evaluate $I_j^e - I_i$ differential because they would have to compare non-monetary present returns with monetary expected returns (see Gugler, 1968, 1969).

In testing the Todaro model Rempel and Todaro (1972) have themselves made amendments which they state as follows: 'Our *a priori* expectations are that the percentage of people in a given area who choose to migrate will vary directly with the relative urban–rural income differential, the extent of clan contacts, the relative index of *per capita* amenity levels and the size of the population of the urban centre, and inversely with the cost of moving' (Rempel and Todaro, 1972: 216). Their overall migration model is expressed as

$$M_{ij}^E = f \left[ \left( \frac{V_j^E - V_i^E}{V_i^E} \right), C_{ij}, CT_{ij}^E, A_i, A_j, T \right] \qquad [4.10]$$

where $M_{ij}$ = migration between $i$ and $j$,
$V_i$ and $V_j$ = expected real income in places $i$ and $j$,
$C_{ij}$ = costs of moving from $i$ to $j$,
$CT_{ij}$ = a measure of clan contacts from area $i$ already resident in area $j$,
$A_i$ and $A_j$ = indices of available amenities in $i$ and $j$,
$T$ = tribal affiliation,
$E$ = a superscript indicating that functional relationships exist within a group having achieved a particular level of educational attainment.

Rempel and Todaro (1972) have illustrated how once again a simple functional theory of migration based on income differences and, on this occasion, expectations is ultimately transformed by the incorporation of a range of other variables which are specific to the particular context in which migration is occurring. The theory symbolised in [4.2] was similarly amended. Most empirical analyses of aggregate migration streams also employ this approach. They base themselves on theoretically derived principles which they then supplement and amend to fit the particular migration flow to be studied and to overcome the constraints imposed by the necessity of measuring explanatory variables. Three examples of multiple regression based aggregate migration models will be used to illustrate these points.

The first and most straightforward example comes from the work of T. P. Schultz (1971) which is but one of a group of empirical studies of inter-regional migration (see Beals, Levy and Moses, 1967; Greenwood, 1969a, b, 1970, 1971a, b; Greenwood and Sweetland, 1972). Schultz analyses the net regional migration streams in Colombia between 1951 and 1964. His model is typical of the empirical approach, but contains borrowings from economics-based theory. In multiple regressin terms it is specified as follows:

$$\frac{M_i}{P_i} = \alpha + \beta_1 W_i + \beta_2 E_{1i} + \beta_3 E_{2i} + \beta_4 L_i + \beta_5 \left(\frac{V_i}{P_i}\right) + \beta_6 T_i + \varepsilon$$

[4.11]

where $M_i$ = net migration to region $i$,
$P_i$ = population of $i$,
$W_i$ = local male agricultural daily wage, including food, in $i$,
$E_{1i}$ and $E_{2i}$ = school enrolment rate for children 5–9 and 10–14, respectively, in $i$,
$L_i$ = estimated growth rate of local potential labour supply in $i$,
$V_i$ = level of political violence in $i$,
$T_i$ = log of time required to travel from $i$ to nearest major city.

The maximum $R^2$ value that Schultz could achieve was 0·498 for the migration of females between combined urban and rural areas, but the conclusion he draws is unequivocal: 'The evidence confirms that inter-regional migration in Colombia responds to market forces drawing rural labour to the cities from regions where the returns to labour are relatively low and the supply of labour is growing relatively rapidly' (T. P. Schultz, 1971: 163; see also Fields, 1979).

The study of Brazilian inter-regional migration by Sahota (1968) is more firmly grounded in theory. Sahota starts with the 'costs and returns' approach; that is,

$$M_{ij} = f(R_{ij}, C_{ij}) = f(W_j, W_i, E_j, E_i, I_j, I_i, D_{ij})   \qquad [4.12]$$

where $M_{ij}$ = migration between $i$ and $j$,
$\quad R_{ij}$ = the potential returns to migrants from $i$ to $j$,
$\quad C_{ij}$ = the costs of migration from $i$ to $j$,
$W_j$ and $W_i$ = wage rates in $j$ and $i$, respectively,
$E_j$ and $\; E_i$ = education rates in $j$ and $i$, respectively,
$\quad I_j$ and $I_i$ = rate of growth of *per capita* income in $j$ and $i$, respectively,
$\quad\quad D_{ij}$ = distance between $i$ and $j$,

with

$$R_{ij} = f(W_j, E_j, I_j)   \qquad [4.13]$$

and

$$C_{ij} = f(W_i, E_i, I_i, D_{ij}).   \qquad [4.14]$$

However, he argues that for practical purposes – that is, in terms of model construction – the effects of adopting the human capital, the selectivity and the *ex post facto* generalisation approaches are similar, since all three focus on the same set of independent variables – income, wages, education, age and distance. Sahota himself adds to this list by including variables such as population density, urbanisation and income dispersion whilst disaggregating the education variable by age groups and employment sectors. The resulting multiple regression models tend to demonstrate the empirical validity of this form of methodology which although essentially eclectic is grounded in neo-classical economic theory. Economic costs and returns appear, on the whole, to dominate the behaviour of migrants, though some relevance for the non-economic 'push' and 'pull' factors is not denied (Sahota, 1968: 243).

The third example comes from a study by geographers of inter-regional migration in Tropical Africa, specifically Uganda. Masser and Gould (1975) employ a model which in functional terms can be expressed as

$$M_{ij} = f(D_{ij}, P_i, P_j, I_i, I_j, U_i, U_j, E_i, E_j)$$

and as a multiple regression model in the form

$$M_{ij} = \alpha - \beta_1 \log D_{ij} + \beta_2 \log P_i + \beta_3 \log P_j$$
$$- \beta_4 \log I_i + \beta_5 \log I_j + \beta_6 \log U_i + \beta_7 \log U_j$$
$$+ \beta_8 \log E_i + \beta_9 \log E_j + \varepsilon$$

where $M_{ij}$ = population born in $i$ and currently resident in $j$,
$\quad D_{ij}$ = distance between $i$ and $j$,
$P_i$ and $P_j$ = population of $i$ and $j$,
$I_i$ and $I_j$ = average income *per capita* in $i$ and $j$,
$U_i$ and $U_j$ = level of urbanisation in $i$ and $j$,
$E_i$ and $E_j$ = proportion of males in $i$ and $j$ who have received some education.

Their complete model had an $R^2$ of $0.74$ whilst after dropping out $E_i$ and $E_j$ $R^2$ was $0.73$ and with only $D_{ij}$, $P_i$ and $P_j$ it was $0.57$. In some respects the Masser and Gould model is similar to those of T. P. Schultz and Sahota mentioned above, but it also epitomises the general perspective adopted by geographers for it is based on the gravity model. Whilst it is certainly reasonable to expect the volume of migration between two places to be inversely related to the distance between them and directly related to the product of their populations, such a notion lacks any basis in causal theory. It is an empirically derived generalisation which has found support by analogy to Newtonian physics and currency amongst forecasters because it usually provides an effective means of establishing high $R^2$ values and hence reducing the magnitude of residuals. In the Masser and Gould (1975: 84) analysis the gravity model accounts for 57 per cent of the variation in $M_{ij}$ while the income, education and urbanisation variables only account for a further 17 per cent.

The issue is essentially one of objective. If the purpose is to derive a model which will maximise $R^2$ and hence minimise residual error then the gravity model is a most suitable starting point, but if, on the other hand, the objective is to construct a causal theory then each variable must be chosen because of its contribution to that theory. In this latter respect the theories symbolised in the models of T. P. Schultz and Sahota are superior to that constructed by Masser and Gould even though in terms of multiple regression analysis the achieved $R^2$ value may be substantially lower. This empirical-modelling perspective which has been particularly prominent in geographical studies of spatial interaction requires close scrutiny because it avoids the question, 'Why does migration occur?' Its prime concern is, 'How can the magnitude of migration streams be predicted?' Whilst answers to the latter question may be based on those to the former, the link is by no means essential. The emphasis on this perspective has tended to divert geographers from attending to the construction of theories which help to generate answers to the first question.

The development and empirical testing of theories of aggregate migration has advanced significantly during the past 25 years. Important innovations have come particularly from economic theories of human capital which have been extended by Todaro and others. At its simplest this theory specifies that potential migrants respond to differentials in real income levels which they adjust to allow for the costs associated with migration. They migrate with the intention of maximising personal economic gains and do so as long as expected net gains are substantial enough. Those who have empirically tested such theories have usually relied upon multiple regression models which they have constructed by introducing, firstly, variables designed to measure costs and returns – income, wages, distance – and, secondly, noting that certain sub-populations with specific characteristics are more likely to respond to economic inequalities, hence the inclusion of independent variables to measure education level and age, and, thirdly, variables peculiar to the specific context, such as tribal affiliation or extent of political violence. It must be remembered, however, that the ultimate cause of migration is the system which is responsible for generating the social and economic inequalities to which the migrants are responding.

The above discussion has demonstrated that most theories of the aggregate migration process are founded on economic theory, whether Marxist or neo-classical, whilst those of individual behaviour owe their origins to psychological theories of motivation and the decision-making process which in their least sophisticated form also assume rational action. How can these two groups of theories be integrated?

## Individuals and groups: towards a synthesis of migration theories

It is usual to assert that whilst one is unable to predict the behaviour of an individual, that of groups is more accessible to prediction. Given this to be the case, what can be learnt about group migration from the experience of individuals and *vice versa*?

In a sense the place utility and the human capital based theories of migration have common origins; they both depend upon the notion of rational action and they emphasise the role of choice, although in both instances this is constrained it is not eliminated as in certain Marxist theories of capitalist development in which labour is expelled from the land (discussed in Roxborough, 1979: 10). Place utility theory has been amended to allow for the behaviour of the boundedly or selectively rational and the satisficer while the human capital theories take on the structure of a probabilistic theory of aggregate response. The place utility matrix symbolises a theory of the decision-making process, whilst aggregate theories usually attempt *ex post facto* explanation, at least in their empirically verifiable multivariate forms. Reconciliation might be based on the use of human capital formulation to study the behaviour of individuals (see Byerlee, 1974: 553) or the translation of decision-making theory to the behaviour of groups, so that migration streams will not merely be viewed as responses to relative economic inequalities.

In practical terms the integration will be eased when survey data provides a source capable of permitting the social, economic and psychological characteristics of individual members of groups – migrants and non-migrants – to be identified; a facility which will enhance the testing of both behavioural and aggregate theories. A 'collective biography' approach, for example, has been employed on a number of occasions. It has the advantage that it enables the researcher to analyse the group as a whole, each individual member of that group and, in consequence, the average member of the group.

Two examples will be used here to illustrate the potential of this form of enquiry. Speare's (1971) study of Taiwanese migration employs costs and returns theory with Todaro-like amendments to examine the propensity of individuals to migrate. Speare bases his analysis on sample surveys of 321 male migrants to Taichung City and 370 male non-migrants residing in the surrounding counties. His model contains seven variables: expected change in income, unemployment, cost of moving, information, home ownership, whether parents are living in Taichung City and whether wife's parents are living there. It predicts that 75·8 per cent of the migrants would, and that 84·3 per cent of the non-migrants would not, migrate on the basis of the seven variables. By social scientific standards these results cast doubt on the assertion expressed at the beginning of this section. The results also revealed that 44·7 per cent of the variance in migration could be attributed to his seven cost-benefit variables, whilst only an extra 4·1 per cent could be accounted for by such 'background' variables as age, education, distance and so forth. Speare's case study gives a clear example of how the costs and returns theory can be used to predict the behaviour of individuals, but it should not be used without some caution for, as Speare (1971: 129–32) points out, 'the costs and benefits of migration are not actually calculated. In fact, our limited data suggest that people have only vague concepts of costs and benefits. Only a small percentage of all migrants knew exactly how much they would earn in the city before they moved and most could only distinguish whether they expected an increase, no change, or a decrease in income to result from the move'; and, 'A great many of the non-migrants we interviewed appear to have never given any serious consideration to the thought of moving anywhere.' The implication to be drawn is that costs and returns theories can be used to predict the migration of individuals as well as that of groups, but they fail to explain the manner in which an individual decides whether or not to migrate merely because that particular decision is not made with specifically optimising criteria.

Similar implications can be drawn from Hay's (1980) study of the probability of individuals migrating from the Testour area of Tunisia. Measurable variables like length of formal education, transferable skills, age and urban contacts are functionally related to urban expected earnings, while level of land-holding is substituted for urban contacts in the functional relationship with rural expected earnings. The overall probability of migrating is related to urban and rural expected earnings and age. One of Hay's findings is that those most likely to migrate – the well-educated young – and those least likely – the poorly-educated elderly – are the least responsive to rural income differences. The results of both Hay's study in Tunisia and that by Speare in Taiwan illustrate the possibilities for extending costs and returns type theories from the aggregate to the individual scales, but neither study is able to investigate the decision-making process at first hand. It is the observed behaviour of individuals that is analysed and not the manner in which individuals form attitudes and then implement them by behaving in particular ways. Just as in Sahota's (1968) study the behaviour of groups is associated statistically with measurable variables so the same procedure is followed through by Speare (1971) and Hay (1980), but in their cases individuals are used.

Speare and Hay type analyses do have a number of distinct advantages, at least for theory testing. Firstly, they use data sets containing important details which can only be found from social surveys and which fail to appear in census reports. Secondly, they avoid the major problem associated with the ecological fallacy. There is no need to infer individual from group behaviour because individuals are the fundamental unit of study. However, they do possess drawbacks. Only relatively localised areas are involved and the sample sizes are often relatively small. In consequence, most theory testing involves placing the mover–stayer dichotomy in a probabilistic framework rather than predicting the magnitude of flows, their origins and destinations. But these micro-scale studies are crucial for the understanding of precisely how migrants behave and in what ways they differ from non-migrants. Their coupling with the form of study undertaken by Lieber (1978) should make it possible to identify the ways in which individuals employ their own particular place utility matrices together with the objective socio-economic characteristics of those migrants, their origins and destinations. But these are attempts to overcome the practical problems of verification and testing rather than the reconciliation or integration of theories.

The common ground between the behavioural and aggregate theories is undeniably considerable. Migration occurs because human beings evaluate the benefits of their current places of residence in comparison with alternative places and if they conclude that any one of the alternatives has long-term advantages which outweigh the short-term disadvantages of relocation then they migrate. Both Wolpert's (1965) place utility matrix and the aggregate theories of migration begin by using the criterion of economic advantages or *expected* economic advantages which are responded to by rational actors. However, while the former concept is easily modified to take account of non-economic advantages the economists' aggregate theories either fail to allow for this category of causal factors or explicitly discount its significance. The first stage in the process of integration must tackle this point. Theories of aggregate migration behaviour must be capable of incorporating non-economic factors rather than treating them as ciphers for monetary returns. Education, life cycle stage, information and especially the 'relatives and friends multiplier' are not merely conditioning variables which help or hinder the process of economic cognition, but substantial reasons for migrating in their own right.

Again, both forms of approach use the rational action argument, but that which focuses particularly on decision making can be altered to incorporate bounded rationality or satisficer behaviour by, for instance, modifying Pred's behavioural matrix. In tests of aggregate theory one is left to infer that because $R^2$ is 0·65 and all the independent variables make a significant contribution then it is those variables themselves which are influencing migration; that it is the evaluation of perpetuating expected income differences that is promoting rural–urban migration, for example. Is one to conclude that the remaining 35 per cent of unexplained variance is due to misspecification problems or to irrationality on the part of migrants or non-migrants in moving to the wrong places or not moving at all? Perhaps this is to ask too much of social scientific theory, but the issue is an important one which might be resolved by allowing for satisficer as well as selectively rational action. As has been shown on a number of occasions, the well-educated young and the poorly-educated elderly behave differently as groups of potential migrants, for the former one requires a theory of rational economic optimisation whilst for the latter a theory of statisficer behaviour would be more appropriate in which a higher weighting is placed on non-economic benefits and costs. This second stage in the integration process would also allow for the incorporation of migrant selectivity by apportioning degrees of rationality or economic responsiveness to groups with particular characteristics.

These two stages would go part of the way to meeting the final objectives of integration; objectives which can be thought of in terms of a three-fold structure. Firstly, the ability to understand the way in which individuals form images of their worlds, assess those images and decide to migrate or not to migrate, together with the evaluatory criteria employed and the factors which control those criteria. Aggregate theory tells us that economic criteria are of prime importance in this image-building and this will provide a convenient starting point. Secondly, it must be possible to transfer this understanding to theories of group behaviour which will ultimately generate predictive models. Again these may be economics based, but they will not be devoid of non-economic attributes. Thirdly, it must also be made possible to apply aggregate theory to the behaviour of individuals with degrees of success acceptable by social scientific standards. The attainment of these three objectives would establish a unified but flexible theory of the migratory behaviour of human beings; as yet they are still unrealised.

# 5
# Transitions and revolutions

Time and again, however well we know the landscape of
love,
and the little church-yard with lamenting names,
and the frightfully silent ravine wherein all the others
end: time and again we go out two together,
under the old trees, lie down again and again
between the flowers, face to face with the sky.
Rainer Maria Rilke, *Time and Again* from *Selected Poems*

Population geography has at its disposal at least two 'grand
theories': one is that of the demographic transition or vital revolution
in which changes in the pattern and level of mortality, fertility and
migration are brought together in one complex system of inter-
linked causes and effects. The objective is to describe and explain
that series of events in the population history of Europe and North
America which has led to the low levels of both mortality and fertility. This truly revolutionary change in the demographic structure
brought about a new régime which is unlikely to be broken as
violently as was the old order in the nineteenth century. Transition
theory has been developed to account for these temporally unique
events, but it also contains elements of a predictive theory which
involves the spatial transfer of experience to the population of Africa,
Asia and Latin America in some future time. The theory is in a sense
revolutionary; it deals with the collapse of old relationships and fore-
tells the creation of new ones. Its theoretical statements are often
imprecise; they tend towards empirical description rather than logical
abstraction. It lacks the precision of a more limited causal theory, yet
one strength may lie in this very weakness for it holds out the
promise of a general historical theory which will deal with temporal
and spatial changes in population structures together with their main
economic and social causes. The specification, criticism and refor-
mulation of such a general theory of revolutionary demographic
change are the aims of this chapter. These aims will be pursued,
firstly, by establishing a fundamental statement of transition theory,

one which can be criticised for both its internal coherence and the validity of the empirical statements to which it gives rise; secondly, by exploring the possibility, suggested by Kingsley Davis (1963), of creating an overall theory of demographic response; and, thirdly, by introducing to population dynamics a yet more generalised theory of change founded on the concepts of historical materialism.

## Thompson–Notestein theory

The origins of transition theory can be traced to the 1929 paper by Warren S. Thompson (1929; see also Thompson, 1944) in which he distinguished between the populations of three specific areas and described their characteristics in terms of birth and death rates. Group A populations were to be found west of a line between Trieste and Danzig (Gdansk) including those of northern Italy and Spain together with the populations of countries settled by emigrants from this area of north-west Europe. (The similarity with Hajnal's (1965) Trieste-Leningrad line and other more traditional deliniations (Anderson, 1974a: 15) is interesting to note.) In this group birth and death rates had declined very rapidly. Group B comprises the populations of southern and eastern Europe where birth and death rate declines were under way. The populations of Africa, Asia and Latin America fell into group C. 'In many of these lands... both birth rates and death rates are quite uncontrolled and we may expect either a rapid increase or almost a stationary population dependent upon the harshness of the "positive" checks to population growth, viz., disease, hunger, war, etc.' (Thompson, 1929: 962). Thompson remarked on the peculiarities of French and Japanese experiences in groups A and C, respectively, and stressed both the time lag which occurred after the decline in the death rate before that of birth rate, and that before the pattern of group A was repeated in group B. The processes creating these differences were only alluded to in passing: modern industrialisation, sanitary conditions, urbanisation and agricultural improvements were mentioned. For group C populations the controlling process was the Malthusian subsistence crisis and the positive check. In India, for instance, the population would grow slowly, but increases due to temporary releases of pressure would be wiped out by famines or epidemics, a fate which Japan could avoid via the modernisation of its industry and some improvements in its agriculture.

Thompson's (1929) contribution was then to point out that there were differences between the population structures of major world regions and that those differences were in a state of flux, but that they were largely determined by leads and lags in the decline of death rates followed by birth rates. Thompson's work was complemented by that of the French demographer Adolphe Landry who, in his study *La Révolution Démographique*, distinguished three demographic régimes: the primitive, the intermediary and the contemporary (Landry, 1934, 1945: 338–46). Transition theory was more fully developed by Frank W. Notestein (1945, 1948, 1950, 1953). His intention was to examine the mechanisms of demographic change, an objective which he pursued in true inductive style by observing the pattern of world and continental population increase since the mid-seventeenth century and assessing the likelihood of future growth. Notestein too identified three 'demographic types'. The 'high growth potential' type occurs where 'mortality is high and variable and is the chief determinant of growth, while fertility is high and thus far has shown no evidence of a downward trend' (Notestein, 1945: 41). The second type, 'transitional growth', exists where birth and death rates are still high and population growth is rapid, but the decline of the birth rate is well underway. The 'incipient decline' type characterises populations in which fertility has fallen or is about to fall below replacement level. There is a certain amount of overlap between Notestein's types and Thompson's groups, although the latter's group B and the former's 'transitional growth' type coincide least satisfactorily (Notestein, 1950: 335).

The real importance of Notestein's 1945 article is that it outlines the mechanism by which the demographic transition had occurred and could take place in the future together with the causes of the inferred changes. As regards the mechanism: 'Growth came from the decline of mortality'; while, 'so far as we can tell from the available evidence, no substantial part of the modern population growth has come from a rise in fertility' (p. 39). The initial decline in mortality was caused, at least in Europe, by a period of peace being followed by, 'a series of agricultural innovations that greatly increased the food supply, which was further augmented by the vast resources of the New World. Industrial innovations began to bring spectacular increases in production. Finally, sanitary and medical advances brought control over the ravaging diseases of childhood and young adult life. In short, the whole process of modernisation in Europe and Europe overseas brought rising levels of living, new controls over disease, and reduced mortality' (p. 39).

According to Notestein's theory fertility decline did not immediately follow that of mortality because the high mortality level of a pre-transition society would have required the creation of social organisations with goals and equipment for the maintenance of high fertility merely to enable the population to survive. These props were only removed gradually. 'Birth rates were reduced largely by means of contraception, but in response to drastic changes in the social and economic setting that radically altered the motives and aims of people with respect to family size' (p. 40). The essential stimuli came from the joint processes of industrialisation and urbanisation so that, 'under the impact of urban life the social aim of perpetuating the family gave way progressively to that of promoting the health, education, and material welfare of the individual child; family limitation became widespread; and the end of the period of growth came in sight' (p. 41).

Notestein's theory can be stated more succinctly in the form of four propositions.

1. The demographic revolution is initiated by the secular decline of mortality.

2. Mortality decline is caused by the cumulative influences of the agricultural, the industrial and the sanitary revolutions which, respectively, lead to better food supplies, an improvement in the factors of production and the standard of living in general, and improvements in public health.

3. Rapid population growth is the result of the temporal lag between the decline of mortality and that of fertility.

4. Fertility decline eventually occurs because the social and economic supports to high fertility are removed. The materialism and individualism associated with the urban way of life give impetus to the rational control of fertility by means of contraceptive practices.

The first essential of this set of theoretical statements is that changes in economic structures, which are associated with industrialisation, bring about an improved standard of living which, firstly, affects mortality and, secondly, leads to rural–urban migration, urbanisation and the creation of an urban society which in turn establishes incentives for the introduction of direct controls on fertility. The second essential, which is implicit in the above propositions but which should be made explicit, is that at least three stages are involved in such a demographic revolution: high mortality and fertility; low mortality and high fertility; low mortality and fertility.

In broad outline Thompson–Notestein theory seeks to explain the causes of the modern rise of population via the effects of modernisation. The demographic revolution is but one of a series of revolutions in the material, social, political and technical spheres of human society which have occurred during the last 200 years.

Thompson–Notestein theory has, however, been adapted, added to and depicted graphically in a whole variety of ways to the extent that as Loschky and Wilcox (1974: 216) remark, 'Because there is such diversity of opinion concerning just what constitutes Transition Theory, it becomes difficult to test the Theory to determine what is and what is not implied by that loose collection of premises.' Most commentators agree with the descriptive element at least, but specifications of the theory's causal elements have become so wide and varied that there is now no one demographic theory. For this reason it is important to fix on a particular version as the focus for criticism. The original Thompson–Notestein theory fulfils that role here.

'In terms of its substantive application, transition theory raises issues in respect to its adequacy as descriptive generalisation, as *ex post facto* explanation, and as prediction' (Hauser and Duncan, 1959: 95). These three issues need to be considered in detail and in turn.

In those countries that have passed through the demographic revolution the pattern of population growth and the associated changes in birth and death rates have tended to follow the model laid out by Thompson–Notestein theory. The phase of high growth potential can be identified quite clearly from the vital statistics of Norway (Drake, 1969; see Woods, 1979: 86), Sweden (Hofsten and Lundström, 1976), Finland (Turpeinen, 1979) and Denmark (Matthiessen, 1972). In each case there are recurrent demographic crises in which the death rate, itself normally high, exceeds the birth rate (see Ch. 3). The same conditions can be identified, although less precisely, in other European countries and Japan. Again the transition phase, in which death rates decline followed by birth rates, is readily observable in nineteenth-century European, North American and Australasian populations. Even incipient decline is evident in Europe in the 1930s and its diagnosis has subsequently been reconfirmed (Council of Europe, 1978). None of this should be at all surprising since Thompson–Notestein theory is itself a generalisation from observed European experience. What is more interesting, however, is the apparent similarity of the pattern of birth and death rate decline in most of the countries. In Europe the major exception to the general model is France. There the birth and death rates not only declined in parallel, but their levels were also relatively close so that a period of rapid population growth did not occur as it did in the rest of

Europe (see Reinhard, Armengaud and Dupâquier, 1968: 328–56).

Even this inconsistency can be subsumed in the general model, as Fig. 5.1 shows, by allowing for variability in the birth and death rate time paths whilst preserving the characteristics of shape. In Fig. 5.1 the French case is given by $d'$ $b'$ whilst very rapid and sustained population growth would be created by $d'''$ $b'''$. There is

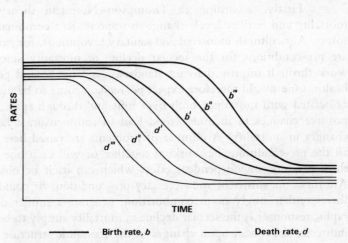

**Fig. 5.1** A variable model of the demographic transition

no reason, however, why $d$ and $b$ should be symmetrical: very rapid mortality decline could be followed by a more gradual reduction in fertility, $d'''$ $b'$, for example. The essential point is that the transition is initiated by mortality decline.

In terms of descriptive generalisation Thompson–Notestein theory has considerable value, at least in the sense that it provides a model of historical trends. The stages element of Thompson–Notestein theory also appears to be useful. Davis (1949: 595–617) and Thomlinson (1965: 21–24), for example, follow Notestein's original terminology; Blacker (1947) defines four stages whilst Clarke (1965: 157), Beshers (1967: 13), Trewartha (1969: 45), Chung (1970: 222), Imhof (1977: 61) and Noin (1979: 223) all identify stages on the basis of similar criteria. However, not all critics have been willing to place populations in the same stages or classify them as being of the same demographic type. For instance, J. S. Davis (1950) has argued that a special 'type' should be created for North America and Australasia; that the populations of these areas do not conform to incipient decline since birth rates have not fallen to the levels of death rates and immigration is still substantial.

The second basis for evaluation, the role of Thompson–Notestein theory as *ex post facto* explanation, does raise more intractible objections. One can at least say that the theory is verifiable, even eminently falsifiable, that it is capable of yielding empirical statements which may be rejected or temporarily accepted. Four objections will be raised here.

Firstly, according to Thompson–Notestein theory both mortality and fertility levels change in response to a combination of forces. Agricultural, industrial and sanitary revolutions, for example, are pre-conditions for the secular decline of mortality since they work through improved living standards, and public and personal health. One would therefore expect *per capita* income to be inversely associated with mortality, both over time and through space, while positive changes in income would lead to commensurate negative changes in mortality. A number of problems are raised here. Must all the pre-conditions be working together or will each one of the three produce an independent effect which can itself be observed? Are these the sufficient and necessary pre-conditions or could other forces, either singly or in combination, generate a similar demographic response? Is the secular decline in mortality simply to be made indirectly dependent upon changes in the economic structure of society?

It is clear from the work of Preston (1975, 1976) that much of the recent increase in life expectancy in the underdeveloped economies cannot be attributed to improvements in *per capita* income, at least at the national level. It is also the case that the demographic transition in Scandinavia appears to have been initiated before that region was subject to the full influence of the industrial revolution (see Grigg, 1980a, b: 217–30) and that the phase of rapid population growth in most of north-west Europe preceded the late nineteenth-century phenomenon of the sanitary revolution. The debate over the relationship between industrialisation and the standard of living has also been a long and ideologically bitter one (see Kuczynski, 1946; and the contributions to Taylor, 1975; Institute of Economic Affairs, 1972). In the long term the shift in factors of production to the industrial sector can and has in the economically developed countries led to sustained advances in gross national product, but the manner in which the resulting personal income has been distributed between individuals and regions has normally been grossly inequitable, at least in the early phases of industrialisation.

There are three points here: that mortality was able to fall before the effects of an industrial revolution could be felt; that the relationship between *per capita* income and mortality is not a simple linear one; and that not all members of a population are bound to benefit from the wealth created by the process of industrialisation. What is not in doubt is that rising absolute living standards, particularly when linked to expanding and guaranteed food supplies, induce a decline in mortality especially when life expectancy is relatively low. The implications of these points are that death rates can decline as a result of rising living standards which may result from either, or linked, agricultural and industrial revolutions, but that mortality can also be reduced independently by the effects of a sanitary or medical revolution.

A second objection to Thompson–Notestein theory as a mode of explanation involves the use of the term *modernisation* which, as we have seen, is a central plank of the whole theory. Notestein (1945), in particular, employs the term in an umbrella sense to cover both social changes and industrialisation. It is, however, important to make the distinction between what can be termed social modernisation and economic growth. The latter involves a sustained and seemingly limitless rise in *per capita* real income and is often associated with the use of new sources of energy and new technology, to which industrialisation usually contributes. In the terminology of Kindleberger and Herrick (1977: 3; see also Mabogunje, 1980: 35–50) economic growth is distinct from economic development, which implies distributional changes as well as growth. Social modernisation, on the other hand, can be defined by reference to the characteristics of 'traditional' and 'modern' societies, by separating out the distinctions between *Gemeinschaft* and *Gesellschaft*. These distinctions have been discussed in detail by Wrigley (1972b), who stresses the emphasis on the individual; the interventionist role of the State; geographical and social mobility; literacy and numeracy; and functional specificity connected with the division of labour in 'modern' society. In short, rational economic behaviour and individual self-interest provide two of the most telling distinguishing characteristics (see also Tipps, 1973).

The potential importance of this distinction between social modernisation and economic growth for Thompson–Notestein theory can be illustrated by Fig. 5.2. There is the possibility that within what Notestein terms modernisation there are two separate forces for change. Economic growth has historically been the prime mover in initiating changes in mortality while social modernisation is responsible for changes in fertility (negative links), but it is clear

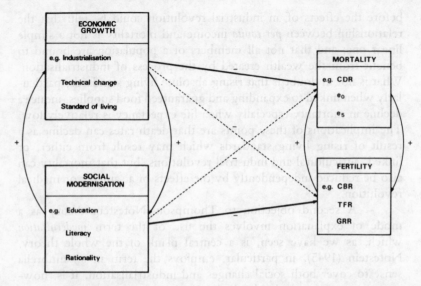

**Fig. 5.2** A model of the associations between economic growth, social modernisation, mortality and fertility

that economic growth and social modernisation are also associated as are mortality and fertility (positive links). This speculation also leads us to the vexed question of the timing of the association between economic growth and social modernisation. As Wrigley (1972b: 244) has remarked, 'We know that modernisation *may* be followed by industrialisation, but not that it *must*, or even that such a sequence of events is likely.' But do we know that industrialisation must be preceded by modernisation, that social modernisation is a prerequisite for sustained economic growth? If the answer to this latter question is yes and the relative strengths of the relationships shown in Fig. 5.2 are appropriate then we have a case for arguing that the crucial role in initiating the demographic revolution should be attributed not to industrialisation, via economic growth and the industrial revolution, but to the complex process of social modernisation. The suspicion must remain that Thompson–Notestein theory under-emphasises the independent importance of social modernisation by combining its contribution with the effects of industrially based economic growth (see also Oechsli and Kirk, 1975).

A third objection concerns the use of the concept of rationality particularly as it is applied to fertility decline in the second or third stages of the transition. Thompson–Notestein theory associates rationality with urbanism, in the sense used by Louis Wirth (1938), which itself involves individualism and materialism. The implications are that rational decision making on fertility is a new phenomenon; that it is connected with the urban way of life; and that as a consequence of urbanisation, itself a function of industrialisation, a growing proportion of a country's population will be affected by its use.

This particular objection has been made most vigorously by Caldwell, (1976; see also Caldwell, 1978) who argues from the assumption that *all* societies are economically rational. His point is that, 'fertility is economically rational only between certain limits that are set by non-economic factors; that there are two types of society, one in which it is economically rational for fertility to be ever lower, but in which a floor is interposed by non-economic considerations, and the other, in which it is rational for it to be ever higher, restrained only by a non-economic ceiling' (Caldwell, 1976: 332). The key factor here is the direction and magnitude of inter-generational wealth flows. When the net flow is from children to parents high fertility is economically rational, but when the net flow is reversed then fertility is economically irrational. This reversal of flow is due mainly to what Caldwell calls 'Westernisation'. By this he means particular social changes connected with emotional and then economic nucleation of the family, which in the form of the European social system is exported to Third World countries along with, or in advance of, the economic system.

More recently, Caldwell (1978) has considered the reversal process in the light of the development of capitalism and the shift from the pre-capitalist familial mode of production to the capitalist non-familial mode. He argues that, 'the real reproductive divide lies between modes of production based largely on networks of relatives and those in which the individuals may sell their labour to complete strangers. It is not factories and steel mills that count in the reduction of fertility; it is the replacement of a system in which material advantage accruing from production and reproduction flows to people who can control or influence reproduction by a system in which those with economic power either gain no advantage from reproduction or cannot control it' (Caldwell, 1978: 568).

Caldwell's point that all societies make decisions on fertility in a rational manner is an important but still controversial one (see Coale, 1973; and Ch. 3). What is perhaps more interesting is the idea that the export of Western attitudes, one element of the 'international demonstration effect' (Santos, 1979: 15), together with the system of world capitalism has shifted downward the ideal family size and has led to the rise of the nuclear family norm. Such a course of events would necessitate the amendment of Notestein's (1945: 51) original statement that, 'the modern nations of the West have imposed on the world's nonindustrial peoples that part of their culture which reduces mortality sufficiently to permit growth, while withholding, or at least failing to foster, those changes in the social setting out of which the reduction of fertility eventually developed in the West'. Altering Thompson–Notestein theory in line with Caldwell's criticisms would allow for the reduction in death rates and birth rates in Africa, Asia and Latin America as responses to Westernisation in both its medical and social manifestations. The universal application of Caldwell's theory of fertility decline does, however, raise certain problems, some of which stem from Caldwell's particular experience of West Africa (see, for instance, Caldwell, 1977; Caldwell and Caldwell, 1978). Whilst one can associate the capitalist non-familial mode of production with the nuclear family the connection between mature capitalism and the secular decline of fertility in the latter part of the nineteenth century raises a particularly interesting problem, one which will be returned to in the last section of this chapter and which was first approached in Chapter 3.

The signficance of Caldwell's (1976, 1978) theoretical notions lies in their emphasis on social factors connected with particular modes of production together with their refusal to regard rationality simply as an innovation of the urban way of life; societies are economically rational between limits set by social objectives.

The fourth and final objection to be discussed here is that Thompson–Notestein theory over-emphasises the dependent nature of population structure. Death rates and birth rates respond to and are affected by a variety of causal forces which are not in themselves influenced by population characteristics, growth rates, distributions and so forth. It is as though the links shown in Fig. 1.1 are all unidirectional, from left to right. Although this cannot be regarded as a major objection, since transition theory must of necessity represent a simplification of a highly complex system, it is important to realise that the structure and distribution of a population can also have a causal influence on social change, economic growth and development. For example, there has been a long debate on the relationship between the rates of population and economic growth; that a moderate increase in the former may be most propitious for a rapid rise in the latter has been one argument (Simon, 1977). There has also been considerable discussion on the associations between the nuclear family structure, the ability to control overall fertility and the likelihood of economic growth, particularly of the industrial kind (see Laslett, 1972). These issues tend to obscure and debase Thompson–Notestein theory by stressing the view that it was only because Western society had a particular set of population characteristics that the agricultural, industrial and sanitary revolutions were able to take place and that once mortality had declined it was a relatively simple matter for fertility to readjust since the mechanisms needed for such a change were already present although not fully utilised.

The four objections raised here to Thompson–Notestein theory – the combination of causal pre-conditions, the use of the terms modernisation and rationality, and the dependent nature of population structure – raise serious doubts about the theory's value as *ex post facto* explanation.

The third basis for criticism – the predictive role of Thompson–Notestein theory – can be considered in two separate ways, that is, 'prediction as prophecy' and 'prediction as testing'. Firstly, is it inevitable that all populations will pass through the form of demographic revolution described by the model? Secondly, are the stages of the transition predictable, will stage two automatically follow stage one and stage three follow stage two? The former question has immense practical importance for the future of world population growth while the latter searches out weaknesses in the form of theory construction itself.

The broad outline of the descriptive model incorporated in Thompson–Notestein theory is being followed by many Third World countries today. The death rate has fallen and the birth rate is beginning to fall. Whilst there is little controversy over the extent and nature of mortality decline; its course has been well documented (see, for example, Davis, 1956; Stolnitz, 1965; Vallin, 1968; Arriaga and Davis, 1969; Preston, 1976), the decline of fertility in Africa, Asia and Latin America has tended to vary in extent from region to region which has meant that while some observers have heralded the onset of a new demographic regime others have been more wary. In the late 1960s Arriaga's (1970) analysis of the Latin American experience fell into this latter category, but more recently Cassen (1976, 1978b), Demeny (1979) and Cavanaugh (1979) have all counselled caution. Amongst those who have identified clear evidence for a substantial and widespread fall in fertility are to be counted Kirk (1971, 1979), Oechsli and Kirk (1975), United Nations (1977), Berelson (1978), Mauldin (1978), Mauldin and Berelson (1978). Unfortunately, however, much of our detailed knowledge of the process of fertility decline in underdeveloped economies is restricted to small island

States where changes can be relatively easily monitored, but whose experience may not be typical of continental areas. Patterns observed in Taiwan (Hermalin, 1976; Sun, Lin and Freedman, 1978), Hong Kong (Freedman and Adlakha, 1968), Singapore (Neville, 1978) and Sri Lanka (Fernando, 1972), for example, need bear little relationship to those of China (Yu, 1978, 1979; Aird, 1978), Indonesia (Jones, 1977; see also Blayo and Vernon, 1977) or India (see Ch. 2).

It is clear that a number of Third World countries are now passing into the final stage of the demographic transition from high to low death and birth rates; that the death rate declined first, so initiating a period of rapid population growth before the birth rate began to fall; but just as there were leads and lags in the way the pattern emerged in the West so there are also temporal and spatial variations to be seen in Africa, Asia and Latin America. Again, at the regional scale marked spatio-temporal patterns can be found. The case of Brazil provides a useful illustration of a country which appears to have had only a relatively small fall in birth rate. The studies reported by Carvalho (1974), Merrick (1974), and Merrick and Graham (1979), although they differ on some details, due mainly to the methods of estimation employed, agree that the Brazilian crude birth rate fell from forty four in the 1950s to thirty seven per 1,000 in 1970. The national fall in CBR amounted to 7·7 per cent between the 1940s and the 1960s, but in the Sao Paulo region the decline was nearly 13 per cent to 33·0, whilst in Bahia and Parana there were slight increases. The lowest CBR, 31·1 per 1,000, was to be found in the Rio de Janeiro and Guanabra region in the 1960s. The inter-regional variation in CBR increased by 37 per cent between 1950 and 1970 (Merrick, 1974: 428). One would expect to see this Brazilian pattern repeated in many large Third World contries. (See Hicks, 1974, and Seiver, 1975, for the case of Mexico.)

Once again the purely descriptive element of Thompson–Notestein theory appears to hold true although one has to allow for variations in timing and levels, variations which are depicted in abstract form in Fig. 5.1. It is of course possible that the patterns prophesied in the theory may be coming about for reasons other than those specified by Notestein. $X$ will occur because of $A$ and $B$. $X$ does occur, but is only partially associated with $A$ and $B$. How, then, should the prediction be regarded?

Three examples must suffice to illustrate the complex issues involved in answering this question. Using a sample of fifty six countries, Rodgers (1979) has developed the notion that mortality is a function of both mean income and the level of income distribution

(Preston, 1975, considered the former). He concludes that, 'the difference in average life expectancy [at birth] between a relatively egalitarian and a relatively inegalitarian country is likely to be as much as five to ten years' (Rodgers, 1979: 350), and argues that such a relationship is 'very robust' and applies to his 'less developed countries' sample as well as the whole sample. In similar style Anker (1978), using a sample of sixty nine underdeveloped countries, concludes that, 'In general, fertility was relatively insensitive to socioeconomic conditions during early stages of economic development. Raising life expectancy at birth and falling female labour force participation rates tended to increase fertility, thus partially offsetting the negative effect on fertility of increases in adult literacy rates and school enrolment rates and decreases in the importance of agricultural employment. After "middle" levels of development, however, fertility becomes fairly sensitive to socio-economic conditions' (Anker, 1978: 68). Oechsli and Kirk (1975) cloud the issues even more by using the terms modernisation (an 'holistic process' made up of an 'interrelated set of social and economic changes', including changes in mortality and fertility) and development seemingly without distinction. 'We can say that modernisation, at some level, is associated with a given mortality level and we can say that the birth rate tends to stay high until some critical level of development is reached and then tends to decline as development proceeds, but we cannot say that development "causes" declining birth and death rates; rather, certain patterns of change in these vital rates are parts of the process of development' (Oechsli and Kirk, 1975: 403).

    All of these examples are of a cross-sectional and empirical nature showing how, in the phrase used above, *X* is only partially associated with *A* and *B*. It is the health revolution, the standard of living and the relative distribution of income which combine to increase life expectancy, but initially this only serves to raise fertility before economic growth advances to a critical level after which time it begins to depress fertility via what has been called social modernisation. In Thompson–Notestein theory this latter element is brought about by urbanisation which, because of urbanism, establishes the rational control of fertility by means of contraception.

    At one level, then, it would seem that the populations of Africa, Asia and Latin America are passing through the form of demographic revolution described by Thompson–Notestein theory, but that this process is neither inevitable nor is it occurring in exactly the way expounded by the theory. It is not inevitable because – and here most observers would agree – demographic changes are at least partially conditional upon the maintenance of economic growth and development neither of which are universal or guaranteed. Two aspects which are now seen to be significant, but which fall outside Thompson–Notestein theory are what Caldwell (1978) calls 'imported Westernisation' and family-planning programmes. The impact of the latter has always proved difficult to demonstrate (see, for example, the contributions to Bogue, 1968; Behrman, Corsa and Freedman, 1969; and more recently, Berelson, 1974; Mauldin and Berelson, 1978), but their potential importance should not be underrated, as the cautionary tale of post-1966 Romania makes clear (Berelson, 1979). Freedman (1979: 11) has identified the problem most succinctly: 'unless there is at least a latent motivation for fewer children and the concept of family limitation is accepted as the normatively legitimate solution to the problem of too many children, providing the means, and services cannot have much effect'. It is this motivation which has been variously attributed to development-modernisation, Westernisation, social modernisation, Malthusian pressure, and changes in social formation linked to mode of production.

Given that it is usually thought unwise to regard history as a source of lessons for the future, Thompson–Notestein theory stands up reasonably well when employed as a prophetic device. It gives a clear description of what appears to be happening in a number of Third World countries and stresses at least one important group of mechanisms which are at work there. Under Hay's criterion this at least would justify its value (see p. 6).

The internal logic of Thompson–Notestein theory has already been considered in passing, but in order to identify an additional source of weakness it is necessary to return to the matter of 'prediction as testing'. Loschky and Wilcox (1974; see also Loschky and Wilcox, 1973) set out to test the internal predictive logic of Thompson–Notestein theory. Using the theory's three stages they 'prove' that the predictions that a society in stage 1 *must* eventually move to stage 2 and that one in stage 2 *must* move to stage 3 are invalid. The theory is, 'not strong enough to force societies to move through the stages' (Loschky and Wilcox, 1974: 223). This does not mean that the progression 1 → 2 → 3 does not occur, but it implies that, for instance, a population could remain in stage 2. Part of the problem here rests with one's initial specification of transition theory, but the general point is a valid one for Thompson–Notestein theory since it does lack a mechanism which will automatically force a population from one stage to the next (see Casetti, 1968). Such a mechanism is to be found in Kingsley Davis's (1963) theory of demographic response, which will be considered in the next section.

In sum Thompson–Notestein theory has proved most resilient to criticism over the period since the 1940s. This resilience has three sources. Firstly, that element of the theory which is a descriptive model of changes in death and birth rates, mortality and fertility, provides an 'ideal type' against which the historical experience of the West and that of African, Asian and Latin American populations in the second-half of the twentieth century can be matched. As is often remarked, no one has yet found an example of a population in which the birth rate declined before the death rate. Secondly, although the theory puts too much emphasis on the effects of that ill-defined force 'modernisation' it is obvious that the factors which do control mortality and fertility are, if only partially and certainly not as simply as Notestein envisaged, a mixture of economic and social. The theory is a half-truth; little more, but certainly no less. Thirdly, while there have been many attempts to develop theories to explain and predict changes in mortality, fertility and migration individually, transition theory deals with the combination of all three during that unique event, the demographic revolution. Hence Thompson–Notestein theory is at once more all-embracing and thus, as a consequence, more vulnerable to attack over details. Because of its function as a 'grand theory' transition theory, although not necessarily the Thompson–Notestein version, needs to be amended rather than totally rejected.

## Demographic response theory

Kingsley Davis's (1963) theory of the 'multiphasic response' focuses attention on the way in which a single stimulus can be responded to in a variety of ways. Whereas Thompson–Notestein theory stresses the association between causes and effect here the emphasis is on cause and effects. The cause, or stimulus, is the increase in a population's natural growth rate which is in turn the result of a secular decline in mortality. However, this stimulus does not create its responses because of growing poverty, as in a Malthusian interpretation, but because of a desire to maintain rising prosperity. Davis (1963: 351) states, perhaps too bluntly, that, 'The answer to the central question about modern demographic history cannot be posed, then, in the framework of ordinary population theory, which assumes the sole "population factor" to be some relation between the population–resources ratio and the collective level

of living. It is doubtful that any question about demographic behaviour can be satisfactorily posed in such terms, because human
beings are not motivated by the population–resources ratio even
when they know about it (which is seldom)'. In short, populations
respond 'without being goaded to by rising poverty'.

The resulting demographic responses manifest themselves in
a variety of forms: delayed marriage, increased celibacy, abortion,
contraception, and overseas and rural–urban migration. Davis illustrates these points from the north-west European and Japanese experiences. In the former the population 'reacted to its persistent excess of births over deaths with virtually the entire range of possible
responses. Regardless of nationality, language, and religion, each in-
dustrializing nation tended to postpone marriage to increase celibacy,
to resort to abortion, to practice contraception in some form, and
to emigrate overseas. The timing and relative importance of the reactions were not identical in the various countries, and of course
methods could not be used that were not then technically feasible for
the public at large (e.g., harmless sterilization); but the remarkable
thing is that all of the northwest European countries reacted, that
they did so in each case with the reappearance of the whole range of
responses, and that virtually the entire panorama was later repeated
in Japan' (p. 351).

Davis also deals explicitly with three related issues and men-
tions two others in passing. The often observed differences between
rural and urban fertility levels are to be seen as reflections of the fact
that while one response for rural-dwellers could be rural–urban
migration, the equivalent for city-dwellers would have to be occupa-
tional mobility which would require formal education and the development of special skills, neither being helped by an 'improvident
marriage or a high marital fertility'. In European societies the delayed marriage response was resorted to more readily and made
more effective where the nuclear family, rather than the extended
family or the joint household system, was the norm. Under such an
arrangement married couples were almost entirely responsible for
their own children. Inheritance customs, on the other hand, are unlikely to 'play any determinative role in demographic change' because they are concerned solely with the matter of discrimination
among potential heirs and not with the total number of heirs.

Two other incidental implications of Davis's theory of multiphasic response are that there may be a hierarchy of responses
which are employed in turn: rural–urban migration, emigration, delayed marriage, celibacy, family limitation in marriage, would be

just some of the possibilities. Secondly, there may be other non-demographic responses which could be employed, particularly by an agrarian society, such as attempting to raise yields, utilising land which had formerly been unused – marsh or heath – or colonising new marginal land.

Davis's theory is useful for a variety of reasons. It holds out the prospect of linking mortality decline with responses which will ultimately, but nonetheless automatically, involve a reduction in fertility without a rise in mortality. That is it provides one way in which a 'forcing' element could be introduced into transition theory. Beyond that it is suggestive of a general theory of demographic change which would also be appropriate outside the bounds of the vital revolution. Rural–urban migration, emigration to America and an increase in the mean age at first marriage in seventeenth-century Europe could, for example, all be interpreted by its use (Grigg, 1980b). Davis's (1963) theory allows cultural, social, economic and political practices to mediate the way in which the responses are employed, their timing and strength. It also makes clear the range of options that are available to achieve the same objective and hence that the same observable pattern can arise from a different combination of causes.

There are problems of course. Davis's theory is partial, it specifies what the responses are responses to – a mortality-induced rise in the natural growth rate – but not how the initial stimulus occurs. The tone is anti-Malthusian, but there is reason to believe that a true Malthusian crisis of population pressure and impending poverty would presage a comparable multiphasic demographic response. It brushes aside the role of inheritance practices as a means of demographic regulation, but Goody (1973, 1976), for instance, has shown how strategies of heirship can have an important influence on the division of land-holdings and hence they are used by even the selectively rational as a means of tackling the problems associated with the production of offspring.

The most important criticism must, however, be related to the nature and working of the initial stimulus. One could, for instance, conceive of a compound theory in which mortality decline is initiated by the mechanism outlined by Notestein (1945), but which generates a combination of responses in the manner of Davis (1963) that ultimately works towards a reduction in fertility rather than an increase in mortality. Glass (1965b) has taken another line by arguing that the stimulus can arise out of any conflict between levels of living and aspirations. This rider has been accepted by Friedlander (1969), who also allows for the possibility that a fall in mortality could result in such a conflict, and adopted by Mosher (1980). Davis's theory can thus be thought of as both an amendment to Thompson–Notestein theory, so allowing for the same form of transition to occur but via a variety of routes, and as a more general model of the consequences of change in one element of the demographic system. The source of the initial stimulus remains, however, a crucial issue.

## Economic, social and demographic transitions

Notestein's (1945) original theory of the demographic transition gave prime mover status to the impact of three revolutions – agricultural, industrial and sanitary – but these can also be viewed as manifestations of a single, although highly complex, transition between distinctive modes of production and social formations, with each mode having its own particular demographic régime. There are of course problems to be faced in taking this view, but they are not necessarily unique. The difficulties of periodisation and of character-ising the distinctive and dominant mode of production in time and space are analogous to those encountered in Thompson–Notestein theory over the definition of stages. The question of the inevitability of transition from mode to mode is similar, at least in the abstract sense, to that of movement between stages (feudal → capitalist → socialist and stages 1 → 2 → 3). Certain questions arise about the mechanisms for such transitions: are they endogenous or exogenous; are they the consequence of gradual evolution, internal conflict or diffusion? By facing these problems population geography will be introduced to a second 'grand theory', that of historical materialism.

This introduction can be most easily accomplished by, firstly, considering the relationship between the contemporary de-mographic régime associated with the capitalist mode of production in the West and the régimes of the pre-capitalist modes which exist in Africa, Asia and Latin America, but which are being affected by the Western capitalist mode. Secondly, the mechanisms which led to the historical transitions between modes, and thus régimes, in Europe will be outlined.

During late capitalism the demographic regime is one in which mortality is low and fertility is near replacement, but fluctu-ates in keeping with economic cycles. The former is low because of the application of medical technology, public health controls and the high standard of the material life of the population. Fertility is low because of the use of contraceptives to implement an ideal family size of two or three children and oscillates in keeping with recurrent boom and slump conditions, by the imposition and relaxation of constraints linked with those conditions via the family wage economy. (The cyclical economic conditions of late capitalism are discussed in detail in Mandel, 1975, and Easterlin 1968; see also Rindfuss and Sweet, 1977; Ermisch, 1979, and the contributions to D. Freedman, 1976.) During the earlier phases of industrial capitalism the technological advances associated with mechanisation together with the organisational developments which form part of the search for profitable returns to capital, combine to affect agricultural productivity and hence food supply. The growth of the factory system and that of wage labour establish forces for urbanisation, whilst both stimulating and facilitating rapid population growth, partly through the relaxation of constraints on marriage. These developments also create a class system of employers and employees, bourgeoisie and proletariat, which determines distinctive demographic responses, particularly with respect to fertility. The bourgeoisie, employing the methods of *Homo economicus*, strengthens its position by adjusting family size to balance falling child mortality and investing in the future human capital of its offspring. The proletariat, whilst responding to the opportunities offered by industrial capitalism, including the long-term rise in absolute living standards, is also affected by a received anti-birth control morality and an increasing demand for female labour to replace men in unskilled work. These tensions are temporarily resolved before the onset of the late capitalist system by changes in adherence to religious ideology and the use of first mechanical and then chemical contraceptives. (Some of these points were first mentioned in Ch. 3.)

Although the exact nature of the pre-capitalist mode appropriate to Africa, Asia and Latin America is still problematic, since Marx himself only dealt with the Asiatic mode (Marx, 1964; see also Engels, 1976; Anderson, 1974b: 463–549; Bradby, 1975; Foster-Carter, 1978; Taylor, 1979: 172–86), it is clear that the capitalist mode has penetrated such areas in a variety of ways and over a number of centuries. Wallerstein (1974; see also Frank, 1978a, b; Wallerstein, 1979), for instance, argues that a European orientated world-economy was established during the sixteenth century by Portuguese, Spanish, French, Dutch and English merchants and soldiers which created a tripartite system of core, periphery and semi-periphery, dominated and articulated from its centre in western Europe. Whilst this may indicate the existence of a mercantilist world-system it does not mean that Europe was capitalist at that stage or that the periphery was fully drawn into capitalism, but it does show that Africa, Asia and Latin America have been affected by an externally controlled market economy for at least 300 years.

During the twentieth century industrial capitalism has been fully introduced to most Third World countries, but again its influence has varied widely depending on such factors as the experience of imperialism, the timing of capitalist penetration and the natural resources of the area. The creation of a class structure, the wage-labour system, rural–urban migration, technological change and, in certain cases, rapid economic growth have all been features of this transition. However, they owe their origins to exogenous forces directed from North America and Europe. The strength of these forces is emphasised by Frank (1969: 11) who concludes in polemical style that, 'no country which has been firmly tied to the metropolis as a satellite through incorporation into the world capitalist system has achieved the rank of an economically developed country, except by finally abandoning the capitalist system', and that these 'satellite countries, regions, localities and sectors are condemned to underdevelopment'.

If difficulties exist over the articulation of pre-capitalist modes of production appropriate to Third World countries then the problems to be faced in characterising associated demographic regimes can be imagined to be of a comparable magnitude. It is likely that whilst no one mode will prove satisfactory, no single régime will in detail encompass the complexity of traditions and cultural backgrounds to be found in Africa, Asia and Latin America. However, Meillassoux (1972, 1981) and Anderson (1974b: 463–549) provide two points of departure.

The essential elements in defining a pre-capitalist mode of production must be the use and ownership of land. Land can be the 'subject of labour' when its produce is simply gathered or hunted and the 'instrument of labour' when cultivation takes place. Meillassoux (1972) claims that in the latter system the production of food is cyclical, one year provides for the next, one generation temporarily supports the next, and that this establishes the basis for, 'the *'family'* as a productive and cohesive unit and of 'kinship' as an ideology' (p. 99). That ultimately, 'control over subsistence is not control of the means of production but of the means of physiological *reproduction*, used to reproduce the life of the human producer' (p. 100). The objective of such societies is, 'reproduction of life as a precondition to production . . . They represent comprehensive, integrated, economic, social and demographic systems ensuring the vital needs of all

the members – productive and non-productive – of the community'
(p. 101). (These associations are discussed in their European context
by Medick (1976: 303).) In Marx's conception of the Asiatic mode
the unit of agricultural production is again the family organised on
the basis of the village community and producing goods largely for
its own consumption, but with some interchange between communities and the supply of local demand for non-agricultural goods
being met by part-time artisans. The fundamental element is, 'the
'tribal or communal property' of land in self-sustaining villages'
(Anderson, 1974b: 484). In this particular mode the State plays a crucial role in the process of production which guarantees its perpetua-
tion and tends to give the entire social formation a stagnant appear-
ance (see also Taylor, 1979: 184).

   Although Marx's analysis is flawed (Anderson, 1974b: 491)
his model, along with Meillassoux's (1972) of what might be called
the 'communal mode of production', provides several pointers to the
relevant demographic régimes which could be current in pre-
capitalist Africa, Asia and Latin America. The family is likely to be
the basic unit of production; it will aim to perpetuate itself within the
context of communal use of land and a largely subsistence economy.
One can go further and argue that fertility will probably reach a
natural level, although this may be well below the biological maximum, and that mortality will be high because of the lack of technical sophistication and the exposure to recurrent environmentally induced crises to which localised economies are prone (see Easterlin,
1978). Migration will be limited in range and volume and will
usually be associated with marriage.

   During the phase of capitalist penetration, which may be
eased by prior exposure to the mercantilist system, several modes of
production and demographic régimes will exist side by side, albeit in
conflict with one another (see Balibar, 1970: 307). In Latin America,
for example, the effect on the pre-capitalist demographic régime of
Spanish and Portuguese intervention was catastrophic due largely
to the introduction of European disease patterns (Sanchez-Albornoz,
1974: 37–85; Zambardino, 1980), but one of its effects was to en-
courage the development of the Atlantic slave trade, which also had
a profound effect on the African régime (Curtin, 1969; Klein, 1978).
Since at least the 1940s the use of advanced drug technology, origi-
nating in North America and Europe, has had a similarly dramatic
effect, but in the opposite direction, with substantial increases in life
expectancy. In both instances demographic change is externally induced, radically alters pre-existing patterns and is associated with

new systems of expropriation or production.

Caldwell (1978; see p. 167) has shown the way in which transition to the capitalist urban–industrial–wage labour based mode of production influences fertility levels by introducing Western views on ideal family size; by reversing the inter-generational wealth flow; and by destroying the pre-capitalist familial mode. Similarly, the initiation of family planning programmes and the distribution of contraceptive devices has on occasions tended to undermine the effective practice of traditional methods of birth control (Caldwell and Ware, 1977). The new demographic régime involves a couple's assessment of benefits on the basis of returns which are likely to accrue to the nuclear family from having a child or additional children. Decision making is free within the constraints of the new economic and social relationships created by the dominant social formation, but both the decision-making unit and the objectives have changed.

Rapid population growth induced by mortality decline has a decisive effect on rural society which is also faced with the commercialisation and subsequent mechanisation of its agricultural base. In such circumstances the traditional demographic responses of rural–urban migration and adjustments in marriage practices are pursued, but with particular emphasis on the former. Migrants search for employment opportunities and respond to rural–urban and inter-regional variations in levels of economic growth. As individuals they behave as though smitten with the new spirit of capitalism by searching out destinations which will yield maximum expected returns and as groups they provide the labour force for those economic sectors and regions in which capital, whether national or international, derives its highest returns. The new capitalist demographic régime requires massive inter-regional and international mobility. (The various scales at which these migratory mechanisms can be demonstrated are discussed in Ch. 4.)

From the point of view of observable spatial variations in mortality, fertility, migration, and hence population growth and distribution the effects of the transformation to the capitalist system show a remarkable range. Mortality and fertility are lowest where penetration has been most successful, often in the smaller states and island communities or those regions founded on great metropolitan centres. Fertility, particularly, has tended to remain high in peripheral areas where the pre-capitalist economic formations have stayed more or less intact or, as in parts of Asia, where resistance emanates from an entire social formation which already contains a well-developed class or caste system, urban centres, a nascent market economy and a sophisticated state political organisation. (See Ch. 2 for the case of the Indian demographic pattern.)

The demographic transition of the Thompson–Notestein model has occurred in parts of the Third World, but still remains to be completed in others. Mortality has fallen partly because of the economic growth induced by capitalism, but mainly as a result of medical and public health technology introduced from the metropolitan region. In the new demographic régime fertility has fallen where the family economy has been most completely replaced by wage-labour in the class-based societies of the rapidly expanding urban areas. Here, private property and the division of labour serve to promote individualism and what in other places have been called modernisation and rationality. Migration provides a means of searching for the rewards promised by the heightened expectations of the new economic system.

Obviously a large number of theoretical problems still remain to be solved in this conception of the demographic transition as one between régimes connected with specific modes of production and levels of technology. For instance, is it to be supposed that the capitalist world-economy will eventually become completely dominant, that there will be no mixed-mode regions as at present, and hence that the demographic régime of late capitalism will be universal? This seems unlikely. For one reason it is probable that the capitalist system will remain adulterated in some way in most Third World regions merely because it has been introduced from outside and, unlike Europe, is not therefore an endogenous formation. Just as there has been a transition from feudalism to capitalism, there will be transitions from specific historical pre-capitalist modes of production, the Asiatic or communal for example, to specific capitalist modes, although these may appear as mere variants of the same 'ideal type'.

In the case of Europe the transition from feudalism to capitalism has remained a subject for heated debate (see Sweezy, 1942; Dobb, 1946; Giddens, 1971: 18–64; Anderson, 1974a, b; Hilton *et al.*, 1976). Whilst few would disagree that at least in England feudalism had largely collapsed by the end of the fifteenth century, the periodisation problem raises great difficulties because full industrial capitalism cannot be identified until the latter part of the eighteenth century. The intervening period was one in which both pastoral and then arable agriculture became commercialised; cottage industries grew up in the countryside; overseas trade expanded and with it

European colonialism; towns significantly increased in size and number from their Medieval bases; in England, Holland and somewhat later in France bourgeois political revolutions took place; and throughout this long intermediate phase wage-labour became more common as the family economy became the family wage economy; and the extraction of profit more exacting.

These matters and their consequences for changes in demographic régimes have been taken up in five recent studies which have all dealt with the relationship between changing family structure and the transition to industrial capitalism. (The general background has been outlined by Dupâquier, 1979.) They will be used here by way of illustration.

In discussing the applicability of his term 'proto-industrialisation' Mendels (1972) has shown the demographic effects which the introduction of small-scale domestic industry can have in partially separating peasant communities from the land; in encouraging a long-term fall in the age at marriage and in establishing short-run fluctuations with market conditions. The consequent population pressure being ideal for the creation of a labour surplus. These points are taken up by Fischer (1973), who emphasises the regional differences between places in which domestic industry was significant in the sixteenth, seventeenth and eighteenth centuries and where population pressure or surplus was relatively great, but he also stresses the importance of land ownership in rural and property ownership in urban areas whilst allowing for the effects of differences between occupations. Thus, in short, 'the achievement of and dependence from property, whether agrarian or urban, and the social status connected with property created a different style of life which made it meaningful to restrict the number of children who would inherit property, status and economic opportunity connected with it, while for the labouring poor it seemed to make no difference in their miserable life'; and so, 'middle-class, property-orientated economic situations and values favoured a rationale for a certain degree of birth control while proletarian situations did not' (Fischer, 1973: 167 and 168).

Medick (1976), particularly, has emphasised the role of the family economy – the familial mode of production – in which the transmission of property through inheritance was unimportant and where the control of parents over the marital activities of their offspring was limited in the proto-industrial system. New nuclear families could be established easily and early without the parental restraint normally administered via inheritance. The returns from child and female labour were also elements which required maximising. The demographic implications of these material relations meant that population was unable to adjust to economic swings. 'The drive toward marriage and intensive reproduction came about – within certain boundaries – more or less independently of the conjuncturally determined demand for labour; even under worsening economic conditions, a retreat to a restrictive, traditional marriage pattern characteristic of peasants and a corresponding mode of reproductive behaviour offered no viable alternative to the rural artisans. The adult proto-industrial worker was not able to exist as an individual; especially, under worsening "material conditions of production", he had to depend to a growing extent upon the "co-operation" of his entire family' (Medick, 1976: 305).

The more empirically orientated studies reported by Levine (1976a, b, 1977) and Braun (1978) on, respectively, Leicestershire and the canton of Zurich give substantial support to the view that the penetration of domestic industry, particularly spinning and weaving, into rural areas not only sought out places with relative population pressure where landless labourers were numerous, but also created for itself a demographic régime which was likely to lead to rapid population growth, at least when compared with a settled land-holding society. Of course both populations were still liable to the ravages of epidemic diseases and starvation resulting from harvest failures, although what Chambers (1957) calls the 'industrial villages' were likely to be most severely affected by the latter (see Ch. 3, p. 92).

The long intermediate phase between the decline of feudalism and the emergence of the capitalist factory system was therefore characterised by a variety of demographic régimes, most of which were particular to specific economic structures, and between which there were observable regional and national differences. The crucial element, as always in pre-capitalist social formations, was the ownership or use of land, but the growth of domestic industries meant that the rather more simple man–land relationship of the feudal system could now be broken without the inevitability of a Malthusian subsistence crisis (see Schofield, 1976; Wrigley and Schofield, 1981).

This transition, which was most clearly evident in western Europe, has been considered from two contrasting view points. The one has invoked demographic response theory by arguing that such innovations as rural industries and urban growth were responses to population pressure. The other emphasises the role of the changing economy and particularly the deployment of trade-derived capital in agriculture and industry which tended to remove the peasant from the land by making that land an object for investment and then to use that land-less or nearly land-less population as a labour source for the domestic production of consumer goods, that is for small-scale commodity production. These two interpretations are not mutually exclusive; population pressure is bound to engender economic and social responses, but the fundamental change lies in the economic structure and it is to this particular aspect that prime mover status must be given. As Medick (1976: 297) remarks, 'Declining marginal returns in the small peasant or sub-peasant economies left only one alternative open to the rural dwellers: the part-time or full-time transition from land-intensive agrarian production to labour-intensive craft production.' It was the search for profit which finally created conditions for the full development of industrial capitalism and under this new system the 'relationships between industrialization and population changes were quite different. Urban industrialization meant the specialization of household members, the separation of the workplace from the home, the separation of household members, and the need for literacy, that is, investment in human capital' (Mendels, 1972: 253).

The transitions between dominant modes of production and those between demographic regimes are inextricably linked. Changes in the former affect patterns of employment, income, location and a whole range of social relationships, as well as being connected with technical innovations, which vitally influence the latter. This historical materialist conception of demographic change remains to date only poorly articulated, yet it promises to provide a series of empirical statements which may be examined in the light of each particular society's historical development. It suggests that Thompson–Notestein theory, which operates at a lower level of abstraction, still provides a useful descriptive model, but that its reliance on modernisation as *the* demographic determinant is misplaced, because it fails to attach due weight to the fundamental importance of the shift to a capitalist, technologically advanced, economy and, above all, the new social formation that that implies. More generally, the theses of historical materialism are derived from political-economy, rather than social biology; they are historical and spatial, rather than universal; and must, therefore, claim precedence over Thompson–Notestein theory, which is itself the natural successor to Malthus.

# Bibliography

**Adams, J. S.** (1969) 'Directional bias in intra-urban migration' *Economic Geography* **45**: 302–23

**Adlakha, A. L.** and **Kirk, D.** (1974) 'Vital rates in India, 1961–71, estimated from census data' *Population Studies* **28**: 381–400

**Aird, J. S.** (1978) 'Fertility decline and birth control in the People's Republic of China' *Population and Development Review* **4**: 225–53

**Anderson, M.** (1971) *Family Structure in Nineteenth Century Lancashire* (Cambridge: Cambridge University Press)

**Anderson, M.** (1976) 'Marriage patterns in Victorian Britain: an analysis based on registration district data for England and Wales, 1861' *Journal of Family History* **1**: 55–78

**Anderson, M.** (1980) *Approaches to the History of the Western Family, 1500–1914* (London: Macmillan)

**Anderson, P.** (1974a) *Passages from Antiquity to Feudalism* (London: New Left Books)

**Anderson, P.** (1974b) *Lineages of the Absolutist State* (London: New Left Books)

**Andorka, R.** (1978) *The Determinants of Fertility in Advanced Societies* (London: Methuen)

**Andrewartha, H. G.** and **Birch, L. C.** (1954) *The Distribution and Abundance of Animals* (Chicago: Chicago University Press)

**Anker, R.** (1978) 'An analysis of fertility differentials in developing countries' *Review of Economics and Statistics* **60**: 58–69

**Appleby, A. B.** (1973) 'Disease or famine? Mortality in Cumberland and Westmorland, 1580–1640' *Economic History Review*, 2nd Series **26**: 403–32

**Appleby, A. B.** (1975) 'Nutrition and disease: the case of London, 1550–1750' *Journal of Interdisciplinary History* **6**: 1–22

**Appleby, A. B.** (1978) *Famine in Tudor and Stuart England* (Liverpool: Liverpool University Press)

**Arriaga, E. E.** (1970) 'The nature and effects of Latin America's non-Western trend in fertility' *Demography* **7**: 483–501

**Arriaga, E. E.** and **Davis, K.** (1969) 'The pattern of mortality change in Latin America' *Demography* **6**: 223–42

**Aston, T. H.** (ed.) (1965) *Crisis in Europe, 1560–1660: Essays from Past and Present* (London: Routledge and Kegan Paul)

**Balibar, E.** (1970) 'On the basic concepts of historical materialism' in Althusser, L. and Balibar, E. *Reading* Capital: 199–308 (London: New Left Books)

**Banks, J. A.** (1954) *Prosperity and Parenthood: A Study of Family Planning Among the Victorian Middle Classes* (London: Routledge and Kegan Paul)

**Beals, R. E., Levy, M. B.** and **Moses, L. N.** (1967) 'Rationality and migration in Ghana' *Review of Economics and Statistics* **49**: 480–86

**Becker, G. S.** (1960) 'An economic analysis of fertility' in National Bureau for Economic Research, *Demographic and Economic Change in Developed Countries*: 209–40 (Princeton, N.J.: Princeton University Press)

**Becker, G. S.** (1962) 'Investment in human capital: a theoretical analysis' *Journal of Political Economy* **70** (Supplement): 9–49

**Becker, G. S.** (1964) *Human Capital* (New York: Columbia University Press)

**Becker, G. S.** (1965) 'A theory of the allocation of time' *Economic Journal* **75**: 493–517

**Becker, G. S.** (1973) 'A theory of marriage, Part I' *Journal of Political Economy* **81**: 813–46

**Becker, G. S.** (1974) 'A theory of marriage, Part II' *Journal of Political Economy* **82** (2, Pt. 2): 11–26

**Becker, G. S.** and **Lewis, H. G.** (1973) 'On the interaction between the quantity and quality of children' *Journal of Political Economy* **81** (Supplement): 279–88

**Behrman, S. J., Corsa, L.** and **Freedman, R.** (eds) (1969) *Fertility and Family Planning: A World View* (Ann Arbor, Mich.: Michigan University Press)

**Bennett, R. J.** (1979) *Spatial Time Series: Analysis, Forecasting, Control* (London: Pion)

**Bennett, R. J.** and **Chorley, R. J.** (1978) *Environmental Systems: Philosophy, Analysis and Control* (London: Methuen)

**Berelson, B.** (1974) 'An evaluation of the effects of population control programmes' in Parry, H. B. (ed.) *Population and its Problems: A Plain Man's Guide*: 133–68 (Oxford: Clarendon Press)

**Berelson, B.** (1978) 'Prospects and programs for fertility reduction: What? Where?' *Population and Development Review* **4**: 579–618

**Berelson, B.** (1979) 'Romania's 1966 Anti-Abortion Decree: the demographic experience of the first decade' *Population Studies* **32**: 209–22

**Beshers, J.** (1967) *Population Processes in Social Systems* (New York: Free Press)

**Bhagwati, J.** and **Srinivasan, T.** (1974) 'On reanalysing the Harris –Todaro model: rankings in the case of sector-specific sticky wages' *American Economic Review* **64**: 502–8

**Biraben, J.-N.** (1979) 'Essai sur l evolution du nombre des hommes' *Population* **34**: 13–25

**Blacker, C.P.** (1947) 'Stages in population growth' *Eugenics Review* **39**: 88–101

**Blaikie, P. M.** (1975) *Family Planning in India: Diffusion and Policy* (London: Arnold)

**Blalock, H. M.** (1961) *Causal Inferences in Nonexperimental Research* (Chapel Hill, N. C.: University of North Carolina Press)

**Blalock, H. M.** (1967) *Toward a Theory of Minority Group Relations* (New York: Wiley)

**Blalock, H.M.** (1969) *Theory Construction: From Verbal to Mathematical Formulations* (Englewood Cliffs, N.J.: Prentice-Hall)

**Blayo, Y.** and **Vernon, J.** (1977) 'La fecondite dans quelques pays d'Asie orientale ' *Population* **32**: 945–75

**Bogue, D. J.** (ed.) (1968) *Progress and Problems of World Fertility Control* in *Demography* **5**: 539–1001

**Bogue, D. J.** (1969) *Principles of Demography* (New York: Wiley)

**Böhning, W. R.** (1972) *The Migration of Workers in the United Kingdom and the European Community* (London: Oxford University Press)

**Bose, A.** (1967) 'Introduction: the study of inter-state variations' in Bose, A. (ed.) *Patterns of Population Change in India, 1951–61*: xxi–li (Bombay: Allied Publishers)

**Boulding, K. E.** (1956) *The Image* (Ann Arbor, Mich.: Michigan University Press)

**Bourgeois-Pichat, J.** (1965) 'The general development of the population of France since the eighteenth century' in Glass, D. V. and Eversley, D.E.C. (eds) *Population in History*: 474–506 (London: Arnold)

**Bourgeois-Pichat, J.** (1967) 'Social and biological determinants of human fertility in non-industrial societies' *Proceedings, American Philosophical Society* **111**: 160–63

**Bowden, P.** (1967) 'Agricultural prices, farm profits, and rents' in Thirsk, J. (ed.) *The Agrarian History of England and Wales, Volume IV, 1500–1640*: 593–695 ('Statistical appendix': 814–70) (Cambridge: Cambridge University Press)

**Bowles, S.** (1970) 'Migration as investment: empirical tests of the human investment approach to geographical mobility' *Review of Economics and Statistics* **52**: 356–62

**Bradby, B.** (1975) 'The destruction of natural economy' *Economy and Society* **4**: 127–61

**Branca, P.** (1975) *Silent Sisterhood* (London: Croom Helm)

**Brass, W.** et al. (1968) *The Demography of Tropical Africa* (Princeton, N. J.: Princeton University Press)

**Brass, W.** (1971) 'On the scale of mortality' in Brass, W. (ed.) *Biological Aspects of Demography*: 69–110 (London: Taylor and Francis)

**Brass, W.** (1975) *Methods of Estimating Fertility and Mortality from Limited and Defective Data*, Occasional Publication, Laboratories for Population Statistics, University of North Carolina (Chapel Hill, N. C.)

**Braudel, F.** (1973) *Capitalism and Material Life, 1400–1800* (London: Weidenfeld and Nicolson)

**Braun, R.** (1978) 'Protoindustrialization and demographic changes in the canton of Zurich' in Tilly, C. (ed.) *Historical Studies of Changing Fertility*: 289–334 (Princeton, N. J.: Princeton University Press)

**Bridbury, A. R.** (1973) 'The Black Death' *Economic History Review*, 2nd Series **26**: 577–92

**Bridbury, A. R.** (1975) *Economic Growth: England in the Later Middle Ages* (Hassocks, Sussex: Harvester Press)

**Bridbury, A. R.** (1977) 'Before the Black Death' *Economic History Review*, 2nd Series **30**: 393–410

**Brown, L. A.** and **Longbrake, D. B.** (1969) 'On the implementation of place utility and related concepts: the intra-urban migration case' in Cox, K. R. and Golledge, R. G. (eds) *Behavioral Problems in Geography: A Symposium*: 169–96, Northwestern University, Studies in Geography No. 17 (Evanston, Ill.)

**Brown, L. A.** and **Longbrake, D. B.** (1970) 'Migration flows in intra-urban space: place utility considerations' *Annals of the Association of American Geographers* **60**: 368–84

**Brown, L. A.** and **Moore, E. G.** (1970) 'The intra-urban migration process: a perspective' *Geografiska Annaler* **52B**: 1–13

**Burnett, P.** (1973) 'The dimensions of spatial choice processes' *Geographical Analysis* **5**: 181–204

**Byerlee, D.** (1974) 'Rural-urban migration in Africa: theory, policy and research implications' *International Migration Review* **8**: 543–66

**Caldwell, J. C.** (1976) 'Toward a restatement of demographic transition theory' *Population and Development Review* 2: 321–66

**Caldwell, J. C.** (1977) 'The economic rationality of high fertility: an investigation illustrated with Nigerian survey data' *Population Studies* 31: 5–27

**Caldwell, J. C.** (1978) 'A theory of fertility: from high plateau to destabilization' *Population and Development Review* 4: 553–77

**Caldwell, J. C.** and **Caldwell, P.** (1977) 'The role of marital sexual abstinence in determining fertility: a study of the Yoruba in Nigeria' *Population Studies* 31: 193–217

**Caldwell, J. C.** and **Caldwell, P.** (1978) 'The achieved small family: early fertility transition in an African city' *Studies in Family Planning* 9(1): 2–18

**Caldwell, J. C.** and **Ware, H.** (1977) 'The evolution of family planning in an African city: Ibadan' *Population Studies* 31: 487–507

**Carvalho, J. A. M.** (1974) 'Regional trends in fertility and mortality in Brazil' *Population Studies* 28: 401–21

**Casetti, E.** (1968) 'A formalization of the demographic transition theory' *Papers and Proceedings, Regional Science Association* 21: 159–64

**Cassen, R. H.** (1976) 'Population and development: a survey' *World Development* 4: 785–830

**Cassen, R. H.** (1978a) *India: Population, Economy, Society* (London: Macmillan)

**Cassen, R. H.** (1978b) 'Current trends in population change and their causes' *Population and Development Review* 4: 331–53

**Cassen, R. H.** and **Dyson, T.** (1976) 'New population projections for India' *Population and Development Review* 2: 101–36

**Castles, S.** and **Kosack, G.** (1973a) *Immigrant Workers and Class Structure in Western Europe* (London: Oxford University Press)

**Castles, S.** and **Kosack, G.** (1973b) 'The function of labour immigration in Western European capitalism' *New Left Review* 73: 3–18 and in Nichols, T. (ed.) (1980) *Capital and Labour: A Marxist Primer*: 117–37 (London: Fontana)

**Cavalli-Sforza, L. L.** and **Bodmer, W. F.** (1971) *The Genetics of Human Populations* (San Francisco: Freeman)

**Cavanaugh, J. A.** (1979) 'Is fertility declining in less developed countries? An evaluation analysis of data sources and population programme assistance' *Population Studies* 33: 283–93

**Chambers, J. D.** (1957) *The Vale of Trent, 1670–1800: A Regional Study of Economic Change*, Economic History Review, Supplement No. 3 (London: Cambridge University Press)

**Chambers, J. D.** (1972) *Population, Economy, and Society in Pre-*

*Industrial England* (London: Oxford University Press)

**Chandrasekhar, S.** (1972) *Infant Mortality, Population Growth and Family Planning in India* (London: Allen and Unwin)

**Choldin, H.** (1973) 'Kinship networks in the migration process' *International Migration Review* 7: 163–75

**Chung, R.** (1970) 'Space-time diffusion of the transition model: the twentieth century patterns' in Demko, G. J., Rose, H. M. and Schnell, G. A. (eds) *Population Geography: A Reader*: 220–39 (New York: McGraw-Hill)

**Clark, L. R.** *et al.* (1967) *The Ecology of Insect Populations in Theory and Practice* (London: Methuen)

**Clark, P.** and **Slack, P.** (1976) *English Towns in Transition, 1500–1700* (London: Oxford University Press)

**Clark, W. A. V.** (1970) 'Measurement and explanation in intra-urban residential mobility' *Tijdschrift voor Economische en Sociale Geografie* **61**: 49–57

**Clark, W. A. V.** and **Avery, K. L.** (1978) 'Patterns of migration: a macroanalytic case study' in Herbert, D. T. and Johnston, R. J. (eds) *Geography and the Urban Environment, Volume 1*: 135–96 (Chichester, Sussex: Wiley)

**Clarke, J. I.** (1965, 2nd edn 1972) *Population Geography* (Oxford: Pergamon)

**Clarkson, L.** (1975) *Death, Disease and Famine in Pre-Industrial England* (Dublin: Gill and Macmillan)

**Cliff, A. D.** *et al.* (1975) *Elements of Spatial Structure: A Quantitative Approach* (Cambridge: Cambridge University Press)

**Coale, A. J.** (1967) 'Factors associated with the development of low fertility: an historic summary' in *Proceedings of the World Population Conference, 1965, Volume 2*: 205–9 (New York: United Nations, Department of Economic and Social Affairs)

**Coale, A. J.** (1969) 'The decline of fertility in Europe from the French Revolution to World War II' in Behrman, S. J., Corsa, L. and Freedman, R. (eds) *Fertility and Family Planning: A World View*: 3–24 (Ann Arbor, Mich.: Michigan University Press)

**Coale, A. J.** (1971) 'Constructing the age distribution of a population recently subject to declining mortality' *Population Index* **37**: 75–82

**Coale, A. J.** (1972) *The Growth and Structure of Human Populations: A Mathematical Investigation* (Princeton, N. J.: Princeton University Press)

**Coale, A. J.** (1973) 'The demographic transition' in *International Population Conference, Liege Volume 1*: 53–72 (Liege: International

Union for the Scientific Study of Population)

**Coale, A. J.** (1979) 'The use of modern analytical demography by T. R. Malthus' *Population Studies* **33**: 329–32

**Coale, A. J., Anderson, B. A.** and **Härm, E.** (1979) *Human Fertility in Russia since the Nineteenth Century* (Princeton, N. J.: Princeton University Press)

**Coale, A. J.** and **Demeny, P.** (1966) *Regional Model Life Tables and Stable Populations* (Princeton, N. J.: Princeton University Press)

**Coale, A. J.** and **Hoover, E. M.** (1958) *Population Growth and Economic Development in Low-Income Countries: A Case Study of India's Prospects* (Princeton, N. J.: Princeton University Press)

**Coleman, D. C.** (1977) *The Economy of England, 1450–1750* (London: Oxford University Press)

**Conrad, P.** (1980) *Imagining America* (London: Routledge and Kegan Paul)

**Council of Europe** (1978) *Population Decline in Europe* (London: Arnold)

**Cousens, S. H.** (1960) 'Regional death rates in Ireland during the great famine, from 1846–1851' *Population Studies* **14**: 55–74

**Coward, J.** (1978) 'Changes in the pattern of fertility in the Republic of Ireland' *Tijdschrift voor Economische en Sociale Geografie* **69**: 353–61

**Cowgill, D. O.** (1949) 'The theory of population growth cycles' *American Journal of Sociology* **55**: 163–70

**Cowgill, U. M.** (1967) 'Life and death in the sixteenth century in the City of York' *Population Studies* **21**: 53–62

**Cox, K. R.** and **Golledge, R. G.** (eds) (1969) *Behavioral Problems in Geography: A Symposium*, Northwestern University, Studies in Geography No. 17 (Evanston, Ill.)

**Croxton, F. E., Cowden, D. J.** and **Klein, S.** (1968, 3rd edn) *Applied General Statistics* (London: Pitman)

**Curtin, P. D.** (1969) *The Atlantic Slave Trade: A Census* (Madison: University of Wisconsin Press)

**Das Gupta, P.** (1971) 'Estimation of demographic measures for India, 1881–1961, based on census age distributions' *Population Studies* **25**: 395–414

**Davis, J. S.** (1950) 'Population and resources: discussion of papers by Frank W. Notestein and P. U. Cardon' *Journal of the American Statistical Association* **45**: 346–9

**Davis, K.** (1949) *Human Society* (New York: Macmillan)

**Davis, K.** (1955) 'Malthus and the theory of population' in Lazarsfeld, P.F. and Rosenberg, M. (eds) *The Language of Social Re-*

*search*: 540–53 (Glencoe, Ill.: Free Press)

**Davis, K.** (1956) 'The amazing decline of mortality in underdeveloped areas' *American Economic Review, Papers and Proceedings* **46**: 305–18

**Davis K.** (1963) 'The theory of change and response in demographic history' *Population Index* **29**: 345–66

**Davis, K.** and **Blake, J.** (1956) 'Social structure and fertility: an analytical framework' *Economic Development and Cultural Change* **4**: 211–35

**Del Panta, L.** and **Livi-Bacci, M.** (1977) 'Chronologie, intensité et diffusion des crises de mortalité en Italie: 1600–1850' *Population* **32** (Numéro Spécial): 401–46

**Demeny, P.** (1979) 'On the end of the population explosion' *Population and Development Review* **5**: 141–62

**De Sapio, R.** (1976) *Calculus for the Life Sciences* (San Francisco: Freeman)

**Dobb, M. (1946)** *Studies in the Development of Capitalism* (rev. edn, 1963) (London: Routledge and Kegan Paul)

**Downs, R. M.** (1970) 'Geographic space perception: past approaches and future prospects' *Progress in Geography* **2**: 65–108 (London: Arnold)

**Drake, M.** (1962) 'An elementary exercise in parish register demography' *Economic History Review*, 2nd Series **14**: 427–45

**Drake, M.** (1969) *Population and Society in Norway, 1735–1865* (Cambridge: Cambridge University Press)

**Drake, M.** (1974) *Historical Demography: Problems and Projects* (Milton Keynes, Bucks.: Open University Press)

**Dublin, L. I.** and **Lotka, A. J.** (1925) 'On the true rate of natural increase' *Journal of the American Statistical Association* **20**: 305–39

**Dupâquier, J.** (1979) 'Population' in Burke, P. (ed.) *The New Cambridge Modern History*, XIII *Companion Volume*: 80–114 (Cambridge: Cambridge University Press)

**Durand, J. D.** (1967) 'The modern expansion of world population' *Proceedings, American Philosophical Society* **111**: 136–59

**Durand, J. D.** (1977) 'Historical estimates of world population: an evaluation' *Population and Development Review* **3**: 253–96

**Easterlin, R. A.** (1968) *Population, Labor Force and Long Swings in Economic Growth: The American Experience* (New York: National Bureau of Economic Research)

**Easterlin, R. A.** (1969) 'Toward a socioeconomic theory of fertility: a survey of recent research on economic factors in American fertility' in Behrman, S. J., Corsa, L. and Freedman, R. (eds) *Fertility* *and Family Planning: A World Survey*: 127–56 (Ann Arbor, Mich.: Michigan University Press)

**Easterlin, R. A.** (1971) 'Does human fertility adjust to the environment?' *American Economic Review* **61**: 399–407

**Easterlin, R. A.** (1973) 'Relative economic status and the American fertility swing' in Sheldon, E. B. (ed.) *Family Economic Behavior: Problems and Prospects*: 170–223 (Philadelphia: Lippincott)

**Easterlin, R. A.** (1975) 'An economic framework for fertility analysis' *Studies in Family Planning* **6**(3): 54–63

**Easterlin, R. A.** (1978) 'The economics and sociology of fertility: a synthesis' in Tilly, C. (ed.) *Historical Studies of Changing Fertility*: 57–133 (Princeton, N. J.: Princeton University Press)

**Easterlin, R. A., Alter, G.** and **Condran, G. A.** (1978) 'Farms and farm families in old and new areas: the northern states in 1860' in Harven, T. K. and Vinovskis, M. A. (eds) *Family and Population in Nineteenth-Century America*: 22–84 (Princeton, N. J.: Princeton University Press)

**Easterlin, R. A.** and **Condran, G. A.** (1976) 'A note on the recent fertility swing in Australia, Canada, England and Wales and the United States' in Richards, H. (ed.) *Population, Factor Movements and Economic Development*: 140–51 (Cardiff: University of Wales Press)

**Easterlin, R. A., Pollak, R. A.** and **Wachter, M. L.** (1980) 'Toward a more general economic model of fertility determination: endogenous preferences and natural fertility' in Easterlin, R. A. (ed.) *Population and Economic Change in Developing Countries*: 81–135 (Chicago: Chicago University Press)

**Engels, F.** (1959) *Outlines of a Critique of Political Economy*, Appendix to Marx, K. *Economic and Philosophic Manuscripts of 1844*: 161–92 (Moscow: Foreign Languages Publishing House)

**Engels, F.** (1976) *Herr Eugen Dühring's Revolution in Science (Anti-Dühring)* (Peking: Foreign Languages Press)

**Ermisch, J. F.** (1979) 'The relevance of the "Easterlin hypothesis" and the "New home economics" to fertility movements in Great Britain' *Population Studies* **33**: 39–58

**Fei, J. C. H.** and **Ranis, G.** (1964) *Development of the Labor Surplus Economy* (Homewood, Ill.: Irwin)

**Fernando, D. F. S.** (1972) 'Recent fertility decline in Ceylon' *Population Studies* **26**: 445–54

**Fernando, D. F. S.** (1974) 'A note on differential fertility in Sri Lanka' *Demography* **11**: 441–56

**Fernando, D. F. S.** (1975) 'Changing nuptiality patterns in Sri

Lanka, 1901–1971' *Population Studies* **29**: 179–90

**Fernando, D. F. S.** (1976) 'Fertility trends in Sri Lanka and future prospects' *Journal of Biosocial Science* **8**: 35–43

**Fernando, D. F. S.** (1977) 'Female educational attainment and fertility' *Journal of Biosocial Science* **9**: 339–51

**Fernando, D. F. S.** (1979) 'Nuptiality, education, infant mortality and fertility in Sri Lanka' *Journal of Biosocial Science* **11**: 133–40

**Fields, G. S.** (1975) 'Rural-urban migration, urban unemployment and job search activities in LDCs' *Journal of Development Economics* **2**: 165–87

**Fields, G. S.** (1979) 'Lifetime migration in Colombia: tests of the expected income hypothesis' *Population and Development Review* **5**: 247–65

**Finley, M. I.** (1980) *Ancient Slavery and Modern Ideology* (London: Chatto and Windus)

**Fischer, W.** (1973) 'Rural industrialization and population change' *Comparative Studies in Society and History* **15**: 158–70

**Flandrin, J.-L.** (1979) *Families in Former Times: Kinship, Household and Sexuality* (Cambridge: Cambridge University Press)

**Flew, A.** (ed.) (1970) *Thomas Robert Malthus*: An Essay on the Principle of Population *and* A Summary View of the Principle of Population (Harmondsworth, Middlesex: Penguin)

**Flinn, M. W.** (1974) 'The stabilisation of mortality in pre-industrial western Europe' *Journal of European Economic History* **3**: 285–318

**Foster-Carter, A.** (1978) 'The modes of production controversy' *New Left Review* **107**: 47–77 and as 'Can we articulate "articulation"?' in Clammer, J. (ed.) (1978) *The New Economic Anthropology*: 210–49 (London: Macmillan)

**Frank, A. G.** (1969) *Capitalism and Underdevelopment in Latin America: Historical Studies of Chile and Brazil* (New York: Monthly Review Press)

**Frank, A. G.** (1978a) *World Accumulation, 1492–1789* (London: Macmillan)

**Frank, A. G.** (1978b) *Dependent Accumulation and Underdevelopment* (London: Macmillan)

**Frederiksen, H.** (1969) 'Feedbacks in economic and demographic transition' *Science* **166:** 837–47

**Freedman, D.** (ed.) (1976) *Fertility, Aspirations and Resources: A Symposium on the Easterlin Hypothesis* in *Population and Development Review* **2**: 411–77

**Freedman, R.** (1979) 'Theories of fertility decline: a reappraisal' *So-*

*cial Forces* **58**: 1–17

**Freedman, R.** and **Adlakha, A. L.** (1968) 'Recent fertility declines in Hong Kong: the role of the changing age structure' *Population Studies* **22**: 181–98

**Freund, J.** (1968) *The Sociology of Max Weber* (London: Allen Lane)

**Friedlander, D.** (1969) 'Demographic responses and population change' *Demography* **6**: 359–81

**Friedlander, D.** (1973) 'Demographic patterns and socioeconomic characteristics of the coal-mining population in England and Wales in the nineteenth century' *Economic Development and Cultural Change* **22**: 39–51

**Gale, S.** (1973) 'Explanation theory and models of migration' *Economic Geography* **49**: 257–74

**Gerth, H. H.** and **Mills, C. W.** (eds) (1948) *From Max Weber: Essays in Sociology* (London: Routledge and Kegan Paul)

**Giddens, A.** (1971) *Capitalism and Modern Social Theory: An Analysis of the Writings of Marx, Durkheim and Max Weber* (Cambridge: Cambridge University Press)

**Glass, D. V.** (1938) 'Changes in fertility in England and Wales, 1851–1931' in Hogben, L. (ed.) *Political Arithmetic*: 161–212 (London: Allen and Unwin)

**Glass, D. V.** (ed.) (1953) *Introduction to Malthus* (London: Watts)

**Glass, D. V.** (1965a) 'Population and population movements in England and Wales, 1700 to 1850' in Glass, D. V. and Eversley, D. E. C. (eds) *Population in History*: 221–46 (London: Arnold)

**Glass, D. V.** (1965b) 'Population growth and population policy' in Sheps, M. C. and Ridley, J. C. (eds) *Public Health and Population Change*: 3–24 (Pittsburgh, Pa.: Pittsburgh University Press)

**Godfrey, E. M.** (1973) 'Economic variables and rural-urban migration: some thoughts on the Todaro hypothesis' *Journal of Development Studies* **10**: 66–78

**Gold, J. R.** (1980) *An Introduction to Behavioural Geography* (London: Oxford University Press)

**Golledge, R. G.** (1967) 'Conceptualizing the market decision process' *Journal of Regional Science* **7**(2) (Supplement): 239–58

**Golledge, R. G.** and **Brown, L. A.** (1967) 'Search, learning and the market decision process' *Geografiska Annaler* **49B**: 116–24

**Goodey, B.** (1971a) *City Scene: An Exploration into the Image of Central Birmingham as seen by Area Residents*, University of Birmingham, Centre for Urban and Regional Studies, Research Memorandum No. 10 (Birmingham)

**Goodey, B.** (1971b) *Perception of the Environment: An Introduction to* *the Literature*, University of Birmingham, Centre for Urban and Regional Studies, Occasional Paper No. 17 (Birmingham)

**Goodey, B.** (1974) *Images of Place*, University of Birmingham, Centre for Urban and Regional Studies, Occasional Paper No. 30 (Birmingham)

**Goody, J.** (1973) 'Strategies of heirship' *Comparative Studies in Society and History* **15**: 3–20

**Goody, J.** (1976) *Production and Reproduction: A Comparative Study of the Domestic Domain* (Cambridge: Cambridge University Press)

**Gosal, G. S.** and **Krishan, G.** (1975) 'Patterns of internal migration in India' in Kosinski, L. A. and Prothero, R. M. (eds) *People on the Move*: 193–206 (London: Methuen)

**Gottfried, R. S.** (1976) 'Epidemic disease in fifteenth century England' *Journal of Economic History* **36**: 267–70

**Gottfried, R. S.** (1978) *Epidemic Disease in Fifteenth Century England: The Medical Response and the Demographic Consequences* (Leicester: Leicester University Press)

**Goubert, P.** (1960) *Beauvais et le Beauvaisis de 1600 à 1730*, 2 Volumes (Volume 2 contains maps and diagrams) École Pratique des Hautes Études – VIᵉ Section, Centre de Recherches Historiques (Paris: S.E.V.P.E.N.)

**Gould, P.** and **White, R.** (1974) *Mental Maps* (Harmondsworth, Middlesex: Penguin)

**Gouldner, A. W.** (1980) *The Two Marxisms: Contradictions and Anomalies in the Development of Theory* (London: Macmillan)

**Gray, R. H.** (1974) 'The decline of mortality in Ceylon and the demographic effects of Malaria control' *Population Studies* **28**: 205–29

**Greenwood, M. J.** (1969a) 'An analysis of the determinants of geographic labour mobility in the United States' *Review of Economics and Statistics* **51**: 189–94

**Greenwood, M. J.** (1969b) 'The determinants of labour migration in Egypt' *Journal of Regional Science* **9**: 283–90

**Greenwood, M. J.** (1970) 'Lagged response in the decision to migrate' *Journal of Regional Science* **10**: 375–84

**Greenwood, M. J.** (1971a) 'An analysis of the determinants of internal labour mobility in India' *Annals of Regional Science* **5**: 137–51

**Greenwood, M. J.** (1971b) 'A regression analysis of migration to urban areas of a less-developed country: the case of India' *Journal of Regional Science* **11**: 253–62

**Greenwood, M. J.** (1973) 'The influence of family and friends on geographic labour mobility in a less developed country: the case of India' *Review of Regional Studies* 3(3): 27–36

**Greenwood, M. J.** and **Sweetland, D.** (1972) 'The determinants of migration between standard metropolitan statistical areas' *Demography* 9: 665–81

**Gregory, D.** (1978) *Ideology, Science and Human Geography* (London: Hutchinson)

**Griffith, G. T.** (1926) *Population Problems of the Age of Malthus* (Cambridge: Cambridge University Press) (2nd edn 1967, London: Frank Cass)

**Grigg, D. B.** (1977) 'E. G. Ravenstein and the "laws of migration"' *Journal of Historical Geography* 3: 41–54

**Grigg, D. B.** (1980a) 'Migration and overpopulation' in White, P. E. and Woods, R. I. (eds) *The Geographical Impact of Migration*: 60–83 (London: Longman)

**Grigg, D. B.** (1980b) *Population Growth and Agrarian Change* (Cambridge: Cambridge University Press)

**Gugler, J.** (1968) 'The impact of labour migration on society and economy in sub-Saharan Africa' *African Social Research* 6: 463–86

**Gugler, J.** (1969) 'On the theory of rural-urban migration: the case of sub-Saharan Africa' in Jackson, J. A. (ed.) *Migration*: 134–55 (Cambridge: Cambridge University Press)

**Gustavus, S. O.** and **Brown, L. A.** (1977) 'Place utilities in a migration decision context' *Environment and Planning A* 9: 529–48

**Habakkuk, H. J.** (1972) *Population Growth and Economic Development since 1750* (Leicester: Leicester University Press)

**Hägerstrand, T.** (1967) *Innovation Diffusion as a Spatial Process* (Chicago: Chicago University Press)

**Haines, M. R.** (1977) 'Fertility, nuptiality and occupation: a study of coal mining populations and regions in England and Wales in the mid-nineteenth century' *Journal of Interdisciplinary History* 8: 245–80

**Haines, M. R.** (1979) *Fertility and Occupation: Population Patterns in Industrialization* (New York: Academic Press)

**Hajnal, J.** (1965) 'European marriage patterns in perspective' in Glass, D. V. and Eversley, D. E. C. (eds) *Population in History*: 101–43 (London: Arnold)

**Hanley, S. B.** and **Yamamura, K.** (1977) *Economic and Demographic Change in Preindustrial Japan, 1600–1868* (Princeton, N. J.: Princeton University Press)

**Harris, J. R.** and **Todaro, M. P.** (1968) 'Urban unemployment in East Africa: an economic analysis of policy alternatives' *East Afri-*

*can Economic Review* **4**: 17–36

**Harris, J. R.** and **Todaro, M. P.** (1969) 'Wages, industrial employment and labour productivity: the Kenyan experience' *East African Economic Review*, New Series **1**: 29–46

**Harris, J. R.** and **Todaro, M. P.** (1970) 'Migration, unemployment and development: a two sector model' *American Economic Review* **60**: 126–42

**Harrison, C. J.** (1971) 'Grain price analysis and harvest qualities, 1465–1634' *Agricultural History Review* **19**: 135–55

**Harvey, D. W.** (1969) 'Conceptual and measurement problems in the cognitive-behavioral approach to location theory' in Cox, K. R. and Golledge, R. G. (eds) *Behavioral Problems in Geography: A Symposium*: 35–67, Northwestern University, Studies in Geography No. 17 (Evanston, Ill.)

**Harvey, D. W.** (1973) *Social Justice and the City* (London: Arnold)

**Harvey, D. W.** (1974) 'Population, resources and the ideology of science' *Economic Geography* **50**: 256–77

**Hatcher, J.** (1977) *Plague, Population and the English Economy, 1348–1530* (London: Macmillan)

**Hauser, P. M.** and **Duncan, O. D.** (eds) (1959) *The Study of Population: An Inventory and Appraisal* (Chicago: Chicago University Press)

**Hawthorn, G.** (1970) *The Sociology of Fertility* (London: Collier-Macmillan)

**Hay, A. M.** (1979) 'Positivism in human geography: response to critics' in Herbert, D. T. and Johnston, R. J. (eds) *Geography and the Urban Environment, Volume 2*: 1–26 (Chichester, Sussex: Wiley)

**Hay, M. J.** (1980) 'A structural equations model of migration in Tunisia' *Economic Development and Cultural Change* **28**: 345–58

**Helleiner, K. F.** (1957) 'The vital revolution reconsidered' *Canadian Journal of Economic and Political Science* **23**: 1–9 and in Glass, D. V. and Eversley, D. E. C. (eds) (1965) *Population in History*: 79–86 (London: Arnold)

**Henry, L.** (1961) 'Some data on natural fertility' *Eugenics Quarterly* **8**: 81–91

**Hermalin, A. I.** (1966) 'The effect of changes in mortality rates on population growth and age distribution in the United States' *Milbank Memorial Fund Quarterly* **44**: 451–69

**Hermalin, A. I.** (1976) 'Empirical research in Taiwan on factors underlying differences in fertility' in Coale, A. J. (ed.) *Economic Factors in Population Growth*: 243–66 (London: Macmillan)

**Herrick, B. H.** (1965) *Urban Migration and Economic Development in Chile* (Cambridge, Mass.: MIT Press)

**Hewitt, M.** (1958) *Wives and Mothers in Victorian Industry* (London: Rockliff)

**Hicks, W.** W (1974) 'Economic development and fertility change in Mexico, 1950–1970' *Demography* **11**: 407–21

**Higman, B. W.** (1976) *Slave Population and Economy in Jamaica, 1807 –1834* (Cambridge: Cambridge University Press)

**Hilton, R.** *et al.* (1976) *The Transition from Feudalism to Capitalism* (London: New Left Books)

**Himes, N. E.** (1936) *Medical History of Contraception* (Baltimore, Md.: Williams and Wilkins)

**Hindess, B.** and **Hirst, P. Q.** (1975) *Pre-Capitalist Modes of Production* (London: Routledge and Kegan Paul)

**Hindess, B.** and **Hirst, P. Q.** (1977) *Mode of Production and Social Formation: An Auto-Critique of* Pre-Capitalist Modes of Production (London: Macmillan)

**Hobsbawm, E. J.** (1954a) 'The general crisis of the European economy in the 17th century' *Past and Present* **5**: 33–70

**Hobsbawm, E. J.** (1954b) 'The crisis of the 17th century – II' *Past and Present* **6**: 44–65

**Hobsbawm, E. J.** (1960) 'The seventeenth century in the development of capitalism' *Science and Society* **24**: 97–112

**Hobsbawm, E. J.** (1964) 'Introduction' to Marx, K. *Pre-Capitalist Economic Formations*: 9–65 (London: Lawrence and Wishart)

**Hofsten, E.** and **Lundström, H.** (1976) *Swedish Population History: Main Trends from 1750 to 1970*, Urval: Skriftserie Utgiven av Statistiska Centralbyrån No. 8 (Stockholm: Statistika Centralbyrån)

**Hoskins, W. G.** (1964) 'Harvest fluctuations and English economic history, 1480–1619' *Agricultural History Review* **12**: 28–46

**Hoskins, W. G.** (1968) 'Harvest fluctuations and English economic history, 1620–1759' *Agricultural History Review* **16**: 15–31

**Huff, J. O.** and **Clark, W. A. V.** (1978) 'Cumulative stress and cumulative inertia: a behavioural model of the decision to move' *Environment and Planning A* **10**: 1101–20

**Hutchinson, G. E.** (1978) *An Introduction to Population Ecology* (New Haven, Conn.: Yale University Press)

**Hvidt, K.** (1975) *Flight to America: The Social Background of 300,000 Danish Emigrants* (London: Academic Press)

**Imhof, A. E.** (1977) *Einführung in die Historische Demographie* (Munich: Verlag C. H. Beck)

**Imhof, A. E.** and **Lindskog, B. J.** (1974) 'Les causes de mortalité en Suède et en Finlande entre 1749 et 1773' *Annales: Économies, Sociétés, Civilisations* **29**: 915–33

**Innes, J. W.** (1938) *Class Fertility Trends in England and Wales, 1876–1934* (Princeton, N. J.: Princeton University Press)

**Institute of Economic Affairs** (1972) *The Long Debate on Poverty* (London: Institute of Economic Affairs)

**Jackson, L. E.** and **Johnston, R. J.** (1974) 'Underlying regularities to mental maps: an investigation of relationships among age, experience and spatial preferences' *Geographical Analysis* **6**: 69–84

**James, P.** (1979) *Population Malthus: His Life and Work* (London: Routledge and Kegan Paul)

**Jerome, H.** (1926) *Migration and Business Cycles* (New York: National Bureau of Economic Research)

**Johnston, R. J.** (1972) 'Activity spaces and residential preferences: some tests of the hypothesis of sectoral mental maps' *Economic Geography* **48**: 199–211

**Johnston, R. J.** (1978) *Multivariate Statistical Analysis in Geography* (London: Longman)

**Jones, G. W.** (1977) 'Fertility levels and trends in Indonesia' *Population Studies* **31**: 29–41

**Kennedy, R. E.** (1976) *The Irish: Emigration, Marriage and Fertility* (Berkeley, Ca.: University of California Press)

**Keyfitz, N.** and **Flieger, W.** (1968) *World Population: An Analysis of Vital Data* (Chicago: Chicago University Press)

**Keynes, J. M.** (1933) 'Robert Malthus: the first of the Cambridge economists' in Keynes, J. M., *Essays in Biography*: 95–149 (London: Macmillan)

**Kindleberger, C. P.** and **Herrick, B. H.** (1977, 3rd edn) *Economic Development* (New York: McGraw-Hill)

**Kirk, D.** (1971) 'A new demographic transition?' in National Academy of Sciences, *Rapid Population Growth, Volume 2, Research Papers*: 123–47 (Baltimore, Md.: Johns Hopkins University Press)

**Kirk, D.** (1979) 'World population and birth rates: agreements and disagreements' *Population and Development Review* **5**: 387–403

**Klein, H. S.** (1978) *The Middle Passage: Comparative Studies in the Atlantic Slave Trade* (Princeton, N. J.: Princeton University Press)

**Knodel, J. E.** (1974) *The Decline of Fertility in Germany, 1871–1939* (Princeton, N. J.: Princeton University Press)

**Knodel, J. E.** (1979) 'From natural fertility to family limitation: the onset of fertility transition in a sample of German villages' *Demography* **16**: 493–521

**Knox, P. L.** and **MacLaran, A.** (1978) 'Values and perceptions in descriptive approaches to urban social geography' in Herbert, D. T. and Johnston, R. J. (eds) *Geography and the Urban Environment, Volume 1*: 197–247 (Chichester, Sussex: Wiley)

**Kolb, A.** (1971) *East Asia* (London: Methuen)

**Krause, J. T.** (1967) 'Some aspects of population change, 1690–1790' in Jones, E. L. and Mingay, G. E. (eds) *Land, Labour and Population in the Industrial Revolution*: 187–205 (London: Arnold)

**Krause, J. T.** (1969) 'English population movements between 1700 and 1850' in Drake, M. (ed.) *Population in Industrialization*: 118–27 (London: Methuen)

**Kuczynski, J.** (1946) *Labour Conditions in Great Britain: 1750 to the Present* (New York: International Publishers)

**Laber, G.** and **Chase, R. X.** (1971) 'Interprovincial migration in Canada as a human capital decision' *Journal of Political Economy* **79**: 795–804

**Lack, D.** (1954) *The Natural Regulation of Animal Numbers* (Oxford: Clarendon Press)

**Lack, D.** (1966) *Population Studies of Birds* (Oxford: Clarendon Press)

**Lamb, H. H.** (1972) *Climate: Present, Past and Future, Volume 1, Fundamentals and Climate Now* (London: Methuen)

**Lamb, H. H.** (1977) *Climate: Present, Past and Future, Volume 2, Climatic History and the Future* (London: Methuen)

**Landry, A.** (1934) *La Révolution Démographique: Études et Essais sur les Problèmes de la Population* (Paris: Sirey)

**Landry, A.** (1945) *Traité de Démographie* (Paris: Payot)

**Langford, C. M.** (1976) *Birth Control Practice and Marital Fertility in Great Britain: A Report on a Survey carried out in 1967–68* (London: Population Investigation Committee, LSE)

**Laslett, P.** (1965) *The World We Have Lost* (London: Methuen)

**Laslett, P.** (ed.) (1972) *Household and Family in Past Time* (Cambridge: Cambridge University Press)

**Ledermann, S.** (1969) *Nouvelles Tables-Types de Mortalité*, Institut National d'Études Démographiques, Travaux et Documents, Cahier No. 53 (Paris: Presses Universitaires de France)

**Lee, E. S.** (1966) 'A theory of migration' *Demography* **3**: 47–57

**Lee, R. D.** (1973) 'Population in pre-industrial England: an econometric analysis' *Quarterly Journal of Economics* **87**: 581–607

**Lee, R. D.** (1974) 'Estimating series of vital rates and age structures from baptisms and burials: a new technique with applications to pre-industrial England' *Population Studies* **28**: 495–512

**Lee, R. D.** (1978) 'Models of preindustrial population dynamics with application to England' in Tilly, C. (ed.) *Historical Studies of*

*Changing Fertility*: 155–207 (Princeton, N. J.: Princeton University Press)

**Leibenstein, H.** (1954) *A Theory of Economic-Demographic Development* (Princeton, N. J.: Princeton University Press)

**Leibenstein, H.** (1974a) 'Socio-economic fertility theories and their relevance to population policy' *International Labour Review* **109**: 443–57

**Leibenstein, H.** (1974b) 'An interpretation of the economic theory of fertility: promising path or blind alley?' *Journal of Economic Literature* **12**: 457–79

**Leibenstein, H.** (1975) 'The economic theory of fertility decline' *Quarterly Journal of Economics* **89**: 1–31

**Leibenstein, H.** (1976) *Beyond Economic Man: A New Foundation for Microeconomics* (Cambridge, Mass.: Harvard University Press)

**Leibenstein, H.** (1978) *General X-Efficiency Theory and Economic Development* (New York: Oxford University Press)

**Le Roy Ladurie, E.** (1969) 'L'aménorrhée de famine (XVIIᵉ–XXᵉ siècles)' *Annales: Économies, Sociétés, Civilisations* **24**: 1589–1601

**Le Roy Ladurie, E.** (1972) *Times of Feast and Times of Famine: A History of Climate since the Year 1000* (London: Allen and Unwin)

**Le Roy Ladurie, E.** (1974) *The Peasants of Languedoc* (Urbana, Ill.: University of Illinois Press)

**Lesthaeghe, R. J.** (1977) *The Decline of Belgian Fertility, 1800–1970* (Princeton, N. J.: Princeton University Press)

**Levine, D.** (1976a) 'Proletarianization, economic opportunity and population growth' in Conze, W. (ed.) *Sozialgeschicte der Familie in der Neuzeit Europas*: 247–53 (Stuttgart: Klett Verlag)

**Levine, D.** (1976b) 'The demographic implications of rural industrialization: a family reconstitution study of Shepshed, Leicestershire, 1600–1851' *Social History* **1**(2): 177–96

**Levine, D.** (1977) *Family Formation in an Age of Nascent Capitalism* (New York: Academic Press)

**Levy, M. B.** and **Wadycki, W. J.** (1973) 'The influence of family and friends on geographic labour mobility' *Review of Economics and Statistics* **55**: 198–203

**Lewis, W. A.** (1954) 'Economic development with unlimited supplies of labour' *Manchester School of Economic and Social Studies* **22**: 139–91

**Lewis-Faning, E.** (1949) *Report of an Enquiry into Family Limitation and Human Fertility in the Past Fifty Years*, Royal Commission on Population, Papers Volume 1 (London: HMSO)

**Lieber, S. R.** (1978) 'Place utility and migration' *Geografiska Annaler*

**60B**: 16–27

**Lindert, P. H.** (1978) *Fertility and Scarcity in America* (Princeton, N.J.: Princeton University Press)

**Lipsey, R. G.** (1966, 2nd edn) *An Introduction to Positive Economics* (London: Weidenfeld and Nicolson)

**Livi-Bacci, M.** (1977) *A History of Italian Fertility during the last Two Centuries* (Princeton, N. J.: Princeton University Press)

**Lloyd, P. J.** (1969) 'Elementary geometric/arithmetic series and early production theory' *Journal of Political Economy* **77**: 21–34

**Loschky, D. J.** and **Wilcox, W. C.** (1973) 'Transition theory: a mode of analysis' *Review of Social Theory* **2**: 16–50

**Loschky, D. J.** and **Wilcox, W. C.** (1974) 'Demographic transition: a forcing model' *Demography* **11**: 215–25

**Lotka, A. J.** (1907) 'Relation between birth rates and death rates' *Science* **26**: 21–2

**Lotka, A. J.** (1922) 'The stability of the normal age distribution' *Proceedings, National Academy of Sciences* **8**: 339–45

**Lotka, A. J.** (1925) *Elements of Physical Biology* (Baltimore, Md.: Williams and Wilkins) reprinted (1956) *Elements of Mathematical Biology* (New York: Dover)

**Lotka, A. J.** (1937) 'Population analysis: a theorem regarding the stable age distribution' *Journal of the Washington Academy of Sciences* **27**: 299

**Lotka, A. J.** (1939) *Théorie Analytique des Associatons Biologiques, Part II. Analyse démographique avec application particulière à l'espèce humaine*, Actualités Scientifiques et Industrielles No. 780 (Paris: Hermann and Cie)

**Lowenthal, D.** (1961) 'Geography, experience, and imagination: towards a geographical epistemology' *Annals of the Association of American Geographers* **51**: 241–60

**Lynch, K.** (1960) *The Image of the City* (Cambridge, Mass.: MIT Press)

**Mabogunje, A. L.** (1970) 'Systems approach to a theory of rural-urban migration' *Geographical Analysis* **2**: 1–18

**Mabogunje, A. L.** (1980) *The Development Process: A Spatial Perspective* (London: Hutchinson)

**Macfarlane, A.** *et al.* (1977) *Reconstructing Historical Communities* (Cambridge: Cambridge University Press)

**Macfarlane, A.** (1978) *The Origins of English Individualism: The Family, Property and Social Transition* (Oxford: Blackwell)

**McEvedy, C.** and **Jones, R.** (1978) *Atlas of World Population History* (Harmondsworth, Middlesex: Penguin)

**McKeown, T.** (1976) *The Modern Rise of Population* (London: Arnold)

**McKeown, T.** (1978) 'Fertility, mortality and causes of death: an examination of the issues related to the modern rise of population' *Population Studies* 32: 535–42

**McKeown, T.** and **Brown, R· G.** (1955) 'Medical evidence related to English population changes in the eighteenth century' *Population Studies* 9: 119–41

**McLaren, A.** (1977) 'Women's work and the regulation of family size' *History Workshop* 4: 70–81

**McLaren, A.** (1978) *Birth Control in Nineteenth-Century England* (London: Croom Helm)

**McLellan, D.** (1973) *Karl Marx: His Life and Thought* (London: Macmillan)

**McNeill, W.** (1977) *Plagues and Peoples* (Oxford: Blackwell)

**Maguire, J.** (1979) 'Contract, coercion, and consciousness' in Harrison, R. (ed.) *Rational Action*: 157–73 (Cambridge: Cambridge University Press)

**Mamdani, M.** (1972) *The Myth of Population Control* (New York: Monthly Review Press)

**Mandel, E.** (1970) *An Introduction to Marxist Economic Theory* (New York: Pathfinder Press)

**Mandel, E.** (1975) *Late Capitalism* (London: New Left Books)

**Mandelbaum, D. G.** (1974) *Human Fertility in India: Social Components and Policy Perspectives* (Berkeley, Ca.: University of California Press)

**Mari Bhat, P. N.** (1977) 'Estimation of vital rates and age distribution under quasi-stability: case of India, 1961, re-examined' *Population Index* 43: 187–205

**Marx, K.** (1964) *Pre-Capitalist Economic Formations* (London: Lawrence and Wishart)

**Marx, K.** (1973) *Grundrissse: Foundations of the Critique of Political Economy* (Harmondsworth, Middlesex: Penguin)

**Marx, K.** (1976) *Capital: A Critique of Political Economy, Volume 1* (Harmondsworth, Middlesex: Penguin)

**Masser, I.** and **Gould, W. T. S.** (1975) *Inter-Regional Migration in Tropical Africa*, Institute of British Geographers, Special Publication No. 8 (London)

**Matras, J.** (1965a) 'The strategy of family limitation: some variations in time and space' *Demography* 2: 351–62

**Matras, J.** (1965b) 'Social strategies of family formation: data for British female cohorts born 1831–1906' *Population Studies* 19: 167

–181

**Matthiessen, P. C.** (1972) 'Replacement for generations of Danish females, 1840/1844–1920/1924' in Glass, D. V. and Revelle, R. (eds) *Population and Social Change*: 199–212 (London: Arnold)

**Mauldin, W. P.** (1978) 'Patterns of fertility decline in developing countries, 1950–75' *Studies in Family Planning* 9(4): 75–84

**Mauldin, W. P.** and **Berelson, B.** (1978) 'Conditions of fertility decline in developing countries, 1965–75' *Studies in Family Planning* 9(5): 89–147

**Medick, H.** (1976) 'The proto-industrial family economy: the structural function of household and family during the transition from peasant society to industrial capitalism' *Social History* 1(3): 291–315

**Meegama, S. A** (1967) 'Malaria eradication and its effects on mortality levels' *Population Studies* 21: 207–37

**Meek, R. L.** (ed.) (1953) *Marx and Engels on Malthus* (London: Lawrence and Wishart)

**Meillassoux, C.** (1972) 'From reproduction to production: a Marxist approach to economic anthropology' *Economy and Society* 1: 93–105

**Meillassoux, C.** (1981) *Maidens, Meal and Money: Capitalism and the Domestic Community* (Cambridge: Cambridge University Press)

**Mendels, F. F.** (1972) 'Proto-industrialization: the first phase of the industrialization process' *Journal of Economic History* 32: 241–61

**Merrick, T. W.** (1974) 'Interregional differences in fertility in Brazil, 1950–1970' *Demography* 11: 423–40

**Merrick, T. W.** and **Graham, D. H.** (1979) *Population and Economic Development in Brazil: 1800 to the Present* (Baltimore, Md.: Johns Hopkins University Press)

**Merton, R. K.** (1967) *On Theoretical Sociology* (New York: Free Press)

**Mincer, J.** (1978) 'Family migration decisions' *Journal of Political Economy* 86: 749–73

**Mitchell, B. R.** (1975) *European Historical Statistics, 1750–1970* (London: Macmillan)

**Miyao, T.** and **Shapiro, P.** (1979) 'Dynamics of rural-urban migration in a changing economy' *Environment and Planning A* 11: 1157–63

**Mosher, W. D.** (1980) 'The theory of change and response: an application to Puerto Rico, 1940 to 1970' *Population Studies* 34: 45–58

**Mosk, C.** (1977) 'Demographic transition in Japan' *Journal of Econo-*

*mic History* **37**: 655–74

**Mosk, C.** (1979) 'The decline of marital fertility in Japan' *Population Studies* **33**: 19–38

**Muth, R. F.** (1971) 'Migration: chicken or egg?' *Southern Economic Journal* **37**: 295–306

**Myers, R. J.** (1940) 'Errors and bias in the reporting of ages in census data' *Transactions, Actuarial Society of America* **41**: 411–15

**Narayan, R. K.** (1977) *The Painter of Signs* (London: Heinemann)

**Nelson, P.** (1959) 'Migration, real income and information' *Journal of Regional Science* **1**: 43–74

**Neville, W.** (1978) 'The birth rate in Singapore' *Population Studies* **32**: 113–33

**Noin, D.** (1979) *Géographie de la Population* (Paris: Masson)

**Notestein, F. W.** (1945) Population: the long view' in Schultz, T. W. (ed.) *Food for the World*: 36–57 (Chicago: Chicago University Press)

**Notestein, F. W.** (1948) 'Summary of the demographic background of problems of underdeveloped areas' *Milbank Memorial Fund Quarterly* **26**: 249–55

**Notestein, F. W.** (1950) 'The population of the world in the year 2000' *Journal of the American Statistical Association* **45**: 335–45

**Notestein, F. W.** (1953) 'Economic problems of population change' in *Proceedings of the Eighth International Conference of Agricultural Economists, 1953*: 13–31 (London: Oxford University Press)

**Oechsli, F. W.** and **Kirk, D.** (1975) 'Modernization and the demographic transition in Latin America and the Caribbean' *Economic Development and Cultural Change* **23**: 391–419

**Olsson, G.** (1965) 'Distance and human interaction' *Geografiska Annaler* **47B**: 3–43

**Olsson, G.** (1967) 'Central place systems, spatial interaction and stochastic processes' *Papers and Proceedings, Regional Science Association* **18**: 13–45

**Olsson, G.** (1969) 'Inference problems in locational analysis' in Cox, K. R. and Golledge, R. G. (eds) *Behavioral Problems in Geography: A Symposium* pp. 14–34, Northwestern University, Studies in Geography No. 17 (Evanston, Ill.)

**Olsson, G.** (1970) 'Explanation, prediction, and meaning variance: an assessment of distance interaction models' *Economic Geography* **46**: 223–33

**Olsson, G.** and **Gale, S.** (1968) 'Spatial theory and human behaviour' *Papers and Proceedings, Regional Science Association* **21**: 229–42

**Palliser, D. M.** (1973) 'Epidemics in Tudor York' *Northern History* **8**: 45–63

**Palliser, D. M.** (1974) 'Dearth and disease in Staffordshire, 1540–1670' in Chalklin, C. W. and Havinden, M. A. (eds) *Rural Change and Urban Growth, 1500–1800*: 54–75 (London: Longman)

**Palloni, A.** (1975) 'Comments on R. H. Gray's 'The decline of mortality in Ceylon and the demographic effects of malaria control'' *Population Studies* **29**: 497–501

**Parkes, A. S.** (1976) *Patterns of Sexuality and Reproduction* (London: Oxford University Press)

**Pearl, R.** (1925) *The Biology of Population Growth* (New York: Knopf)

**Pearl, R.** and **Reed, L. J.** (1920) 'On the rate of growth of the population of the United States since 1790 and its mathematical representation' *Proceedings, National Academy of Science* **6**: 275–88

**Peel, J.** (1963) 'The manufacture and retailing of contraceptives in England' *Population Studies* **17**: 113–25

**Petersen, W.** (1964) *The Politics of Population* (London: Gollancz)

**Petersen, W.** (1979) *Malthus* (London: Heinemann)

**Pierce, R. M.** and **Rowntree, G.** (1961) 'Birth control in Britain: Part II, Contraceptive methods used by couples married in the last thirty years' *Population Studies* **15**: 121–60

**Pinchbeck, I.** (1930) *Women Workers and the Industrial Revolution, 1750–1850* (London: Routledge)

**Platt, C.** (1978) *Medieval England* (London: Routledge and Kegan Paul)

**Popper, K. R.** (1965) *The Logic of Scientific Discovery* (New York: Harper and Row)

**Popper, K. R.** (1972) *Objective Knowledge* (Oxford: Clarendon Press)

**Post, J. D.** (1977) *The Last Great Subsistence Crisis in the Western World* (Baltimore, Md.: Johns Hopkins University Press)

**Postan, M. M.** (1950) 'Some economic evidence of declining population in the later Middle Ages' *Economic History Review*, 2nd Series **2**: 221–46

**Postan, M. M.** (1972) *The Medieval Economy and Society* (London: Weidenfeld and Nicolson)

**Potts, M., Diggory, P.** and **Peel, J.** (1977) *Abortion* (Cambridge: Cambridge University Press)

**Pred, A.** (1967) *Behavior and Location: Foundations for a Geographic and Dynamic Location Theory, Part I*, Lund Studies in Geography, Series B, Human Geography No. 27 (Lund: Gleerup)

**Pred, A.** (1969) *Behavior and Location: Foundations for a Geographic and Dynamic Location Theory, Part II*, Lund Studies in Geography, Series B, Human Geography No. 28 (Lund: Gleerup)

**Preston, S. H.** (1975) 'The changing relation between mortality and level of economic development' *Population Studies* **29**: 231–48

**Preston, S. H.** (1976) *Mortality Patterns in National Populations* (New York: Academic Press)

**Preston, S. H., Keyfitz, N.** and **Schoen, R.** (1972) *Causes of Death: Life Tables for National Populations* (New York: Seminar Press)

**Ranis, G.** and **Fei, J. C. H.** (1961) 'A theory of economic development' *American Economic Review* **51**: 533–65

**Rao, S. L. N.** (1973) 'On long-term mortality trends in the United States, 1850–1968' *Demography* **10**: 405–19

**Razzell, P. E.** (1965) 'Population change in eighteenth century England: a re-appraisal' *Economic History Review*, 2nd Series **18**: 312–32

**Razzell, P. E.** (1974) 'An interpretation of the modern rise of population in Europe – a critique' *Population Studies* **28**: 5–17

**Redford, A.** (1926) *Labour Migration in England, 1800–1850* (3rd edn, 1976) (Manchester: Manchester University Press)

**Reinhard, M. R., Armengaud, A.** and **Dupâquier, J.** (1968) *Histoire Générale de la Population Mondiale* (Paris: Éditions Montchrestein)

**Remple, H.** and **Todaro, M. P.** (1972) 'Rural-to-urban labour migration in Kenya' in Ominde, S. H. and Ejiogu, C. N. (eds) *Population Growth and Economic Development in Africa*: 214–31 (London: Heinemann)

**Rindfuss, R. R.** and **Sweet, J. A.** (1977) *Postwar Fertility Trends and Differentials in the United States* (New York: Academic Press)

**Rodgers, G. B.** (1979) 'Income and inequality as determinants of mortality: an international cross-sectional analysis' *Population Studies* **33**: 343–51

**Rogers, C. D.** (1975) *The Lancashire Population Crisis of 1623* (Manchester: Manchester University Extra Mural Department)

**Rossi, P. H.** (1955) *Why Families Move: A Study of the Social Psychology of Urban Residential Mobility* (New York: Free Press)

**Rowntree, G.** and **Pierce, R. M.** (1961) 'Birth control in Britain: Part I, Attitudes and practices among persons married since the First World War' *Population Studies* **15**: 3–21

**Roxborough, I.** (1979) *Theories of Underdevelopment* (London: Macmillan)

**Rubin, E.** (1960) 'The quantitative data and methods of the Rev. T. R. Malthus' *American Statistician* **14**: 28–31

**Runciman, W. G.** (1968) 'Class, status and power?' in Jackson, J. A. (ed.) *Social Stratification*: 25–61 (Cambridge: Cambridge University Press)

**Rushton, G.** (1969) 'Analysis of spatial behaviour by revealed space preference' *Annals of the Association of American Geographers* **59**: 391 –400

**Russell, J. C.** (1948) *British Medieval Population* (Albuquerque, N. M.: University of New Mexico Press)

**Russell, J. C.** (1966a) 'The preplague population of England' *Journal of British Studies* **5**(2): 1–21

**Russell, J. C.** (1966b) 'The effects of pestilence and plague, 1315– 1385' *Comparative Studies in Society and History* **8**: 464–73

**Ryder, N. B.** (1969) 'The emergence of a modern fertility pattern: United States, 1917–66' in Behrman, S. J., Corsa, L. and Freedman, R. (eds) *Fertility and Family Planning: A World View*: 99–103 (Ann Arbor, Mich.: Michigan University Press)

**Sabot, R. H.** (1979) *Economic Development and Urban Migration: Tanzania, 1900–1971* (Oxford: Clarendon Press)

**Sahota, G.S.** (1968) 'An economic analysis of internal migration in Brazil' *Journal of Political Economy* **76**: 218–45

**Sánchez-Albornoz, N.** (1974) *The Population of Latin America: A History* (Berkeley, Ca.: University of California Press)

**Santos, M.** (1979) *The Shared Space: The Two Circuits of the Urban Economy in Underdeveloped Countries* (London: Methuen)

**Sauvy, A.** (1969) *General Theory of Population* (London: Weidenfeld and Nicolson)

**Schofield, R. S.** (1972) '"Crisis" mortality' *Local Population Studies* **9**: 10–22

**Schofield, R. S.** (1976) 'The relationship between demographic structure and environment in pre-industrial western Europe' in Conze, W. (ed.) *Sozialgeschicte der Familie in der Neuzeit Europas*: 147–60 (Stuttgart: Klett Verlag)

**Schofield, R. S.** (1977) 'An anatomy of an epidemic: Colyton, November 1645 to November 1646' in *The Plague Reconsidered*: 95–126 (Local Population Studies Supplement) (Matlock, Derbyshire: Local Population Studies Society)

**Schultz, T. P.** (1971) 'Rural–urban migration in Colombia' *Review of Economics and Statistics* **53**: 157–63

**Schultz, T. W.** (1961) 'Investment in human capital' *American Economic Review* **51**: 1–17

**Schultz, T. W.** (1962) 'Reflections on investment in man' *Journal of Political Economy* **70** (Supplement): 1–8

**Schultz, T. W.** (ed.) (1974) *The Economics of the Family: Marriage, Children and Human Capital* (Chicago: Chicago University Press)

**Schwartz, A.** (1973) 'Interpreting the effect of distance on migration' *Journal of Political Economy* **81**: 1153–69

**Scott, J. W.** and **Tilly, L. A.** (1975) 'Women's work and the family in nineteenth-century Europe' *Comparative Studies in Society and History* **17**: 37–64

**Seiver, D. A.** (1975) 'Recent fertility in Mexico: measurement and interpretation' *Population Studies* **29**: 341–54 (also **31**: 175–7)

**Sharlin, A.** (1978) 'Natural decrease in early modern cities: a reconsideration' *Past and Present* **79**: 126–38

**Sharpe, F. R.** and **Lotka, A. J.** (1911) 'A problem in age-distribution' *Philosophical Magazine*, Series 6 **21**: 435–8

**Shaw, R. P.** (1975) *Migration Theory and Fact: A Review and Bibliography of Current Literature*, Regional Science Research Institute, Bibliography Series No. 5 (Philadelphia)

**Shryock, H. S.** and **Siegel, J. S.** (1976) *The Methods and Materials of Demography* (Condensed Edition) (New York: Academic Press)

**Simon, J. L.** (1977) *The Economics of Population Growth* (Princeton, N. J.: Princeton University Press)

**Sjaastad, L. A.** (1962) 'The costs and returns of human migration' *Journal of Political Economy* **70** (Supplement): 80–93

**Slack, P.** (1979) 'Mortality crises and epidemic disease in England, 1485–1610' in Webster, C. (ed.) *Health, Medicine and Mortality in the Sixteenth Century*: 9–59 (Cambridge: Cambridge University Press)

**Smith, R. M.** (1978) 'Population and its geography in England, 1500–1730' in Dodgshon, R. A. and Butlin, R. A. (eds) *An Historical Geography of England and Wales: 199–237* (London: Academic Press)

**Smith, T. C.** (1977) *Nakahara: Family Farming and Population in a Japanese Village, 1717–1830* (Stanford, Ca.: Stanford University Press)

**Smulevich, B. Y.** (1978) 'Bourgeois population theories' in Valentey, D. I. (ed.) *The Theory of Population*: 384–93 (Moscow: Progress Publishers)

**Speare, A.** (1970) 'Home ownership, life cycle stage and residential mobility' *Demography* **7**: 449–58

**Speare, A.** (1971) 'A cost-benefit model of rural to urban migration in Taiwan' *Population Studies* **25**: 117–30

**Spencer, B., Hum, D.** and **Deprez, P.** (1976) 'Spectral analysis and the study of seasonal fluctuations in historical demography' *Journal of European Economic History* **5**: 171–90

**Spengler, J. J.** (1972) 'Malthus's total population theory: a restatement and reappraisal' in Spengler, J. J., *Population Economics*: 3–65 (Durham, N. C.: Duke University Press)

**Spengler, J. J.** (1976) 'Alfred James Lotka's vision of the population problem' in Richards, H. (ed.) *Population, Factor Movements and Economic Development* : 120–38 (Cardiff: University of Wales Press)

**Stolnitz, G. J.** (1965) 'Recent mortality trends in Latin America, Asia and Africa: review and re-interpretation' *Population Studies* **19**: 117–38

**Stone, L.** (1977) *The Family, Sex and Marriage in England, 1500–1800* (London: Weidenfeld and Nicolson)

**Sun, T. H., Lin, H. S.** and **Freedman, R.** (1978) 'Trends in fertility, family size preferences, and family planning practice: Taiwan, 1961–76' *Studies in Family Planning* **9**(4): 54–70

**Sweezy, P. M.** (1942) *The Theory of Capitalist Development* (New York: Monthly Review Press)

**Taeuber, I. B.** (1958) *The Population of Japan* (Princeton, N. J.: Princeton University Press)

**Taeuber, I. B.** (1960) 'Japan's demographic transition re-examined' *Population Studies* **14**: 28–39

**Tannous, A. I.** (1942) 'Emigration, a force of social change in an Arab village' *Rural Sociology* **7**: 62–74

**Taylor, A. J.** (ed.) (1975) *The Standard of Living in Britain in the Industrial Revolution* (London: Methuen)

**Taylor, J. G.** (1979) *From Modernization to Modes of Production: A Critique of the Sociologies of Development and Underdevelopment* (London: Macmillan)

**Teitelbaum, M. S.** (forthcoming) *The British Fertility Decline* (Princeton, N. J.: Princeton University Press)

**Thomas, B.** (1954) *Migration and Economic Growth: A Study of Great Britain and the Atlantic Economy* (Cambridge: Cambridge University Press)

**Thomlinson, R.** (1965) *Population Dynamics: Causes and Consequences of World Demographic Change* (New York: Random House)

**Thompson, W. S.** (1929) 'Population' *American Journal of Sociology* **34**: 959–75

**Thompson, W. S.** (1944) *Plenty of People* (Lancaster, Pa.: Jaques Cattell Press)

**Tillott, P. M.** (ed.) (1961) *Victoria County History of Yorkshire: The City of York* (London: Oxford University Press)

**Tilly, L. A.** and **Scott, J. W.** (1978) *Women, Work and Family* (New York: Holt, Rinehart and Winston)

**Tilly, L. A., Scott, J. W.** and **Cohen, M.** (1976) 'Women's work and European fertility patterns' *Journal of Interdisciplinary History* **6**: 447–76

**Tipps, D. C.** (1973) 'Modernization theory and the comparative study of societies: a critical perspective' *Comparative Studies in Society and History* **15**: 199–226

**Todaro, M. P.** (1969) 'A model of labor migration and urban unemployment in less developed countries' *American Economic Review* **59**: 138–48

**Todaro, M. P.** (1976) *Internal Migration in Developing Countries: A Review of Theory, Evidence, Methodology and Research Priorities* (Geneva: International Labour Office)

**Todaro, M. P.** (1977) *Economic Development in the Third World: An Introduction to Problems and Policies in a Global Perspective* (London: Longman)

**Todaro, M. P.** (1980) 'Internal migration in developing countries: a survey' in Easterlin, R. A. (ed.) *Population and Economic Change in Developing Countries*: 361–90 (Chicago: Chicago University Press)

**Tranter, N. L.** (1973) *Population Since the Industrial Revolution: The Case of England and Wales* (London: Croom Helm)

**Trewartha, G. T.** (1969) *A Geography of Population: World Patterns* (New York: Wiley)

**Turpeinen, O.** (1979) 'Fertility and mortality in Finland since 1750' *Population Studies* **33**: 111–14

**United Nations** (1955) *Age and Sex Patterns of Mortality: Model Life Tables for Underdeveloped Countries*, Department of Economic and Social Affairs, Bureau of Social Affairs, Population Studies No. 22 (New York)

**United Nations** (1967) *Methods of Estimating Basic Demographic Measures from Incomplete Data*, Department of Economic and Social Affairs, Bureau of Social Affairs, Population Studies No. 42 (New York)

**United Nations** (1977) *Levels and Trends of Fertility Throughout the World, 1950–70*, Department of Economic and Social Affairs, Bureau of Social Affairs, Population Studies No. 59 (New York)

**United States Bureau of the Census** (1975) *Historical Statistics of the United States: Colonial Times to 1970* (Washington D. C.)

**Vallin, J.** (1968) 'La mortalité dans les pays du Tiers Monde: évolution et perspectives' *Population* **23**: 845–68

**van de Walle, E.** (1972) 'Marriage and marital fertility' in Glass, D. V. and Revelle, R. (eds) *Population and Social Change*: 137–51 (London: Arnold)

**van de Walle, E.** (1974) *The Female Population of France in the Nineteenth Century: A Reconstruction of 82 Départements* (Princeton, N. J.: Princeton University Press)

**van de Walle, E.** (1978) 'Alone in Europe: the French fertility decline until 1850' in Tilly, C. (ed.) *Historical Studies of Changing Fertility*: 257–88 (Princeton, N. J.: Princeton University Press)

**van de Walle, E.** (1979) 'France' in Lee, W. R. (ed.) *European Demography and Economic Growth*: 123–43 (London: Croom Helm)

**Vinovskis, M. A.** (ed.) (1979) *Studies in American Historical Demography* (New York: Academic Press)

**Visaria, P. M.** (1969) 'Mortality and fertility in India, 1951–61' *Milbank Memorial Fund Quarterly* **47**: 91–116

**Visaria, P. M.** and **Jain, A. K.** (1976) *Country Profiles: India* (New York: The Population Council)

**Wallerstein, I.** (1974) *The Modern World-System: Capitalist Agriculture and the Origins of the European World-Economy in the Sixteenth Century* (New York: Academic Press)

**Wallerstein, I.** (1979) *The Capitalist World-Economy* (Cambridge: Cambridge University Press)

**Webber, M. J.** (1972) *Impact of Uncertainty on Location* (Cambridge, Mass.: MIT Press)

**Westoff, C. F.** and **Ryder, N. B.** (1977) *The Contraceptive Revolution* (Princeton, N. J.: Princeton University Press)

**Whelpton, P. K., Campbell, A. A.** and **Patterson, J. E.** (1966) *Fertility and Family Planning in the United States* (Princeton, N. J.: Princeton University Press)

**White, P. E.** and **Woods, R. I.** (eds) (1980) *The Geographical Impact of Migration* (London: Longman)

**Willcox, W. F.** (ed.) (1929) *International Migrations, Volume 1, Statistics* (New York: National Bureau of Economic Research)

**Willcox, W. F.** (ed.) (1931) *International Migrations, Volume 2, Interpretations* (New York: National Bureau of Economic Research)

**Wirth, L.** (1938) 'Urbanism as a way of life' *American Journal of Sociology* **44**: 1–24

**Wolpert, J.** (1965) 'Behavioural aspects of the decision to migrate' *Papers and Proceedings, Regional Science Association* **15**: 159–69

**Woods, R. I.** (1979) *Population Analysis in Geography* (London: Longman)

**Wright, N. H.** (1968) 'Recent fertility change in Ceylon and prospects for a national family planning program' *Demography* **5**: 745–56

**Wrightson, K.** and **Levine, D.** (1979) *Poverty and Piety in an English Village: Terling, 1525–1700* (New York: Academic Press)

**Wrigley, E. A.** (1965) 'Changes in the philosophy of geography' in Chorley, R. J. and Haggett, P. (eds) *Frontiers in Geographical Teaching*: 3–20 (London: Methuen)

**Wrigley, E. A.** (1966a) 'Family limitation in pre-industrial England' *Economic History Review*, 2nd Series **19**: 82–109

**Wrigley, E. A.** (ed.) (1966b) *An Introduction to English Historical Demography* (London: Weidenfeld and Nicolson)

**Wrigley, E. A.** (1969) *Population and History* (London: Weidenfeld and Nicolson)

**Wrigley, E. A.** (1972a) 'Mortality in pre-industrial England: the example of Colyton, Devon, over three centuries' in Glass, D. V. and Revelle, R. (eds) *Population and Social Change*: 243–73 (London: Arnold)

**Wrigley, E. A.** (1972b) 'The process of modernization and the Industrial Revolution in England' *Journal of Interdisciplinary History* **3**: 225–59

**Wrigley, E. A.** (1975) 'Baptism coverage in early nineteenth-century England: the Colyton area' *Population Studies* **29**: 299–316

**Wrigley, E. A.** (1977) 'Births and baptisms: the use of Anglican baptism registers as a source of information about the numbers of births in England before the beginning of civil registration' *Population Studies* **31**: 281–312

**Wrigley, E. A.** and **Schofield, R. S.** (1981) *The Population History of England: 1541–1871: A Reconstruction* (London: Arnold)

**Wynne-Edwards, V. C.** (1962) *Animal Dispersion in Relation to Social Behaviour* (Edinburgh: Oliver and Boyd)

**Wynne-Edwards, V. C.** (1965) 'Self-regulating systems in populations of animals' *Science* **147**: 1543–8

**Wyon, J. B.** and **Gordon, J. E.** (1971) *The Khanna Study: Population Problems in the Rural Punjab* (Cambridge, Mass.: Harvard University Press)

**Yu, Y. C.** (1978) 'The demographic situation in China' *Population Studies* **32**: 427–47

**Yu, Y. C.** (1979) 'The population policy of China' *Population Studies* **33**: 125–42

**Yule, G. U.** (1925) 'The growth of population and the factors which control it' *Journal of the Royal Statistical Society* **88**: 1–58

**Zaba, B.** (1979) 'The four-parameter logit life table system' *Population Studies* **33**: 79–100

**Zambardino, R. A.** (1980) 'Mexico's population in the sixteenth century: demographic anomaly or mathematical illusion?' *Journal of Interdisciplinary History* **11**: 1–27

# Index